SAS ESSENTIALS

SAS ESSENTIALS
A Guide to Mastering SAS for Research

ALAN C. ELLIOTT

WAYNE A. WOODWARD

JOSSEY-BASS
A Wiley Imprint
www.josseybass.com

Published by Jossey-Bass
A Wiley Imprint
989 Market Street, San Francisco, CA 94103-1741—www.josseybass.com

Readers should be aware that Internet Web sites offered as citations and/or sources for further information may have changed or disappeared between the time this was written and when it is read.

Limit of Liability/Disclaimer of Warranty: While the publisher and author have used their best efforts in preparing this book, they make no representations or warranties with respect to the accuracy or completeness of the contents of this book and specifically disclaim any implied warranties of merchantability or fitness for a particular purpose. No warranty may be created or extended by sales representatives or written sales materials. The advice and strategies contained herein may not be suitable for your situation. You should consult with a professional where appropriate. Neither the publisher nor author shall be liable for any loss of profit or any other commercial damages, including but not limited to special, incidental, consequential, or other damages.

Jossey-Bass books and products are available through most bookstores. To contact Jossey-Bass directly call our Customer Care Department within the U.S. at 800-956-7739, outside the U.S. at 317-572-3986, or fax 317-572-4002.

Jossey-Bass also publishes its books in a variety of electronic formats. Some content that appears in print may not be available in electronic books.

Library of Congress Cataloging-in-Publication Data
Elliott, Alan C., 1952-
    SAS essentials : a guide to mastering SAS for research / Alan C. Elliott and Wayne A. Woodward.
        p.   cm.
    Includes bibliographical references and index.
    ISBN 978-0-470-46129-7 (pbk.)
        1. SAS (Computer file)   2.   Mathematical statistics—Data processing.   I. Woodward, Wayne A.   II. Title.
    QA276.4.E423   2010
    519.50285—dc22

                                                                    2009031926

Printed in the United States of America
FIRST EDITION

PB Printing   10 9 8 7 6 5 4 3 2 1

CONTENTS

FIGURES AND TABLES

FIGURES

TABLES

PREFACE

SAS Essentials is a ground-up introduction to SAS statistical software as it is used for research analysis in an applied statistics course. The book can be used in an SAS computer lab associated with an introductory statistics course, as a stand-alone SAS introductory course, or as a self-paced tutorial. Each chapter is designed so that the material can usually be covered in a one-hour computer lab class.

Although there are millions of SAS installations around the world, there is a steep learning curve involved in mastering the program. This book is a straightforward approach developed from more than fifteen years of teaching introductory SAS courses for scientific researchers and more than fifty combined years of teaching and consulting by the authors.

This book uses a hands-on programming approach to teaching SAS. It includes techniques for entering and manipulating data combined with step-by-step instructions for analyzing the data using commonly taught introductory applied statistical techniques.

Data sets for the examples can be downloaded from a Web site described in Chapter 1: "Creating a Folder for Storing Your SAS Files." This book uses examples based on SAS 9.2 for Windows. However, the vast majority of the examples will work with any Windows version of SAS.

ACKNOWLEDGMENTS

There is more to SAS than a programming language and more to the output than p-values. With that in mind, this book integrates information from discussions with colleagues over several years who contributed ideas to the selection of content for this book. Several colleagues helped by reading early versions and providing suggestions on various topics from their area of expertise. These include Terry D. Bilhartz, PhD (Sam Houston State University), Linda Hynan, PhD (UT Southwestern Medical Center, Dallas) and Cecil Hallum (Sam Houston State University).

We are also indebted to the fine editorial and production staff at Josey Bass/Wiley Publications and for the reviewers that provided valuable insights and suggestions. In particular we'd like to thank Andy Pasternack, Seth Schwartz, and Kelsey McGee for their help in getting this work into print.

Above all we wish to thank our wives, E'Lynne and Beverly for their patience and support through the long process of writing and rewriting the book.

Alan C. Elliott and Wayne A. Woodward
Dallas, Texas

THE AUTHORS

Alan C. Elliott has been a faculty member at the University of Texas Southwestern Medical Center at Dallas, currently in the Center for Biostatistics and Clinical Science, for more than 25 years. He holds masters degrees in business administration (MBA) and applied statistics (MAS). He has authored or coauthored a number of scientific articles and more than a dozen books on a wide variety of subjects including the *Directory of Microcomputer Statistical Software, Microcomputing with Applications, Getting Started in Internet Auctions, Currents in American History,* and the *Statistical Analysis Quick Reference Guide.* He has taught courses in statistics, research methods and computing (including SAS and SPSS) at the university for more than fifteen years and has been a collaborator on numerous medical research projects.

Wayne A. Woodward received his PhD (1974) in mathematical statistics from Texas Tech University. He is professor of Statistics and chair of the Department of Statistical Science at Southern Methodist University. He was elected as fellow of the American Statistical Association in 1996 and in 2003 was named an Altshuler University Distinguished Teaching Professor at SMU. In 2004 he received the Don Owen Award, given annually by the San Antonio chapter of the American Statistical Association, for recognition of his contributions in the areas of research, consulting, and service to the statistical community. He was named the 2006–2007 United Methodist Church Scholar/Teacher of the Year at SMU. Wayne is an active researcher, having published more than 60 research articles. His primary research interests lie in the area of statistical time series analysis with applications in the analysis of brain imaging and EEG data and in outlier detection.

SAS ESSENTIALS

CHAPTER

GETTING STARTED

LEARNING OBJECTIVES

- To be able to use the SAS software program in a Windows environment
- To understand basic information about getting data into SAS and running a SAS program
- To be able to run a simple SAS program

Research involves the collection and analysis of data. The SAS system is a powerful software program designed to give researchers a wide variety of both data management and data analysis capabilities. Although SAS has millions of users worldwide, it is not the simplest program to learn. With that in mind, we've created this book to provide you with a straightforward approach to learning SAS that can help you surmount the learning curve and successfully use SAS for data analysis.

Two main concepts are involved in learning SAS: first, how to get data into SAS and ready for analysis, and second, how to perform the desired data analysis. This chapter introduces you to the SAS system's use in the Microsoft Windows environment and provides examples of using SAS to analyze data.

USING SAS IN A WINDOWS ENVIRONMENT

SAS runs on a number of computer platforms (operating systems), including mainframes and personal computers whose operating systems are UNIX, Mac OS X, Linux, and Windows. This book is based on SAS's use in the Windows environment, although most of what is covered is the same on any computer. We assume that you have already installed SAS on your computer. Most differences across computers have to do with file references. Before discussing the SAS program, we'll review some of the basic file-handling features of Windows.

Creating a Folder for Storing Your SAS Files

Because there are several versions of Windows currently in use, we present general guidelines that should work in any one of them. To follow our examples, we recommend that you store the data and SAS files provided with this book in a folder named SASDATA. In fact, the examples in this text will assume that all example files used in this book are at the root of your hard drive, in a folder whose full path is C:\SASDATA.

In your own research, you may choose to store your SAS files in a folder with any name that makes sense to you, such as C:\RESEARCH. You can also create subfolders for each analysis—such as C:\RESEARCH\SMITH or C:\RESEARCH\JONES.

To copy the example files for this book to the C:\SASDATA folder on your own computer, do the following:

1. Download the example files from the following Website:
   http://www.alanelliott.com/sas

2. Follow the installation instructions provided on the Web site. Doing so creates the C:\SASDATA folder on your computer and copies the example files to that folder. (The Web site may also include updates concerning the information in this book.)

The examples in the book are designed to use data in the folder C:\SASDATA—in other words, in a folder on your computer's hard drive. You can also put the example files on any rewritable medium such as a flash drive—just remember to adjust the file names and file paths given in this book accordingly if you store your files in a location other than C:\SASDATA.

Beginning the SAS Program

There are at least two ways to start the SAS program. If the SAS icon appears on your Windows desktop, simply double-click it to launch SAS. If the SAS icon is not on your desktop, go to the Start button and select Start ⇨ Programs ⇨ SAS (English) to launch SAS. Henceforth we will refer to this simply as the SAS icon.

Understanding the SAS Windows Interface

Once you begin the SAS program, you will see a screen similar to that shown in Figure 1.1. (The SAS program appearance may be slightly different depending on which versions of Windows and SAS you're using.)

FIGURE 1.1. *Initial SAS screen*

The normal opening SAS screen is divided into three visible windows. The top right window is the **Log** window, and at the bottom right is the **Editor**. The third window, which appears as a vertical element on the left, is called the **SAS Explorer/Results** window. There are other SAS windows that are not currently visible. These include the **Output** and **Graph** windows. (A tab for the Output window does appear on the initial screen.) To open a SAS window that is not currently visible, click its tab at the bottom of the screen. Briefly, here are the purposes of these windows.

> **Editor:** Also called the Enhanced Editor or Windows Programming Editor (WPGM), this is the area where you write SAS code. It is like a simple word processor. When you open a previously saved SAS program, its contents will appear in this window. SAS code is stored in plain ASCII text, so files saved in the ASCII format from any other editor or word processor may be easily opened in this editor. You can also copy (or cut) text from another editor or word processor and paste it into the Editor window.

> **Log:** When you run a SAS program, a report detailing how (and if) the program ran appears in the Log window. Typically, when you run a SAS program, you first look at the contents of the Log window to see if any errors in the program were reported. The Log highlights errors in red. You should also look for warnings and other notes in the Log window which tell you that some part of your program may not have run correctly.

> **SAS Explorer/Results:** This window appears at the left of the screen and contains two tabs (shown at the bottom of the window): The Results tab displays a tree-like listing of your output, making it easy to scroll quickly to any place in your output listing. The Explorer tab (currently shown in Figure 1.1) displays the available SAS libraries, where SAS data files are stored. A SAS library is a nickname to an actual physical location on disk, such as `C:\SASDATA`. This will be described in detail in Chapter 3.

> **Output:** Once you run a SAS program that creates analysis output, the Output window is automatically displayed. This window contains the results (also called the listing) of your SAS job. If it does not appear, click the Output tab to display this window.

> **Graph:** If your SAS program creates graphic output, SAS will display a Graph window containing that output. Usually such output is displayed by default. If it does not appear, click the Graph tab (not shown in Figure 1.1) to display this window.

Do not close any of the windows that make up the SAS interface. Move from window to window by clicking on the tabs (which are analogous to the tabs on the Windows taskbar) or by pressing an appropriate function key. If you close one of the windows, its tab at the bottom of the SAS screen will disappear and you will need to go to the View pull-down menu and select the appropriate window name to redisplay the element that you closed.

YOUR FIRST SAS ANALYSIS

Now that you have installed SAS and copied the SAS example data files to your computer, it's time to jump in and perform a quick analysis to see how the program works. (You have downloaded the example files, haven't you? If not, go back to the "Creating a Folder for Storing Your SAS Files" section and do so.) The following steps show you how to open a SAS program file, analyze the data in the file, and create statistical output.

Our first example is a quick overview of how SAS works. You should not be concerned if you don't know much about the information in the SAS program file at this point. The remainder of the book teaches you how to create and run SAS programs.

HANDS-ON
EXAMPLE

In this example you'll run your first SAS analysis.

1. Launch SAS by double-clicking the SAS icon on your desktop or by selecting Start ⇨ Programs ⇨ SAS. (To put the SAS program icon on your desktop, consult your Windows documentation.) SAS initially appears as shown in Figure 1.1. (If a tutorial or some other initial dialog box appears, dismiss it.)

2. Open a program file. This example uses a file named FIRST.SAS. To open this file, first make sure that your active window is the Editor window. (Click anywhere in the Editor window to make it the active window.) On the menu bar, select File ⇨ Open Program to open the file C:\SASDATA\ FIRST.SAS. You may need to navigate to the C:\SASDATA folder to open this file.

(Continued)

3. Examine the opened file, the contents of which appear in the Editor window. Maximize the Editor window so you can see more of the program code. Figure 1.2 shows the Editor window maximized. We'll learn more in later chapters about what these lines of code mean.

FIGURE 1.2. *The FIRST.SAS file opened*

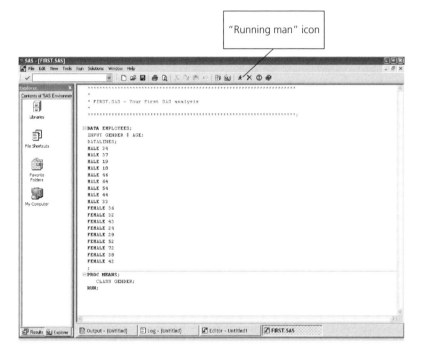

4. Run the SAS job. On the menu bar, select Run ⇨ Submit, click the "running man" icon on the toolbar, or press F8. The SAS instructions in the file are carried out (or, in computer terminology, the commands are executed). The SAS program creates analysis output that automatically appears in the Output window.

5. View the output. If the job runs without errors (which it should in this case), the Output window is displayed, showing the analysis output created by the program. The Output window is shown maximized in Figure 1.3.

FIGURE 1.3. *Output for FIRST.SAS*

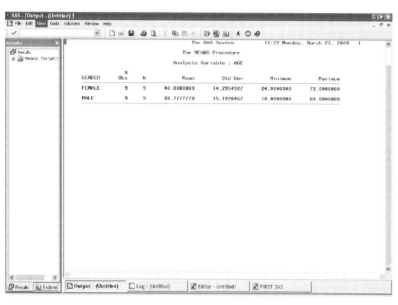

a. The analysis requested in this SAS program is a task to calculate basic statistics (PROC MEANS) for each group (GENDER) in the data set.

b. Notice the Results window on the left in Figure 1.3—it contains a single item called **Means: The SAS System** (the full name is truncated in the image). As you perform more analyses in SAS, this list will grow. You can quickly display the results of any previous analysis by clicking the item in the list.

6. Print the output. Make sure the Output window is active by pressing F7 or clicking anywhere in that window, then print the contents of the Output window by clicking the printer icon on the toolbar or by selecting File ⇨ Print on the menu bar.

7. Save the output. To save the results shown in the Output window, on the menu bar select File ⇨ Save As and enter an appropriate name for the output file, such as FIRST OUTPUT. The file will be saved as FIRST OUTPUT .LST. (The .LST extension is automatically added to the file name.) (You must be in the Output window for the file to be saved properly.)

(Continued)

8. Save the SAS program (instruction file) that created the output by going to the Editor window and clicking the tab named FIRST.SAS, shown at the bottom right of Figure 1.3. With the program on the screen, select File ⇨ Save As and enter a name such as MYFIRST. This saves the file as MYFIRST .SAS. (The .SAS extension is automatically added to the file name.)

9. Clear the output from the SAS windows to get ready for the next example. In the Output window, right-click and select Edit ⇨ Clear All from the pop-up menu. Do the same for the Log window. In the Editor window, right-click and select Clear All. (We'll learn a shortcut to this process later in this chapter.)

The Save As command saves the contents of whatever window is currently active. Thus, if you are in the Output window, it saves the output as an *.1st (listing) file; if you are in the Log window, it saves the contents of that window as an *.log file; and if you are in the Editor window it saves the code as an *.sas (SAS program code) file.

That's it! You've run your first SAS job. But wait, there's more. Now that you have one SAS job under your belt, its time to try another one. This time, you'll make a small change to the program before you run it.

Before running each Hands-on Example, clear the Output, Log, and Editor windows so you will not mix up data from a previous example. To clear each window, use the right-click technique previously described, or go to the window and on the menu bar select Edit ⇨ Clear All. In the section "Using SAS Function Keys" in this chapter we will create a way to shorten this process.

In this example you will make a small change in the program and see how that change alters the output.

1. In the Editor window, open the file `SECOND.SAS`. (It should be in your `C:\SASDATA` folder.)

2. Under the comment line that reads

   `* PUT YOUR TITLE ON THE NEXT LINE;`

   type this new line:

   `TITLE "HELLO WORLD, MY NAME IS ` *your name*`.";`
     Enter your own name instead of *your name*. Make sure you include the quotation marks and end the statement with a semicolon (;).

3. Run the SAS program, examine the output, and print the results.

HOW SAS WORKS

Look at the `SECOND.SAS` program file to see how SAS works. It is really very simple. The lines in the file are like the items on a grocery list or a "to do" list. You create a list of things you want SAS to do and when you submit the job, SAS does its best to carry out your instructions. The basic steps are:

1. Enter data into SAS. (This is called the `DATA` step.)

2. Tell SAS what analysis to perform. (This is called `PROC`s, for procedures.)

3. Observe the output. (This is called `OUTPUT`.)

Figure 1.4 illustrates this process.

   This book follows the process shown in Figure 1.4. It contains a number of sample SAS programs that show you how to get data into SAS, analyze the data using SAS procedures, and read the output.

   To end the SAS program, select File ⇨ Exit on the menu bar. Make sure you've saved all files you wish to save before ending the program. (The program will prompt you to save files if you have not previously done so.)

FIGURE 1.4. *How SAS works*

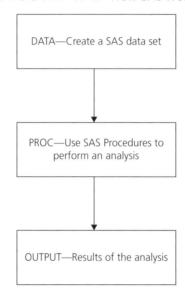

TIPS AND TRICKS FOR RUNNING SAS PROGRAMS

This section contains tips and tricks that can help you if something in your program goes wrong. Now that you have seen two sample SAS jobs, you should have an idea of how SAS programs are constructed. This section provides general rules for writing SAS programs.

Within a SAS program, each statement begins with an identifying keyword (DATA, PROC, INPUT, CARDS, RUN, etc.) and ends with a semicolon (;). For example:

```
DATA TEMP;
PROC PRINT DATA=TEMP;
```

SAS statements are free-format—they do not have to begin in any particular column. Thus,

- Statements can begin anywhere and end anywhere.

- **One statement can continue over several lines** with a semicolon at the end of the last line signaling the end of the statement.

■ **Several statements may be on the same line**, with each statement terminated with a semicolon.

■ **Blanks**, as many as you want but at least one, may be used to separate the components (words) in a SAS program statement.

■ Case (lower- and upper-) *doesn't* matter in most SAS statements.

■ **Case *does matter* in data and quoted information.** When you enter character data values (such as M or m for "male"), case will matter when you are sorting or selecting the data. Also, the contents of a title or footnote are placed in quotation marks and are printed in the output using the uppercase and lowercase characters you indicate in the program code.

■ **The most common error in SAS programming is a misplaced (or missing) semicolon.** Pay careful attention to the semicolons at the end of the statements; they tell SAS that the statement is completed.

■ **A second common error is a missing RUN statement.** You *must* end every program with a RUN statement (in the Windows version of SAS). If you do not end the program with a RUN statement, your program may not terminate normally, and your last statement may not be completed.

■ **A third common error in a SAS program is the presence of unmatched quotation marks**. If you enter a title without matching quotation marks, you will see an error message in your Log file such as "The TITLE statement is ambiguous due to . . . unquoted text." This error can cause subsequent statements in your code to be misinterpreted by SAS.

■ **A search for errors in a program log should be from the top down.** It is inevitable that you will write programs that contain errors in syntax. When you get lots of errors in a SAS run, always fix the errors from the top down in your program code, because often the early errors lead to confusion that results in the later errors.

■ **If program errors cause problems that result in SAS's "freezing up" or not completing the steps in your program,** you can abort SAS's processes by pressing Ctrl+Break and selecting the "Cancel Submitted Statements" option from the dialog box that appears.

■ **If you cannot resolve a problem within SAS**, *save your files*, restart SAS, and reopen the files. Try to find the code that caused the problem, and then re-run your program.

■ **The structure of your SAS programs should be easy to read.** Notice how the example programs in this book are structured—how some statements are indented for easy reading and how the code contains comments. Pay attention to the formatting of future examples. These commonly accepted (and recommended) program formatting techniques can help you or your colleagues in the future when you go back to read code that was written months or years before.

Now that you've experienced running simple programs in SAS, you will want to know more about the syntax and conventions for entering and running a SAS program. Following is a brief introduction to some of the SAS program requirements you need to know.

Using the SAS Enhanced Editor

You may have noticed that different parts of the coding in the FIRST.SAS file appear in various colors in the SAS Enhanced Editor. This editor is designed to help you write your SAS code and to prevent many potential errors. The color coding is designed to help you clearly see step-boundaries (major SAS commands), keywords, column and table names, and constants.

For example, in a SAS program:

Green is used for comments.

Dark Blue is used for the keyword in major SAS commands.

Blue is used for keywords that have special meaning as SAS commands.

A yellow highlight is used for data.

A boundary line separates each step.

If you make a mistake in coding your SAS job, the appropriate colors will not appear. In fact, statements that SAS does not understand typically appear in red, which helps you locate potential problems with your code.

Using SAS Function Keys

You can use keyboard function keys to move from window to window or to execute certain tasks in SAS. Some people prefer the use of function keys (rather than mouse clicks) as a quicker way of selecting program options. Table 1.1 lists some of the SAS function keys you can use throughout this book.

You can also customize these keys. For example, to display the full set of function key commands, on the menu bar select Tools ⇨ Options ⇨ Keys.

TABLE 1.1. **SAS Function Keys**

Function Key	SAS command	Result
F2	RESHOW	Reshows window interrupted by system command
F3	END; /*GSUBMIT BUFFER=DEFAULT*/	Submits SAS statements in clipboard
F4	RECALL	Recalls current SAS code to editor
F5	PROGRAM (PGM)	Displays Editor window
F6	LOG	Displays Log window
F7	OUTPUT	Displays Output window
F8	ZOOM OFF;SUBMIT	Submits (runs) the current SAS program
F9	KEYS	Displays Keys window
F10	Not defined	
F11	COMMAND BAR	Moves cursor to command bar
F12	Not defined	

HANDS-ON
EXAMPLE

In earlier examples you cleared the information from the Output and Log windows manually. In this example you will create a new F12 function key command that will clear these windows and return you to the Editor window. The F12 key you're about to define uses three SAS commands: CLEAR OUTPUT, CLEAR LOG, and WPGM. The CLEAR command clears the contents of the Output and Log windows, and the WPGM command returns you to the Windows Programming Editor.

Follow these instructions to create a new F12 function key definition.

1. On the menu bar select Tools ⇨ Options ⇨ Keys.

2. Next to the blank F12 option, enter CLEAR OUTPUT; CLEAR LOG; WPGM. (Do not include the period that ends the previous sentence.) Press the Enter key to lock in the new command.

3. Exit the Keys window and try out this function key by re-running one of the previous examples. With the output displayed on the screen, press F12. The output will be cleared, the log file information will be cleared, and the Editor window will be displayed, still containing the current program code. Thus, this command allows you to quickly clear the Log and Output windows without deleting the program code. This new command will be used in some of our future examples.

Use the F12 SAS function key you created to clear the contents of the Output and Log windows between examples.

Using the SAS Menus

The SAS pull-down menu items differ depending on which window is currently active (Editor, Output, Log). To see the options change, click each window to make it active and notice the changes to the menu choices at the top of the main SAS window.

The SAS window you will use most is that of the Editor, because that is where you will write and edit SAS code. Therefore, we'll spend a little time describing the menus for the Editor window.

File: Used for opening and saving files and for printing.

Edit: Used to copy, cut, and paste text, as well as to find and replace text.

View: Allows you to go back and forth between viewing the Editor window, the Log window, and the Output window.

Tools: Allows you to open programs for graphics and text editing, along with other options available to customize the program to your preferences.

Run: Allows you to run (submit) a SAS program; also provides access to remote SAS options.

Solutions: Contains options to advanced procedures not discussed in this text.

Window: As in most Windows programs, allows you to choose display options for opened windows such as tile and cascade; also allows you to select (make active) a particular window, such as the Log or Output window.

Help: Contains options for the SAS help system as well as online documentation. (See the section "Getting SAS Help on the Web" later in this chapter.)

Understanding Common File Extensions

Another piece of information you need to be aware of when learning and using SAS concerns the type of files used and created by SAS or mentioned in this book. Like most Windows files, they have specific file name extensions that indicate what application is associated with them (e.g., the way a `*.doc` extension indicates a Microsoft Word file).

SAS code file (`filename.sas`): This is an ACSII text file and may be edited using the SAS Editor, Notepad, or any text editor that can read an ASCII file.

SAS log file (`filename.log`): This ASCII text file contains information such as errors, warnings, and data set details for a submitted SAS program.

SAS listing file (`filename.lst`): This ASCII file contains the output (listing) of a SAS job.

SAS data file (`filename.sas7bdat`): This file contains a SAS data set, including variable names, labels, and the results of calculations you may have performed in a DATA step. You cannot open or read this file except in SAS or in a few other programs that can read SAS data files.

Raw data files (`filename.dat` or `filename.txt` or `filename.csv`): These ASCII (text) files contain raw data that can be imported into SAS or edited in an editor such as Notepad.

Excel file (`filename.xls`): The data in a Microsoft Excel file (when properly formatted into a table of columnar data) can be imported into SAS using the File ⇨ Import menu selection. Other data files such as those produced by Microsoft

Access (*.mdb) and Lotus 1-2-3 (*.wks) can be imported into SAS in a similar way.

Getting SAS Help on the Web

SAS help is available from the SAS Help pull-down menu (Help ⇨ SAS Help and Documentation). When you select this option, SAS displays a help file as shown in Figure 1.5 (with the SAS Products option expanded). As with other software help systems, you can choose to search for keywords (using the Search tab), or you can scroll through the tree-like list to select topics of interest.

In Figure 1.5 note that the SAS Products section has been expanded to display links to help with a number of SAS program components. The options called Base SAS and SAS/STAT are references to the information discussed in this text. Specifically, details about the statistical procedures (PROCs) discussed in this book are documented in these two sections of the Help file.

FIGURE 1.5. *Help file display*

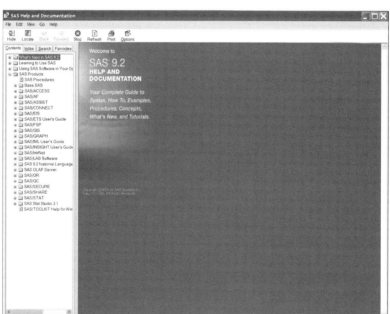

SUMMARY

This chapter provided an overview of SAS and examples of how to run an existing SAS program. In the following chapters we will discuss the components of a SAS program, including how to enter data, how to request analyses, and how to format and read output.

EXERCISES

1.1. Enter code and run a SAS program.

Enter the following SAS code into the Editor window and run the program. Make sure the Editor window is clear of all other information before you begin.

```
DATA TEMP;
INPUT ID SBP DBP SEX $ AGE WT;
DATALINES;

1 120 80 M 15 115
2 130 70 F 25 180
3 140 100 M 89 170
4 120 80 F 30 150
5 125 80 F 20 110

;
RUN;
PROC PRINT DATA=TEMP;
TITLE 'Exercise 1.1 - Your Name';
RUN;
PROC MEANS;
RUN;
```

Include your name in the TITLE line. Observe the results in the Output window. To save the output to a file, make sure the Output window is active and select File ⇨ Save As, or you can select and copy the contents of the Output window and paste the output into an e-mail or word processor document. (We recommend that you change the output font to Courier or Courier New if you paste the output into a full-fledged word processor such as Microsoft Word.)

Hints for running this program:

a. Begin SAS.

b. Enter the SAS code into the Editor window. Pay attention to the color coding to make sure all of your code has been entered correctly.

c. Before running the program, save the SAS code under the name C:\SASDATA\MYEXERCISE1.1.SAS.

d. Run the program. (Click the "running man" icon or select Run ⇨ Submit on the menu bar.)

e. Check the Log window for errors.

f. If there are errors in the Log file, proceed to the next step; if not, go to step k.

g. Press F12 to clear the Log and Output windows if you have previously defined the F12 key. If not, in the Log and Output windows right-click and from the pop-up menu select Edit ⇨ Clear All to erase the current contents of those windows. (This is so that you won't accidentally try to fix an old error.)

    h.   Return to the Editor window.

    i.   Make corrections in the Editor window and re-save the code.

    j.   Go back to step d.

    k.   Examine the output.

    l.   You may optionally print, save, or e-mail the output as directed by your instructor.

    m.   Optionally end SAS.

1.2. Change the contents of a SAS program.

Enter the following SAS code into the Editor window and run the program. Make sure the Editor, Log, and Output windows are clear of all other information before you begin. (You can clear the Log and Output windows by pressing F12 if you have previously defined that key.)

```
DATA RECOVERY;
INPUT LNAME $ RECTIME;
DATALINES;
JONES 3.1
SMITH 3.6
HARRIS 4.2
MCCULLEY 2.1
BROWN 2.8
CURTIS 3.8
JOHNSTON 1.8
;
RUN;
PROC PRINT DATA=RECOVERY;
Title 'Exercise 1.2 - Your Name';
RUN;
PROC MEANS DATA=RECOVERY;
RUN;
```

Include your name in the TITLE line. Observe the results in the Output window.

CHAPTER

2

GETTING DATA INTO SAS

LEARNING OBJECTIVES

- To enter data using freeform list input
- To enter data using the compact method
- To enter data using column input
- To enter data using formatted input
- To enter data using the INFILE technique
- To enter multiple-line data

Before you can perform any analysis, you must have data. SAS contains powerful tools you can use to enter, import, and manage your data. This chapter introduces the most commonly used methods for getting data into SAS. Additional techniques are covered in the next chapter.

The primary way to enter and manipulate data in SAS is with the SAS DATA step. Entering and manipulating data are the primary topics of the next two chapters. In the initial SAS examples, you may have noticed that the programs begin with the keyword DATA, followed by lines of code defining the data for analysis. As noted in Chapter 1, this is called the DATA step. Within the DATA step, data are manipulated, cleaned, and otherwise prepared for analysis. Depending on how carefully the data have been collected and entered, this process can be quick and simple or long and detailed. Either way, the DATA step is the primary way to get your data into SAS.

Table 2.1 is an overview of how the SAS DATA step works and what will be discussed in the next few chapters.

USING THE SAS DATA SETS

A SAS data set is a collection of information that is in a form ready for SAS to use. Therefore, an important task for you to learn is how to read, manipulate, and manage SAS data sets. The following sections describe how to create a SAS data set, beginning with simple examples and later describing more complex data set creation techniques.

TABLE 2.1. Overview of the SAS DATA step

TASK	HOW DO YOU DO IT?
Getting data: initiating/creating a new SAS data set, either by reading a list of data or by using data that are in another file	Within the DATA step, use a SAS DATA statement as discussed in Chapter 2 (this chapter).
Saving data: storing data in a permanent location on your hard drive	Within the DATA step, write the created data set to a location on disk directly or by using a SAS library as discussed in Chapter 3.
Preparing data for analysis: cleaning and manipulating your data set to get it ready for analysis	Within the DATA step, create variable labels, assign missing values, create new variables, and assign labels to data categories as discussed in Chapter 4.

In the SAS language, the `DATA` statement signals the creation of a new data set. For example, a `DATA` statement in SAS code may look like this:

```
DATA MYDATA;
```

The keyword `DATA` tells SAS to create a new data set. The word `MYDATA` in the `DATA` statement is the name assigned to the new data set. (You can choose any name for a SAS data set that conforms to SAS naming conventions, as described in the section "Rules for SAS Variable Names" in this chapter.) Thus, the SAS `DATA` statement has two major functions:

- It signals the beginning of the `DATA` step.

- It assigns a name (of your choice) to the data set created in the `DATA` step. The general form of the `DATA` statement is:

```
DATA datasetname;
```

The SAS `datasetname` in the `DATA` statement can have several forms.

- The SAS data set name can be a single name (used for **temporary data sets**, those kept only during the current SAS session). For example:

```
DATA TEMP;
DATA EXAMPLE;
DATA OCT2007;
```

- Or, the SAS data set name can be a two-part name. The two-part name tells SAS that this **permanent data set** will be stored on disk beyond the current SAS session in a SAS library indicated by the prefix name (the name preceding the dot). For example:

```
DATA PERM.CLASS;
DATA RESEARCH.JAN2008;
DATA CLASS.EX1;
DATA JONES.EXP1;
```

Thus in the first example, the prefix `PERM` is the name of the SAS library and `CLASS` is the name of the SAS data set. Details about creating libraries and permanent data sets are provided in the next chapter.

- A SAS data set name can also refer directly to the Windows name of a file on your hard disk. For example:

```
DATA "C:\SASDATA\SOMEDATA";
DATA "C:\MYFILES\DECEMBER\MEASLES";
```

This naming convention refers to a permanent SAS data set and will be illustrated in the next chapter.

■ Or, the SAS data set name can be omitted entirely. This technique is used for temporary data sets, which are kept only during the current SAS session. For example:

```
DATA;
```

In this case, SAS will name the data set for you. On the first occurrence of such a DATA step, SAS will name the data set DATA1, then DATA2, and so so.

Thus, the DATA statement is the usual beginning for every SAS program. In the next sections and chapters, you will see some of the power of the DATA statement in reading and preparing data for analysis. The general syntax for the SAS DATA statement is:

```
DATA datasetname;
    <code to enter data>;
    <code to create new variables>;
    <code to assign missing values>;
    <code to output data>;
        <code to assign labels to variables>;
        <and other data tasks>;
```

Each of these components of the DATA statement will be discussed in some detail, although covering the full extent of the DATA statement's capabilities would take a book several times the length of this volume.

UNDERSTANDING SAS DATA SET STRUCTURE

Once you read data into SAS, the program stores the data values as a data set (also called a data table) as a collection of data values arranged in a rectangular table. Table 2.2 is a visual illustration of how SAS internally stores a typical data set—columns are data variables (each named) and rows are subjects, observations, or records.

TABLE 2.2. **SAS Data set (table) structure**

	ID	SBP	DBP	GENDER	AGE	WT
OBS1	1	120	80	M	15	115
OBS2	2	130	70	F	25	180
...	.	.	.	.	.	.
OBS100	100	120	80	F	20	110

Although the structure of this table may look similar to the way data are stored in a Microsoft Excel spreadsheet, there are some important differences.

■ Each **column** represents a variable and is designated with a variable name (ID, SBP, etc.). Every SAS variable (column) must have a name, and the names must follow certain naming rules.

■ Each **row**, marked here as obs1, obs2, and so on, indicates observations or records. An observation consists of data observed from one subject or entity.

In the section "Creating a SAS Library Using a Dialog Box" in Chapter 3 you will see how to display a SAS data table in spreadsheet mode.

RULES FOR SAS VARIABLE NAMES

Each variable (column) in the SAS data set (table) must have a name, and the names must follow certain rules. This is different from Excel, which imposes no restriction on how (or if) to name columns of data. However, many of the rules for SAS are similar to those for a data table created in Microsoft Access. Each SAS variable name

■ Must be 1–32 characters long but must not include any blanks.

■ Must start with the letters A through Z or an underscore (_). A name may not include a blank.

■ May include numbers (but not as the first character).

■ May include upper- and lowercase characters (variable names are case-insensitive).

■ Should be descriptive of the variable (optional but recommended).

Here are some examples of correct SAS variable names:

```
GENDER
AGE_IN_1999 (notice underscores)
AGEin1999
_OUTCOME (notice the leading underscore)
HEIGHT_IN_CM (notice underscores)
WT_IN_LBS (notice underscores)
```

And here are some examples of incorrect SAS variable names:

```
AGE IN 2000
2000MeaslesCount
S S Number
Question 5
WEIGHT IN KG
AGE-In-2000
```

These variable names are incorrect because some include blanks (S S Number, AGE IN 2000, Question 5, WEIGHT in KG), start with something other than a letter or an underscore (2000MeaslesCount), or contain special characters other than the underscore (AGE-In-2000).

> SAS versions earlier than version 7 had stricter naming rules. Notably, names could be only up to eight characters long.

UNDERSTANDING THREE SAS VARIABLE TYPES

SAS is designed to differentiate among three basic types of variables: numeric, text, and date.

■ **Numeric variables** (default): A numeric variable is used to designate values that could be used in arithmetic calculations or are grouping codes for categorical variables. For example, the variables SBP (systolic blood pressure), AGE, and WEIGHT are numeric. However, an ID number, phone number, or Social Security number should not be designated as a numeric variable.

■ **Character (text, string) variables**: Character variables are used for values that are not used in arithmetic calculations. For example, a variable that uses M and F as codes for gender would be a character variable. For character variables, case matters, because to the computer a lowercase f is a different character from an uppercase F. It is important to note that a character variable may contain numeric digits. As mentioned previously, a Social Security number (e.g., 450-67-7823) or an ID number (e.g., 143212) should be designated as a character variable because their values should never be used in mathematical calculations. When designating a character variable in SAS, you must indicate to SAS that it is of character type. This is illustrated in upcoming examples.

■ **Date variables**: A date value may entered into SAS using a variety of formats, such as 10/15/09, 01/05/2010, JAN052010, and so on. As you will see in upcoming examples, dates are handled in SAS using format specifications that tell SAS how to read or display the date values. For more information about dates in SAS, see Appendix B.

METHODS OF READING DATA INTO SAS

The next few sections illustrate several techniques for entering data (creating a data set) in SAS. These are not the only ways to enter data into SAS, but they are the most common. The methods discussed are:

- Reading data using freeform list input

- Reading data using the compact method

- Reading data using column input

- Reading data using formatted input

Methods of importing data from other file formats (such as Excel) are discussed in the next chapter.

Reading Data Using Freeform List Input

A simple way to enter data into SAS is as freeform input. In this method, variable names in the DATA step are indicated by a list following the INPUT statement keyword. For example:

```
DATA MYDATA;
INPUT ID SBP DBP GENDER $ AGE WT;
```

The DATA statement names the SAS data set (as discussed above), and the INPUT statement tells SAS the names of the variables in the data set. Notice the $ following the variable name GENDER. In freeform input, this indicates to SAS that the variable GENDER is of character type (because values for this variable are M and F).

Once the data set name and variables have been defined, you must specify to SAS how to find and read in the data. One of the simplest methods for reading in a short data set is with freeform input. Freeform input requires that the data values for each subject or entity be listed one after another on a single row or line, separated by at least one blank. For example:

```
1 120 80 M 15 115
2 130 70 F 25 180
3 140 100 M 89 170
4 120 80 F 30 150
5 125 80 F 20 110
```

The first line contains the data for a single subject. The first data value (1) in that line corresponds to the first variable (ID) in the INPUT statement. The second value (120) corresponds to SBP, and so on. Each data value on each line is separated by at least one blank.

In a SAS program, a special keyword, DATALINES, tells SAS that the upcoming lines contain data. The following code (DFREEFORM.SAS) is an example of freeform input:

```
DATA MYDATA;
INPUT ID $ SBP DBP GENDER $ AGE WT;
DATALINES;
```

```
1 120 80 M 15 115
2 130 70 F 25 180
3 140 100 M 89 170
4 120 80 F 30 150
5 125 80 F 20 110
;
PROC PRINT;
RUN;
```

This program reads in five lines of data and creates a listing of the data (PROC PRINT) that is displayed in the Output window. Here are the components of this SAS program in the order in which they should occur:

1. The DATA statement tells SAS to create a data set. In this case, the data set is named MYDATA.

2. The INPUT statement indicates the variable names for the data set.

3. The DATALINES statement tells SAS that the next few lines contain data.

4. Each data line contains the values for one subject, and the values in the data line correspond to the variables named in the INPUT statement; and those data values must be separated on the line by at least one blank.

5. The semicolon following the data indicates the end of the data values. When SAS encounters the semicolon, it stops reading data values and creates an internal SAS data set table like the one illustrated by Table 2.3.

TABLE 2.3. A sample SAS data set

OBS	ID	SBP	DBP	GENDER	AGE	WT
1	1	120	80	M	15	115
2	2	130	70	F	25	180
3	3	140	100	M	89	170
4	4	120	80	F	20	150
5	105	125	80	F	20	110

Notice that the columns of the data set table match the variable names in the `INPUT` statement.

6. The `PROC PRINT` statement tells SAS to create a listing of the data. We'll learn more about `PROC PRINT` in the section "Using PROC PRINT" in Chapter 5.

7. The `RUN` statement tells SAS to finish this section of the program. Without the `RUN` statement, SAS may expect that more instructions are pending, and it will not finish the procedure. Therefore, SAS programs *must* conclude with a `RUN` statement. One of the most common errors in writing a SAS program is to omit the `RUN` statement. Don't let this happen to you!

Advantages of freeform list input Some of the advantages of freeform list input are:

■ It's easy, with very little to specify.

■ Rigid column positions are not required, making data entry easy.

■ If you have a data set in which the data are separated by blanks, this is the quickest way to get your data into SAS.

Rules and restrictions for freeform list input The following rules and restrictions govern freeform list input:

■ Every variable on each data line must be in the order specified by the `INPUT` statement.

■ Data values must be separated by at least one blank. (We'll learn about data with other delimiters in the Going Deeper section "Using Advanced INFILE Statement Options" in this chapter.)

■ Blank spaces representing missing variables are not allowed. Having missing values in the data causes values to be out of sync. If there are missing values in the data, a dot (.) should be placed in the position of that variable in the data line. (We'll learn about other missing value techniques in the section "Using IF to Assign Missing Values" in Chapter 4.) For example, a data line with `AGE` missing might read:

```
4 120 80 F . 150
```

■ Data values for character variables are restricted:

   ■ No embedded blanks are allowed within the data value for a character field (e.g., `MR ED`).

   ■ A character field can have a maximum length of eight characters.

HANDS-ON EXAMPLE

In this example you will enter data using the freeform data entry technique.

1. In the Editor window, open the file DFREEFORM.SAS. (The code was shown above.) Run the program.

2. Observe that the output listing (shown here) illustrates the same information as in Table 2.3.

Obs	ID	SBP	DBP	GENDER	AGE	WT
1	1	120	80	M	15	115
2	2	130	70	F	25	180
3	3	140	100	M	89	170
4	4	120	80	F	30	150
5	5	125	80	F	20	110

This tells you that SAS has properly read in your data and created a SAS data set that can now be used for further analysis.

Reading Data Using the Compact Method

A second version of freeform input allows you to have several subjects' data on a single line. This technique is often used in textbooks to save space. For example, here is a typical way in which a freeform data set is read into SAS:

```
DATA WEIGHT;
INPUT TREATMENT LOSS;
DATALINES;

1 1.0
1 3.0
1 -1.0
```

```
1 1.5
1 0.5
1 3.5
2 4.5
2 6.0
2 3.5
2 7.5
2 7.0
2 6.0
2 5.5
3 1.5
3-2.5
3-0.5
3 1.0
3  .5
;
PROC PRINT;
RUN;
```

To save space, the data can be compacted using an @@ option in the INPUT statement to tell SAS to continue reading each line until it runs out of data.

```
DATA WEIGHT;
INPUT TREATMENT LOSS @@;
DATALINES;

1 1.0 1 3.0 1 -1.0 1 1.5 1 0.5 1 3.5
2 4.5 2 6.0 2 3.5 2 7.5 2 7.0 2 6.0 2 5.5
3 1.5 3 -2.5 3 -0.5 3 1.0 3 .5

;
PROC PRINT;
RUN;
```

Notice the @@ on the INPUT line. This second version of the input procedure takes up less space. Other than the addition of the @@ indicator, this data entry technique has the same benefits and restrictions as the previous freeform input method.

HANDS-ON EXAMPLE

In this example you will edit a freeform data entry program to use the compact entry method.

1. Open the file DFREEFORM.SAS, which was used in the previous example. Run the program and examine the data listing in the Output window. Press F12 to clear the Output and Log windows, then return to the Editor window. (If you have not defined the function key F12, refer to the section "Using SAS Function Keys" in Chapter 1.)

2. On the INPUT line, place a space and @@ after the WT and before the semicolon.

3. Modify the data so there are two subjects per line. For example, the first two lines become:

```
1 120 80 M 15 115 2 130 70 F 25 180
```

4. Run the program and verify that the data are listed correctly in the Output window. (The output should be the same as before.)

Reading Data Using Column Input

Another technique for reading data into SAS is called column input. This data entry technique should be used when your data consist of fixed columns of values that are not necessarily separated by blanks. For example, consider the following data:

```
1120 80M15115
2130 70F25180
3140100M89170
4120 80F30150
5125 80F20110
```

This column format is a common setup for data that are read from scientific instruments or data collection devices.

Because the freeform technique will not work with these data, SAS allows you to specify which columns in the raw data set contain each variable's values. You must know the starting column and ending columns for each variable's values. The INPUT statement uses the following format:

```
INPUT variable startcol-endcol ...;
```

A specific example of the column data entry technique is:

```
DATA MYDATA;
INPUT ID $ 1 SBP 2-4 DBP 5-7 GENDER $ 8 AGE 9-10 WT 11-13;
```

Notice that the primary difference between this column input statement and the freeform list input statement is the inclusion of column ranges telling SAS where in the data set to find the information for each variable. (The $ after ID and GENDER specifies that they are character-type [text] variables.)

Here is an example program (DCOLUMN.SAS) using the column input format. This program reads in data and calculates descriptive statistics for the numeric variables using PROC MEANS (which will be discussed in detail in the section "Using PROC MEANS" in Chapter 6).

```
DATA MYDATA;
INPUT ID $ 1 SBP 2-4 DBP 5-7 GENDER $ 8 AGE 9-10 WT 11-13;
DATALINES;
1120 80M15115
2130 70F25180
3140100M89170
4120 80F30150
5125 80F20110

;
RUN;
PROC MEANS;
RUN;
```

Notice in the INPUT statement that each variable name is followed by a number or a range of numbers that tells SAS where to find the data values in the data set. The numbers for ID are found in column 1. The values for SBP are found in the column range from 2 to 4, and so on.

Advantages of column input   Some of the advantages of column input are:

- Data fields can be defined and read in any order in the INPUT statement, and unneeded columns of data can be skipped.

- Blanks are not needed to separate fields.

- Character values can range from 1 to 200 characters. For example:

```
INPUT DIAGNOSE $ 1-200;
```

- For character data values, embedded blanks are no problem (e.g., John Smith).

■ You can input only the variables you need and skip the rest. This is handy when your data set (perhaps downloaded from a large database) contains variables you're not interested in using. Read only the variables you need.

Rules and restrictions for column input   The following rules and restrictions govern column input:

■ Data values must be in fixed column positions.

■ Blank fields are read as missing.

■ Character fields are read right-justified in the field.

■ Column input has more specifications than list input. You must specify the column ranges for each variable.

You should also be aware of how SAS reads in and interprets column data. For example, the INPUT statement shown in the following code indicates that the character value data for GENDER appear in columns 1 to 3. If the value is really only one character wide, SAS reads in the value in the column and right-justifies the character data. (The numbers 1234 . . . at the top of each example represent column positions.)

```
INPUT GENDER $ 1-3;

1 2 3 4 5 6 7                    1   2    3   4
    M
  M                ---> All read as    M
M
```

In a similar way, numeric values can appear anywhere in the specified column range. Consider the use of the following INPUT statement to read values for the numeric variable X:

```
INPUT X 1-6;

1   2   3   4   5   6   7
            2   3   0
        2   3   .   0
    2   .   3   E   1
2   3
-   2   3
```

SAS reads the information in columns 1 to 6 and interprets the information as a number. The above numbers are read as 230, 23, 23 (2.3E1 is a number written in scientific notation: 2.3 times 10 to the 1st power = 23), 23, and -23.

HANDS-ON
EXAMPLE

This example illustrates the column data input method.

1. In the Editor window, open the file DCOLUMN.SAS. Run the program. The following information is shown in the Output window:

```
                    The MEANS Procedure

Variable  N         Mean      Std Dev      Minimum       Maximum

SBP       5  127.0000000    8.3666003  120.0000000  140.0000000

DBP       5   82.0000000   10.9544512   70.0000000  100.0000000

AGE       5   35.8000000   30.2605354   15.0000000   89.0000000

WT        5  145.0000000   31.6227766  110.0000000  180.0000000
```

   Notice that because ID and GENDER are character variables, information about them is not included in this table of descriptive statistics. It does not make sense to calculate a mean from text information.

2. Suppose you are interested only in the variables SBP and AGE in this data set. Modify the INPUT statement to include only SBP and AGE:

   INPUT SBP 2-4 AGE 9-10;

3. Run the modified program. The data in the columns not specified are ignored during data input, and the statistics reported are only those for SBP and AGE.

Reading Data Using Formatted Input

Another technique for reading in data from specific columns is called formatted input. This technique allows you to specify information about how SAS will interpret data as they are read into the program. SAS uses the term INFORMAT to specify an input specification that tells it how to read data. (A FORMAT specification tells SAS how to output data into a report, which is discussed in the section "Using FORMATs for Output" in this chapter.) Using an INFORMAT is helpful when you are reading data that might be in an otherwise hard-to-read format, such as date and dollar values. The syntax for formatted input is:

    DATA MYDATA;

```
INPUT @col variable1 format. @col variable2 format. ...;
```

where @col is a pointer that tells SAS from which column to start reading the information about a particular variable. Here is a specific example:

```
DATA MYDATA
INPUT @1 SBP 3. @4 DBP 3. @7 GENDER $1. @8 WT 3.
      @12 OWE COMMA9.;
```

In this example, notice that the information for each variable contains three components. Thus, for the first variable the information is:

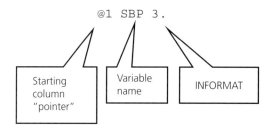

1. **The pointer** (the @ sign) tells SAS to read data for this variable beginning in the indicated column (in this case column 1).

2. **The variable name** (SBP) tells SAS that the name of this first variable is SBP.

3. **The INFORMAT** (3.) tells SAS that data at this location in each row are numbers containing three digits.

Notice the dot following the 3. INFORMAT designation. All INFORMATs and FORMATs end with a dot (.) or contain a dot. The number tells SAS the number of characters to be read. In this example, the other types of INFORMATs shown are the $1. INFORMAT, which tells SAS that GENDER is a character variable of width 1, and the COMMA9. INFORMAT, which tells SAS that the variable OWE is a number that might contain commas and dollar signs. The INFORMAT COMMA9. indicates that the data value to be read in contains nine digits. In fact, FORMATs and INFORMATs all end with a number (such as 9. or 9.2). The number specifies how many characters are in the format—that is, the number of characters (or digits) to be read in for an INFORMAT or to be written out for a FORMAT. For example, the FORMAT 9. indicates a number nine digits in length. Also, the FORMAT 9.2 indicates a number nine digits in length that contains two decimal points.

Pay special attention to the last variable in the INPUT statement, OWE. The values for this variable are difficult to read using any other technique because the data values contain dollar signs ($) and commas. (Try reading this data into Excel— it's very difficult.) The COMMA9. INFORMAT tells SAS to read in numbers that contain dollar signs and commas and to convert the values into numbers. Here is an example program (DINFORMAT.SAS) that uses the example INPUT statement:

```
DATA MYDATA;
INPUT @1 SBP 3. @4 DBP 3. @7 GENDER $1. @8 WT 3.
      @12 OWE COMMA9.;
DATALINES;
120 80M115 $5,431.00
130 70F180 $12,122
140100M170 7550
120 80F150 4,523.2
125 80F110 $1000.99
;
PROC PRINT;
RUN;
```

Notice that the OWE variable contains some particularly nasty-looking pieces of information that many programs would have trouble reading. With SAS it's a breeze. As you use SAS more, you will find that using INFORMATs can be a valuable time saver in getting data ready for analysis.

Advantages and restrictions of formatted input   Some of the advantages and restrictions of formatted input are:

- Advantages and restrictions are similar to those for column input.

- The primary difference between the column input and formatted input techniques is the ability to read in data using INFORMAT specifications.

- Formatted input is particularly handy for reading date and dollar values.

Table 2.4 shows a list of commonly used SAS FORMATs and INFORMATs. Note that in SAS terminology, an INFORMAT is used to input data. As mentioned earlier, when data are output using these criteria, the output is called a FORMAT. The code (such as 5. or COMMA9.) for an INFORMAT or a FORMAT is the same. For a complete listing of INFORMATs and FORMATs, refer to SAS help or to SAS documentation.

TABLE 2.4. Example SAS FORMATs and INFORMATs

FORMAT/INFORMAT	MEANING
5.	Five columns of data as numeric data.
$5.	Character variable with width 5, removing leading blanks.
$CHAR5.	Character variable with width 5, preserving leading blanks.
COMMA6.	Six columns of numeric data and strips out any commas or dollar signs (*i.e.*, **$40,000 is read as 40000**).
COMMA10.2	Reads or writes 10 columns of numeric data with 2 decimal places (strips commas and dollar signs.) $19,020.22 is **read as 19020.22. 1022** is written as 1,022.00.
DOLLAR10.2	FORMAT to write out numeric data in dollar format. 19020.22 **output as $19,020.22**.
MMDDYY8.	Date as **01/12/99**. (Watch out for Y2K issue.)
MMDDYY10.	Date as 04/07/2004
DATE7.	Date as **20JUL01**
DATE9.	Date as **12JAN1999**. (No Y2K issue.)
WORDDATE12.	Output date as **Jan 8, 1999** format.
WORDDATE18.	Output date as **November 12, 2004** format.
WEEKDATE29.	Output date as **Thursday, November 23, 2000** format

Using FORMATs for Output

Because the topic of FORMATs has been illustrated for the purpose of entering data, we present an example that uses INFORMATs to read in data and a FORMAT to output data. Remember that:

- Use INFORMAT to *read in data*.

- Use FORMAT to output or print out data.

- SAS INFORMATs and FORMATs always end with a period or number, such as DATE9., $11., COMMA9., or 9.2

HANDS-ON
EXAMPLE

In this example you use the INFORMAT method of reading data into a SAS data set.

1. In the Editor window, open the file DINFORMAT.SAS (program file shown above) and run the program. The output should look like this:

Obs	SBP	DBP	GENDER	WT	OWE
1	120	80	M	115	5431.00
2	130	70	F	180	12122.00
3	140	100	M	170	7550.00
4	120	80	F	150	4523.20
5	125	80	F	110	1000.99

2. Modify the INPUT statement by replacing the INFORMAT comma9. with $9.. This tells SAS to read in the data for the variable OWE as character data rather than as numeric data.

3. Run the modified program and observe the output. How has it changed? Note that the new OWE variable read in with the $9. FORMAT cannot be used in any calculation because it is not numeric.

A FORMAT statement within the DATA step is used to tell SAS how data will be presented in output. The FORMAT statement, which appears in the DATA step, uses the following syntax:

```
FORMAT VAR1 FORMAT1. VAR2 VAR3 VAR4 FORMAT2.etc... .;
```

FORMAT is the SAS keyword that begins the statement. VAR1 is a variable name to which a format is to be applied and FORMAT1. is the name of the FORMAT (such as 3., COMMA6., DATE9., etc.) to apply to VAR1. FORMAT2. applies to VAR2, VAR3, and VAR4. You may define any number of FORMATs to variables within this statement. The following code illustrates the use of the FORMAT statement:

```
DATA MYDATA;
INPUT @1 NAME $11. @12 BDATE DATE9.;
FORMAT BDATE WORDDATE12.;   * Assigns an output format
                                to BDATE;

DATALINES;
Bill        08JAN1952
Jane        02FEB1953
Clyde       23MAR1949

;
PROC PRINT;
RUN;
```

In this SAS program, the INFORMAT DATE9. is used to read in a data value called BDATE. (Refer to Table 2.4 to see how the data in the data set match the DATE9. INFORMAT.) The FORMAT statement tells SAS to use the output format WORDDATE12. whenever the BDATE variable is output.

Notice that the date format has been changed from the cryptic *08JAN1952* format on input to a more readable *Jan 8, 1952* format on output.

HANDS-ON
EXAMPLE

In this example you will use INFORMATs to read in date values and FORMATs to write out date values.

1. In the Editor window, open the file DINFORMAT2.SAS (program file shown above) and run the program. The output should look like this:

Obs	NAME	BDATE
1	Bill	Jan 8, 1952
2	Jane	Feb 2, 1953
3	Clyde	Mar 23, 1949

In the FORMAT statement, change the format for BDATE to WEEKDATE29., re-run the program. (Be sure to include the period at the end of the format specification.) How does that change the output?

3. Enter a new line of data containing your first name and your birthdate. Make sure your new data line up (i.e., are in the same columns) with the current data. Re-run the program. On what day of the week were you born?

4. Put an asterisk before the FORMAT line. An asterisk changes a SAS statement into a comment that is ignored when a program is run. Re-run the edited SAS program—how does that change the output? Why? (The answer is that SAS stores dates as integers, and when there is no format assigned to a date variable, the internal representation of the date is output instead of a date value. See Appendix C for more information about dates.)

Reading External Data Using INFILE

In the examples used so far, the DATALINES statement has been used to tell SAS that data records follow the program statements in the DATA step. If your data are already in a computer file, you can instruct SAS to read the records from the computer file using the INFILE statement.

For example, in this world of data, data everywhere, data sets are available by download from a number of sources. Data are often in a text (raw data) file where the values are in fixed columns. Thus, in these situations you can use either the column input or formatted input technique to read the data into SAS. In practice, because these data sets may contain hundreds or thousands of rows (thus making it difficult to embed them into your SAS code), you should read the data from these files using the INFILE technique.

The INFILE statement is used to identify an external ASCII (text) file in SAS. It is an alternative to the DATALINES statement. The general form for the INFILE statement is:

```
INFILE filespecification options;
```

For example, the file EXAMPLE.DAT contains 50 lines of data in ACSII format. (You can look at this data file using Notepad or any text editor or word processor.) The first few lines are:

```
       AGE  TIME1   TIME2 TIME3
101 A   12  22.3  25.3  28.2  30.6  5  0
102 A   11  22.8  27.5  33.3  35.8  5  0
104 B   12  22.8  30.0  32.8  31.0  4  0
110 A   12  18.5  26.0  29.0  27.9  5  1
```

Here is an example SAS program that reads in the first five columns of this data file:

```
DATA MYDATA;
INFILE 'C:\SASDATA\EXAMPLE.DAT';
INPUT  ID $ 1-3 GP $ 5 AGE 6-9
    TIME1 10-14 TIME2 15-19
    TIME3 20-24;
PROC MEANS;
RUN;
```

Notice that the INFILE statement must appear in the code *before* the INPUT statement that reads the data lines. When run, this code produces the following output:

```
                    The MEANS Procedure
Variable   N        Mean      Std Dev      Minimum      Maximum

AGE       50   10.4600000   2.4261332   4.0000000   15.0000000

TIME1     50   21.2680000   1.7169551   17.0000000   24.2000000

TIME2     50   27.4400000   2.6590623   21.3000000   32.3000000

TIME3     50   30.4920000   3.0255942   22.7000000   35.9000000
```

Notice that there is no DATALINES statement—the INFILE statement eliminates the need for it. Once you have defined an INFILE statement, SAS automatically reads the data from that file using your specification in the INPUT statement. To summarize:

■ **Data in the program code:** Use a DATALINE statement.

■ **Data read from external source:** Use an INFILE statement.

In this example you will read in data from an external file and limit the number of variables read into the SAS data set.

1. Open the SAS program file DINPUT.SAS.

```
DATA MYDATA;
INFILE 'C:\SASDATA\EXAMPLE.DAT';
INPUT  ID $ 1-3 GP $ 5 AGE 6-9 TIME1 10-14 TIME2 15-19 TIME3 20-24;
PROC MEANS;
RUN;
```

   Run the program and observe the output shown above.

2. Modify the INPUT statement to read in only the variables ID, GP, AGE, and TIME3.

3. Re-run the program and observe the difference in output. Note that the new output includes statistics for AGE and TIME3. Why are statistics for ID and GP not included in the output?

GOING DEEPER: MORE TECHNIQUES FOR ENTERING DATA

SAS includes myriad ways to read in data. Techniques covered thus far are the most common methods. The following additional techniques can also be helpful when your data are listed in multiple records per subject and when your data are in comma-delimited format.

Reading Multiple Records per Observation

Occasionally, data will be stored in such a way that multiple lines (or records) are required to hold one subject's information. SAS is able to associate observations that span more than one line to one subject. Suppose input records are designed so that each subject's information is contained on three lines:

```
10011 M 15 115
    120 80 254
    15 65 102
10012 F 25 180
   130 70 240
    34 120 132
```

```
10013 M 89 170
    140 100 279
    19 89 111
etc.
```

One method for reading these data into a SAS data set is to have three consecutive INPUT statements. Each INPUT statement advances to the next record (but stays with the same subject). Thus, each of the three records in the data file becomes one "subject" in the SAS data set:

```
INPUT ID $ SEX $ AGE WT;
INPUT SBP DBP BLDCHL;
INPUT OBS1 OBS2 OBS3;
```

Another method for reading in these data uses the / indicator to advance to the next line. Each time a / is seen in the INPUT statement, it tells SAS to go to the next physical record in the data file to find additional data for the same subject:

```
INPUT ID $ SEX $ AGE WT/ SBP DBP BLDCHL/ OBS1 OBS2
    OBS3;
```

A third way to read these data is by using the #n indicator to advance to the first column of the nth record in the group. In this case, #2 means jump to the second line in the data file. The highest #n tells SAS how many lines are used for each subject:

```
INPUT ID $ SEX $ AGE WT #2 SBP DBP BLDCHL #3 OBS1 OBS2
    OBS3;
```

or in another order:

```
INPUT #2 SBP DBP BLDCHL #1 ID $ SEX $ AGE WT #3 OBS1
    OBS2 OBS3
```

An advantage of this technique is that you can read the data lines into SAS in any order, as specified by the #n. Note that all of these methods require that there be *the same number of records for each subject*. If there are differing numbers of records per subject, SAS can still read in the data, but that technique is beyond the scope of this book.

An example of a program (DMULTLINE.SAS) to read multiple-line data into SAS is the following:

```
DATA MYDATA;
INPUT ID $ SEX $ AGE WT/ SBP DBP BLDCHL/ OBS1 OBS2
    OBS3;
DATALINES;
```

```
10011 M 15 115
   120 80 254
   15 65 102
10012 F 25 180
   130 70 240
   34 120 132
10013 M 89 170
   140 100      279
   19 89 111
;
```

PROC PRINT;
RUN;

In this case, we used the / advance indicator technique to read the three data lines.

Using Advanced INFILE Statement Options

When you acquire a data set from another source that you intend to read into SAS using an INFILE statement, the data set may not be in the exact format you need. To help you read in external data, SAS includes a number of options you can use to customize your INFILE statement. They include the following:

DLM

> Allows you to define a delimiter to be something other than a blank. For example, if data are separated by commas, include the option DLM ',' in the INFILE statement.

DSD

> Instructs SAS to recognize two consecutive delimiters as a missing value. For example, the information M,15,,115 would be read as M, 15, Missing, 115. Also, it permits the use of a delimiter within quoted strings. For example, the data value "Robert Downey, Jr." would be read properly, meaning that SAS wouldn't interpret the comma in the name as signaling a new value.

MISSOVER

> Tells SAS that if it encounters the end of a data line without finding enough data to match all of the variables in the INPUT statement to go to the next line and start reading the remaining variables from the INPUT statement from that next line.

FIRSTOBS=

> Tells SAS on what line you want it to start reading your raw data file. This is handy if your data file contains one or more header lines or if you want to skip the first portion of the data lines.

OBS=
Indicates which line in your raw data file should be treated as the last record to be read by SAS.

There are a number of other options, but these are the most commonly used. Here is an example of how some of these options can be included in the INFILE statement to read data from a file. Suppose the first few lines in a data file (EXAMPLE.CSV) are:

```
GROUP,AGE,TIME1,TIME2,TIME3,Time4,SOCIO
A,12,22.3,25.3,28.2,30.6,5
A,11,22.8,27.5,33.3,35.8,5
B,12,22.8,30.0,32.8,31.0,4
A,12,18.5,26.0,29.0,27.9,5
B,9,19.5,25.0,25.3,26.6,5
B,11,23.5,28.8,34.2,35.6,5
```

Note that this is a comma-delimited data file. The first line is a header containing variable names. Suppose you want to read the first 25 lines of data from this file. (The file contains 50 lines of data.) The following code (DINFILE.SAS) will accomplish that:

```
DATA MYDATA;
INFILE 'C:\SASDATA\EXAMPLE.CSV' DLM=',' FIRSTOBS=2
       OBS=26;
INPUT GROUP $ AGE TIME1 TIME2 TIME3 Time4 SOCIO;
PROC MEANS;
RUN;
```

Notice that the DLM=',' option tells SAS that the data are comma delimited. The FIRSTOBS=2 option instructs SAS to start reading the data with the second line, and OBS=26 tell SAS to end with line 26, which means that it will read in the first 25 lines of data. The PROC MEANS produces the output

```
                          The MEANS Procedure
```

Variable	N	Mean	Std Dev	Minimum	Maximum
AGE	25	9.8800000	2.5547342	4.0000000	14.0000000
TIME1	25	21.0408400	1.7025391	17.0000000	23.5000000
TIME2	25	27.2400000	2.4166092	21.3000000	30.5000000
TIME3	25	29.9520000	3.3461570	22.7000000	34.4000000
Time4	25	30.3320000	3.8348968	21.2000000	35.8000000
SOCIO	25	4.0400000	1.3988090	1.0000000	5.0000000

SUMMARY

One of the most powerful features of SAS, and a reason it is used in many research and corporate environments, is that it is very adaptable for reading in data from a number of sources. This chapter showed only the tip of the iceberg. More information about getting data into SAS is provided in the next chapter. For more advanced techniques, see the SAS documentation.

EXERCISES

2.1. Input data into SAS.

a. Open the SAS file EX_2.1.SAS.

```
DATA CHILDREN;
* WT is in column 1-2, HEIGHT is in 4-5 and AGE is in 7-8;
* Create an INPUT statement that will read in this data set;
INPUT     ;
DATALINES;
64 57 8
71 59 10
53 49 6
67 62 11
55 51 8
58 50 8
77 55 10
57 48 9
56 42 10
51 42 6
76 61 12
68 57 9
;
Title "Exercise 2.1 - your name";
PROC PRINT;
RUN;
```

b. Notice that the INPUT statement is incomplete. Using one of the input techniques discussed in this chapter, complete the INPUT statement and run the resulting program.

2.2. Complete the INPUT statement using column input.

The file EX_2.2.SAS contains a partial SAS program that includes data in the following defined columns:

VARIABLE NAME	COLUMN	TYPE
ID	1-5	Text
AGE	6-7	Numeric
GENDER	8	Text (M or F)
MARRIED	9	Text (Y or N)
WEIGHT IN POUNDS	10-12	Numeric

a. Complete the SAS code snippet shown below using the column input technique.

```
DATA PEOPLE;
INPUT ID $ 1-5 ; * finish INPUT statement;
DATALINES;
0000123MY201
0002143FY154
0004333FN133
0005429MN173
0013249FY114
;
Title "Exercise 2.2 - your name";
PROC PRINT;
RUN;
```

E: bpdata.dat

b. Run the program. Verify that the output lists the data correctly.

2.3. Complete the INPUT statement using formatted input.

The SAS program EX_2.3.SAS contains a data file with the following defined columns:

VARIABLE NAME	COLUMN	TYPE
ID	1-5	Text
GENDER	6	Text (M or F)
MARRIED	7	Numeric 0,1
BDATE	8-16	Date

a. Complete the SAS code snippet shown below using the formatted input technique. Refer to Table 2.4 to determine which date INFORMAT to use. For the output FORMAT, use the format that outputs dates in the Thursday, November 23, 2000 format.

```
DATA BIRTHDATES;
INPUT ID $ 1-5 ;            * finish INPUT statement;
FORMAT BDATE someformat.;  * finish OUTPUT FORMAT
                                     statement;
DATALINES;
00001M112JAN1979
00021F003MAR1959
00043F018JUL1981
00054M022DEC1968
00132F110JUL1952

;
Title "Exercise 2.3 - your name";
PROC PRINT;
RUN;
```

2.4. Read an external data file.

The file BPDATA.DAT is a raw (ASCII text) data file that contains data with the following defined columns:

VARIABLE NAME	COLUMN	TYPE
ID	1	Text
SBP	2-4	Numeric
DBP	5-7	Numeric
GENDER	8	Text (M or F)
AGE	9-10	Numeric
WEIGHT	11-13	Numeric

a. Complete the following SAS code snippet (EX_2.4.SAS) to read in this data set. The data are in the file named C:\SASDATA\BPDATA.DAT.

```
DATA BPDATA;
INFILE 'inputfilename'; * Finish the INFILE statement;
INPUT ID 1 SBP 2-4 ;    * Finish the input statement;
Title "Exercise 2.4 - your name";
PROC MEANS;
RUN;
```

b. Make sure you include your name in the title statement.

c. Run the program and observe the results.

2.5. Going Deeper: Read a large external file.

In this exercise you will read data from an external raw data file (TRAUMA. CSV) in comma-separated-values (CSV) format that contains thousands of records. The first few records look like this:

```
SUBJECT,AGE,GENDER,PLACE,STATUS
1868,12.1,Female,Street,Alive
1931,18.7,Female,Street,Alive
1950,16.6,Female,Street,Alive
1960,8.5,Female,Street,Alive
2019,6.7,Male,Unknown,Alive
2044,7.8,Male,Street,Alive
```

Notice that the first line (row) in this file contains a header with variable names.

a. Complete the SAS code snippet (EX_2.5.SAS):

```
DATA TRAUMA2;
INFILE 'filename' DLM=  FIRSTOBS= ; * Finish the INFILE
                                      statement;
INPUT SUBJECT $ AGE  GENDER $ PLACE $ STATUS $;
TITLE "Exercise 2.5 - your name";
PROC MEANS;
RUN;
```

Finish this incomplete code by doing the following:

I.   Enter the appropriate filename in the INFILE statement.

II. Place an appropriate value after the DLM = statement.

III. Place an appropriate value after the FIRSTOBS= statement.

IV. Notice in the INPUT statement that the only numeric variable is AGE.

V.   Run the corrected program.

You should get the following output:

```
            The MEANS Procedure
          Analysis Variable : AGE
```

N	Mean	Std Dev	Minimum	Maximum
16242	10.6396010	5.8030633	0	21.0000000

VI. How many records are in this data set?

b. Revise the program slightly: This time include an OBS= statement so the program will read in only the first 50 records (not including the header line).

```
DATA TRAUMA2;
INFILE 'filename' DLM=  FIRSTOBS=  OBS = ; * Finish
                                              statement;
INPUT INC_KEY $ AGE  GENDER $ INJSITE $ DISSTATUS $;
Title "Exercise 2.5b - your name";
PROC PRINT; * Note change to PROC PRINT;
RUN;
```

I.   Enter the appropriate filename in the INFILE statement.

II.   Place an appropriate value after the DLM= statement.

III.   Place an appropriate value after the FIRSTOBS= statement.

IV.   Place the value 51 in the OBS= statement (to read in only the first 50 records—remember that record 1 is skipped).

V.   Change the PROC MEANS to PROC PRINT.

VI.   Run the revised program. The Output window should include a listing of the first 50 records in the data set.

CHAPTER

3

READING, WRITING, AND IMPORTING DATA

LEARNING OBJECTIVES

- To be able to work with SAS libraries and permanent data sets
- To be able to read and write permanent SAS data sets
- To be able to interactively import data from another program
- To be able to define SAS libraries using program code
- To be able to import data using code
- To be able to discover the contents of a SAS data set

Research data sets are growing by leaps and bounds. Some institutions, government agencies, and businesses gather information from individual transactions, which can result in hundreds of thousands of data values each day. Whether the data set you are working with has millions of records or a few hundred isn't the point of this chapter. The point is that once you read in your data, you will want to store it in a way that makes it easy to retrieve for analysis. That means that you may want to store more than raw data values. You'll want your data set to include variable names, labels for your variables, manipulations you've done to get it ready for analysis, and other information.

WORKING WITH SAS LIBRARIES AND PERMANENT DATA SETS

It can be time consuming to reenter or re-create variables, labels, recodings, and calcu-lations each time you run an analysis. To simplify matters, SAS allows you to create a permanent data set that, once created, is easy to access and use. Keep in mind that a SAS data set is different from a SAS program (code) file. The code files, which we used in the previous chapter, contain a listing of SAS commands and raw data values and can be used to create a SAS data set, but the code file is not a SAS data set. Keep the following points in mind. SAS data sets:

- are created by a `DATA` statement (there are other ways of creating a SAS data set that we'll learn later in this chapter)

- are an internal representation of the data created by the `DATA` statement

- contain more than the data values—they can contain variable names, labels, the results of codings, calculations, and variable formats

- are referred to by a name that indicates whether the data set is temporary or permanent

All of the SAS data sets created in Chapter 2 were temporary. That is, when the SAS program ends, the data set goes away. This chapter shows you how to create a SAS data set that is permanently stored in a folder on your hard disk (or flash drive, network drive, or other storage medium).

The technique for saving a SAS data set as a file in a folder location is different from what is used in most Windows applications. Instead of using the File ⇨ Save paradigm, you store a SAS data set using code in a SAS program. To illustrate how this works, you need to know the basic differences between a temporary and a permanent SAS data set:

- **A temporary SAS data set is** named with a single-level name, such as `MEASLES` or `MAR2000`. It is created in a `DATA` statement and is available for analysis only during one active session of SAS. When you exit the SAS program, all temporary data sets are erased.

- **A permanent SAS data set** is a file saved on your hard disk and is designated with a two-part name, such as `RESEARCH.SOMEDATA` or `MYSASLIB.MEASLES2009`.

The prefix to the data set is called the SAS library name. The library name is a nick-name for a location on your hard disk (such as C:\SASDATA) where you store your SAS data sets. You may also refer to a permanent SAS data set using a Windows file path, such as C:\SASDATA\SOMEDATA or C:\RESEARCH\MEASLES2009. The following information describes how to use both techniques.

> Technically, all SAS data sets have two-part names. Any SAS data set name using a single-level name, such as MEASLES, is seen internally by SAS as the data set WORK.MEASLES. The WORK prefix is the default temporary library name used by SAS. Any data set with the WORK prefix is a temporary data set and is erased when you exit the SAS program.

This section presents information on how to read and write permanent SAS data sets in the Windows environment, and in this chapter's Going Deeper sections we'll present a technique that is used in both Windows and other operating systems. Figure 3.1 provides a graphical representation of how reading data into SAS works.

READING AND CREATING PERMANENT SAS DATA SETS USING THE WINDOWS FILE NAME TECHNIQUE

The Windows file name technique for creating a permanent SAS data set is straight-forward. Instead of using a temporary SAS data set name such as PEOPLE (as in the examples in Chapter 2) in the SAS DATA statement, use a Windows file name. For example, instead of using

```
DATA PEOPLE;
```
use
```
DATA "C:\SASDATA\PEOPLE";
```

How you implement this in a SAS program is illustrated in the following example. Consider this SAS code (WRITE.SAS):

FIGURE 3.1. *Reading and storing data in SAS*

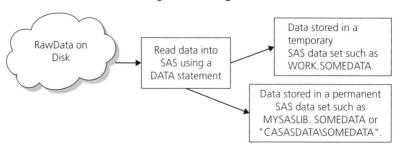

```
DATA "C:\SASDATA\PEOPLE";
INPUT ID $ 1 SBP 2-4 DBP 5-7 GENDER $ 8 AGE 9-10
  WT 11-13;
DATALINES;
1120 80M15115
2130 70F25180
3140100M89170
4120 80F30150
5125 80F20110
;
RUN;
PROC MEANS;
RUN;
```

This code creates a data set called PEOPLE on your hard drive in the C:\SASDATA folder, and the Window file name of this permanent file is PEOPLE.SAS7BDAT. To summarize:

- The statement **DATA** PEOPLE; creates an internal SAS data set that is temporary. (It vanishes when you exit SAS.)

- The statement **DATA** "C:\SASDATA\PEOPLE"; creates a permanent SAS data set stored on your hard drive.

In fact, you can substitute the Windows file name specification anywhere you can use the SAS data set name specification. This is illustrated in several of the upcoming examples.

HANDS-ON
EXAMPLE

This example illustrates how to write data to a permanent SAS data set.

1. In the Editor window, open the file WRITE.SAS. Note that the data statement contains a Windows file designation in quotation marks:

    ```
    DATA "C:\SASDATA\PEOPLE";
    ```

2. Run this program. Click the Log tab at the bottom of the SAS screen and find the following note:

    ```
    NOTE: The data set C:\SASDATA\PEOPLE has 5 observations and
    6 variables.
    ```

    (Continued)

> This NOTE in the Log window indicates that a data set named PEOPLE was created at the Windows hard drive location C:\SASDATA.
>
> 3. Because the data set name in SAS is C:\SASDATA\PEOPLE, it follows that the data are stored in the C:\SASDATA folder. To verify this, open your C:\SASDATA folder. Verify that the C:\SASDATA folder contains a file named PEOPLE.SAS7BDAT. The .SAS7BDAT file extension indicates to the Windows operating system the type of file, and in this case it indicates that this file is a SAS data set. (The .SAS7BDAT file extension may not be visible in Windows Explorer, depending on whether your Windows folder options include displaying file extensions.)

READING DATA FROM PERMANENT SAS DATA SETS

In a similar way, a Windows file name can be used to read a permanent SAS data set (a file with the .SAS7BDAT extension). For example, suppose you have a data set in the C:\SASDATA folder named SOMEDATA.SAS7BDAT. To access that data in SAS, you could include the full Windows file path in a DATA= statement in any SAS PROC statement. For example:

```
PROC MEANS DATA='C:\SASDATA\SOMEDATA';RUN;
```

HANDS-ON
EXAMPLE

In this example you will read data from an existing SAS data set.

1. In the Editor window, open the file READFILE.SAS. The entire program consists of a single line of code:

```
PROC MEANS DATA='c:\sasdata\somedata';RUN;
```

Note that the DATA= statement includes the information

```
DATA='c:\sasdata\somedata';
```

2. Run this program and observe that SAS used the data from the file SOMEDATA.SAS7BDAT to calculate descriptive statistics on the numeric variables from that data set. This method of reading SAS data sets works only in the Windows environment.

READING AND CREATING PERMANENT SAS DATA SETS USING A SAS LIBRARY

In the previous section, you read and wrote SAS data sets to and from a Windows folder (`C:\SASDATA`) by specifying a Windows file name (`C:\SASTATA\SOMEDATA`), which indicated the complete file name for the `SOMEDATA.SAS7BDAT` file. Another technique for reading and writing SAS data sets has been used by SAS in other computer operating systems since before the advent of Windows, and it is commonly employed by SAS users in both Windows and other operating systems. It involves creating a shortcut name to a drive location called (in SAS terminology) a library name. This library name is a *nickname* (similar to a Windows shortcut name) for a drive location (in Windows terminology, a folder). For example, suppose you have a folder named

> `C:\RESEARCH\COUNTYDATA\MEASLES\YR2009\`

in which you have stored one or more permanent SAS data sets, one of which is `ZIPCODES.SAS7BDAT`. Instead of referring to the entire file path

> `C:\RESEARCH\COUNTYDATA\MEASLES\YR2009\ZIPCODES.SAS7BDAT`

in your `DATA` statement, you can create a nickname (for example, `DATA09`) that can be used as a shortcut for referring to a specific SAS data set in this folder. Thus, the data file named `ZIPCODES.SAS7BDAT` in the `DATA09` library is referred to in SAS (using the much-shortened name) as `DATA09.ZIPCODES`. The `DATA09` prefix is a nickname for in the folder `C:\RESEARCH\COUNTYDATA\MEASLES\YR2009\`, and `ZIPCODES` is the SAS data file name. Examples and exercises in this book use a SAS library with the following characteristics:

- The location of the hard drive folder: `C:\SASDATA`
- The SAS library name: `MYSASLIB`

Note that if you've chosen to place the sample files for this book in a different folder, you need to make appropriate adjustments in the Hands-on Examples and chapter exercises.

This section describes how to create the relationship linking a hard drive location to a SAS Library name. Two important points to grasp are:

- **Every SAS library has a name** such as `MYSASLIB`, `RESEARCH`, `MYDATA`, and so on.

- Every SAS library name **is a nickname** that points to a specific folder such as `C:\SASDATA`, `N:\NETWORK\DRIVE`, `I:\MYFLASH\DRIVE`, and so on.

Within the SAS program, every SAS data set has two parts to its name. For example, the SAS data set referred to as `MYSASLIB.MAY2000` consists of

- The **library** named `MYSASLIB`
- The **data set** named `MAY2000`

This SAS naming convention is used for SAS data sets in all types of computers and operating systems—mainframes, Windows, Mac OS X, UNIX, and so on. Once you learn how to use SAS in Windows, you can easily transfer that skill to any other computer platform.

To summarize, once you've created a SAS library named `MYSASLIB` that points to `C:\SASDATA`, the data set you refer to as `MYSASLIB.MAY2000` is stored on your hard drive using the name `C:\SASDATA\MAY2000.SAS7BDAT`.

CREATING A SAS LIBRARY USING A DIALOG BOX

The easiest way to create a SAS library in Windows (with a custom name of your own choosing) is to use the New Library dialog box shown in Figure 3.2. To display this dialog box, make the SAS Explorer window active (click the Explorer tab at the bottom of the left window in the main SAS screen). Select File ⇨ New, click the Library option, and then click OK.

In the Name field, enter the name you want to assign to the library. In this book, the shortcut name `MYSASLIB` is used. In the Path field, enter the location of the directory. In this book, the files are assumed to be in the `C:\SASDATA` folder on the hard drive. You will typically not change anything in the Engine drop-down or the Options field. Once you've created the `MYSASLIB` library, all SAS data files in `C:\SASDATA` become a part of the library.

FIGURE 3.2. *New Library dialog box*

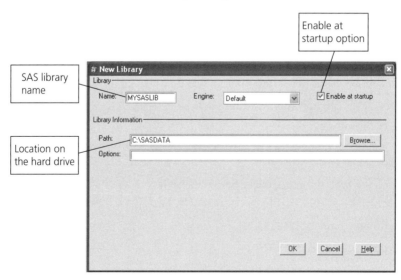

Notice the option Enable at startup. If you intend to use this library name repeatedly, you should choose this option by checking the box next to it. Choosing the Enable at startup option tells SAS to remember the library name and location and to reactivate it each time the SAS program is started.

HANDS-ON
EXAMPLE

In this example you will define a SAS library and give it a nickname.

1. Make the SAS Explorer window active (click the Explorer tab at the left bottom on the main SAS screen). The title bar at the top of the window should read Contents of 'SAS Environment' (this window is similar to Windows Explorer). (If you are not currently in the SAS Environment window, select View ⇨ Up one level as many times as are required to get to this window.) Select File ⇨ New, select the Library option, and click OK. The dialog box shown in Figure 3.2 appears.

2. Enter `MYSASLIB` in the Name field and `C:\SASDATA` in the Path field and check the Enable at startup option. (Or you can use a path to a flash drive or any other location where your SAS data set is stored.) Click OK to dismiss the dialog box.

3. On the left side of your SAS screen, click the Explorer tab. You should see a Libraries icon that resembles a filing cabinet, as shown in Figure 3.3.

FIGURE 3.3. *The SAS Library icon*

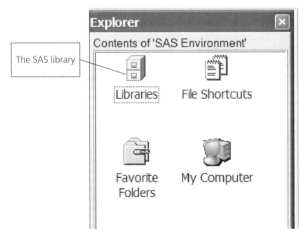

Double-click the Libraries icon. *(Continued)*

4. A new window called Active Libraries appears. This window shows which SAS library names have been defined. If you performed the previous steps correctly, you will see a library named MYSASLIB. Double-click the MYSASLIB icon to display the contents of MYSASLIB window. In that window you will see a list of the permanent SAS data sets (i.e., files that have an .SAS7BDAT extension) that are in the C:\SASDATA folder. One of the permanent SAS data sets listed is named SOMEDATA.

5. Double-click the SOMEDATA icon. A window like the one illustrated in Figure 3.4 is displayed.

FIGURE 3.4. *SAS Viewtable*

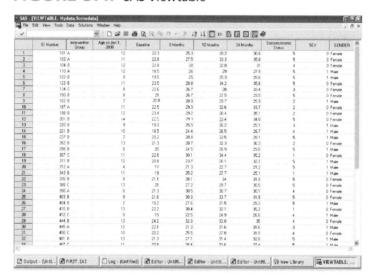

6. This spreadsheet window is called the SAS Viewtable. It displays the contents of a SAS data set.

7. Close the MYSASLIB.SOMEDATA data set by selecting File ⇨ Close or by clicking the X at the top right of the window.

8. Return to the Editor window and open the file LIBNAME1.SAS, which contains the following short SAS program:

```
PROC MEANS DATA=MYSASLIB.SOMEDATA;
RUN;
```

9. Run this program. In the Output window you'll see that SAS has calculated and reported descriptive statistics for the numeric values in the MYSASLIB. SOMEDATA data set. (You may have to click the Output tab to see the results.)

Any SAS data file (with an .SAS7BDAT extension) that you copy into the Windows folder linked to a SAS library name automatically becomes a part of that SAS library. Thus, if you acquire an .SAS7BDAT file from some source, all you have to do to make that file available in the SAS `MYSASLIB` library is to copy that file (using Windows Explorer) to the `C:\SASDATA` folder.

This Hands-on Example illustrated how to create a SAS library shortcut name and how to use that name to refer to a SAS data set in a `PROC` statement. One reason for creating a SAS library nickname linked to a folder is to provide you with a location to place imported data files. The next section illustrates that procedure.

IMPORTING DATA FROM ANOTHER PROGRAM

In Chapter 2, we showed how to read data from a raw (ASCII) text file using the `INPUT` statement. SAS can also read in or import data from a variety of other formats. This can be done using a step-by-step Wizard whose use is illustrated in this section. The imported data set can be stored in a temporary or a permanent SAS data set. Importing data using program code is described in a Going Deeper section later in the chapter.

Interactively Importing Microsoft Excel Data

Before importing Microsoft Excel data, examine the Excel file to verify that it is ready to import into SAS. The file should meet these two criteria:

- The first row should contain the names of the SAS variables and should adhere to SAS naming conventions. (These were discussed in Chapter 2.)

- Each column in the spreadsheet should contain data corresponding to the variable name in row 1 and should be consistent with the desired variable type. For example an `AGE` variable column should contain only numbers. If an age is unknown, the entry should be a designated missing value code (such as `-99`) or left blank. Blanks in the spreadsheet will be read in SAS as a default missing value of . (dot).

If the Excel file does not satisfy these criteria, modify it to conform to the requirements before proceeding to import the data into SAS. For a more thorough discussion of preparing Excel data for importing, see Elliott et al. (2006). Figure 3.5 shows an Excel file (`EXAMPLE.XLS`) ready to be imported. Note that for each column, row 1 contains the name of the variable (in SAS variable format) and each column contains data consistent with the data type of the variable.

To import these data, you can use the SAS Import Wizard by selecting File ⇨ Import data. The initial screen of the Import Wizard is displayed in Figure 3.6.

FIGURE 3.5. *Excel data ready for import*

	A	B	C	D	E	F	G	H
1	GROUP	AGE	TIME1	TIME2	TIME3	TIME4	STATUS	
2	A	12	22.3	25.3	28.2	30.6	5	
3	A	11	22.8	27.5	33.3	35.8	5	
4	B	12	22.8	30.0	32.8	31.0	4	
5	A	12	18.5	26.0	29.0	27.9	5	
6	B	9	19.5	25.0	25.3	26.6	5	
7	B	11	23.5	28.8	34.2	35.6	5	
8	C	8	22.6	26.7	28.0	33.4	3	
9	B	8	21.0	26.7	27.5	29.5	5	
10	B	7	20.9	28.9	29.7	25.9	2	
11	A	11	22.5	29.3	32.6	33.7	2	
12	B	12	23.4	29.2	30.4	35.1	2	
13	B	14	22.5	29.3	33.4	34.8	5	
14	B	9	19.3	25.5	26.2	25.1	3	

FIGURE 3.6. *Initial screen of the SAS Import Wizard*

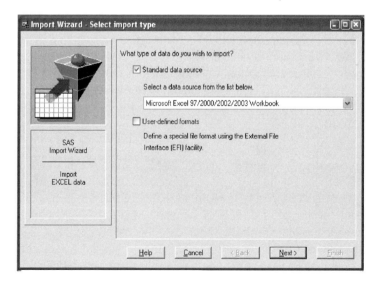

The Wizard prompts you to enter the following information:

- Type of file to import (in this case Excel 97/2000/2002/2003 Workbook [.xls])

- The name of the Excel file to import (such as C:\SASDATA\EXAMPLE.XLS)

- The SAS library where you want to store the imported data; select the WORK library to import the data into temporary storage or a library name to store the data in a permanent file

HANDS-ON EXAMPLE

In this example you will use the SAS import wizard to import data from an Excel file.

1. Begin the SAS Import Wizard by selecting File ⇨ Import data.

2. From the Select a data source drop-down list, select the type of file you want to import. See Figure 3.6. In this case select Microsoft Excel 97/2000/2002/2003 Workbook. After you've selected the type of file to import, click Next.

3. Enter the name of the Excel file to import: In the Connect to MS Excel dialog box, enter the path of the file, or click the Browse button and locate the file. As shown in Figure 3.7, indicate the file path C:\SASDATA\ CARLIST.XLS. Click OK.

FIGURE 3.7. *Selecting an Excel file name*

4. Select the table to import: The next dialog box prompts you to specify the table you want to import. An Excel file can contain several worksheets. At this prompt, select the CARS$ table. Click Next.

5. Assign a SAS file name and indicate where the data should be stored. As discussed earlier in this chapter, every SAS data set is stored in a location called a library. You can select either the temporary library (WORK) or a

(Continued)

permanent library name. In this case, select the WORK library and name the data set (member name) CARLIST as shown in Figure 3.8.

FIGURE 3.8. *Selecting the library and member name*

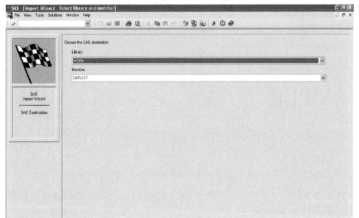

6. Click Next. SAS asks if you want to create a file that contains the code that could be used to create this data set. Skip this option by clicking Finish. The data in the CARLIST.XLS file are imported into SAS and are assigned the SAS data set name CARLIST. To verify that the SAS data set has been created:

   a. Click the Explorer tab at the bottom left of the SAS screen. (If necessary, select View ⇨ Up one level until you are at the Contents of SAS Environment window.)

   b. Click the Libraries icon, then the Work icon. You should see a data set (table) named CARLIST.

   c. Double-click the CARLIST table icon, and a table appears that contains the data imported from the CARLIST.XLS file. This data set is now ready to use in SAS. Note that because it is in the WORK library, it is a temporary data set.

7. In the Editor window, enter the following code:

```
PROC PRINT DATA=CARLIST;RUN;
```

Run the program. Here are the first few records of the output listing:

Obs	Auto	MPG	CYLINDERS	SIZE	HP	WEIGHT	ACCEL	ENG_TYPE
1	Buick Estate Wagon	16.9	8	350	155	4.360	14.9	1
2	Ford Country Sq. Wagon	15.5	8	351	142	4.054	14.3	1
3	Chevy Malibu Wagon	19.2	8	267	125	3.605	15.0	1
4	Chrys Lebaron Wagon	18.5	8	360	150	3.940	13.0	1
5	Chevette	30.0	4	98	68	2.155	16.5	0
6	Toyota Corona	27.5	4	134	95	2.560	14.2	0
7	Datsun 510	27.2	4	119	97	2.300	14.7	0
8	Dodge Omni	30.9	4	105	75	2.230	14.5	0
9	Audi 5000	20.3	5	131	103	2.830	15.9	0

etc...

8. Re-import this Excel data file. This time, select the library named MYSASLIB (instead of WORK) and name the SAS data set AUTOLIST. When you have imported the Excel file into a SAS data set, its name becomes MYSASLIB. AUTOLIST and it is stored in a permanent file (on your hard drive as the file named C:\SASDATA\AUTOLIST.SAS7BDAT). (Optional: Use Windows Explorer to verify that this file is on your hard drive.) (Note: To import a data set into a permanent file [library], you must have a defined SAS library name.)

9. Calculate descriptive statistics for the data using the SAS code below. Why is it necessary to use the name MYSASLIB.AUTOLIST instead of AUTOLIST in this case?

```
PROC MEANS DATA=MYSASLIB.AUTOLIST; RUN;
```

10. What is the difference between the SAS data sets CARLIST and MYSASLIB. AUTOLIST? (CARLIST is a temporary data set; MYSASLIB.AUTOLIST is a permanent data set.) If you didn't know, go back and re-read the sections on temporary and permanent SAS data sets.

GOING DEEPER: MORE WAYS TO MANAGE DATA

In this Going Deeper section we discuss the following topics:

■ Creating a SAS library using program code

■ Importing Excel data using SAS code

■ Viewing the contents of a SAS data set

Creating a SAS Library Using Program Code

Creating a SAS library using the technique illustrated in the section "Creating a SAS Library Using a Dialog Box" is easy, but sometimes it is handy to create a SAS library "on the fly" within a SAS program. Creating a library within the code makes it active within only a single SAS session. When you exit SAS, the library nickname is "forgotten" by SAS, although any data sets you've created are permanently stored in your folder referred to by the library. You may use these permanent SAS data sets again by re-creating a library nickname pointing to the Windows folder where the data file is stored.

The following SAS code creates a SAS library name called MYLIB2 at the location C:\SASDATA:

```
LIBNAME MYLIB2 "C:\SASDATA";
```

When SAS reads this code at the beginning of your SAS program, the libname (library name) MYLIB2 is created and can subsequently be used as a part of a permanent data set name. For example, suppose you have a data set named RESEARCH.SAS7BDAT in the folder C:\SASDATA. Once you define the libname MYLIB2 pointing to that folder, you will refer to that data set using the SAS data set name MYLIB2.RESEARCH.

Note that for illustrative purposes we are creating the library named MYLIB2 that is purposefully different from the MYSASLIB library that is used in the rest of the book (all the same files are in both libraries because they both point to the same location on disk). There is no conflict in creating two SAS library names that point to the same folder on your drive, although in practice you would not normally have two such library names.

HANDS-ON
EXAMPLE

In this example you will define a SAS library in code and use the library name to read in a SAS data file.

1. In the SAS Explorer, display the window named Contents of SAS Environment. Refer to previous examples if you don't remember how to display this window. Double-click the Libraries icon, shown previously in Figure 3.3.

2. A new window named Active Libraries appears. Examine the active library names. There should not be a library named MYLIB2.

3. In the Editor window, open the file `LIBNAME2.SAS`, which contains the following code:

```
LIBNAME MYLIB2 "C:\SASDATA";
RUN;
```

4. Run this program. The `LIBNAME` statement creates the SAS library nickname `MYLIB2` but does not create any output. Examine the Active Libraries window in the SAS Explorer. There is now a library icon named `MYLIB2`. The folder represented by the filing cabinet icon indicates that SAS created the `MYLIB2` library.

5. Double-click the `MYLIB2` icon and verify that the library includes one or more SAS data sets (including the data sets `SOMEDATA` and `CARS2`). Note that this new library contains the same data sets as the `MYSASLIB` library because they are both defined as nicknames for "pointing to" `C:\SASDATA`.

6. In the Editor window, add the following code to `LIBNAME2.SAS`. Run the program. SAS calculates descriptive statistics for the numeric variables in the `MYLIB2.SOMEDATA` data set.

```
PROC MEANS DATA=MYLIB2.SOMEDATA;
RUN;
```

The `MYLIB2` library nickname continues to be active and available for use until you exit the SAS program. The library nickname `MYSASLIB`, created with the dialog box, using the Enable at startup option, is remembered by SAS each time the program begins.

GOING DEEPER: IMPORTING MICROSOFT EXCEL DATA USING SAS CODE

Instead of using the Import Wizard to import Excel data, you can use SAS code. This technique is handy when you are importing a number of similar files. For example, suppose your Excel data changes over time and you need to re-import it whenever it changes. When the SAS program is run, it reads the new data from the Excel file and creates a SAS data set that you can use in an analysis.

The following program, `IMPORTEXAMPLE.SAS`, imports the Excel spreadsheet `EXAMPLE.XLS` and creates a SAS data set named `WORK.FROMXL`.

```
PROC IMPORT OUT= FROMXL
            DATAFILE= "C:\SASDATA\EXAMPLE.XLS"
            DBMS=EXCEL REPLACE;
      SHEET="Database";
      GETNAMES=YES;
RUN;
```

This code contains several options that have not been previously discussed.

- ■ `PROC IMPORT` is a SAS procedure you can use to import data from a variety of file formats.

- ■ The `OUT=` option defines the name of the SAS file (in this case because a permanent library name is not a part of the name, the resulting temporary SAS data set will be named `FROMXL` or, more precisely, `WORK.FROMXL`).

- ■ The `DATAFILE=` option indicates the location of the original Excel file.

- ■ The `DBMS=` option indicates the type of data source file to be imported. Table 3.1 lists the types of files SAS can import.

- ■ The `REPLACE` option instructs SAS to replace the old dataset with the same name.

TABLE 3.1.   SAS DBMS data sources

DBMS identifier	Data source	File extension
`ACCESS`	Microsoft Access database	`.MDB`
`DBF`	dBASE file	`.DBF`
`WK1`	Lotus 1 spreadsheet	`.WK1`
`WK3`	Lotus 3 spreadsheet	`.WK3`
`WK4`	Lotus 4 spreadsheet	`.WK4`
`EXCEL`	Excel version 4 or 5 spreadsheet	`.XLS`
`EXCEL4`	Excel version 4 spreadsheet	`.XLS`
`EXCEL5`	Excel version 5 spreadsheet	`.XLS`
`EXCEL97`	Excel 97 spreadsheet	`.XLS`
`DLM`	delimited file (default delimiter is a blank)	`.*`
`CSV`	delimited file (comma-separated values)	`.CSV`
`TAB`	delimited file (tab-delimited values)	`.TXT`

- The `SHEET=` option designates the name of the Excel table to import.

- The `GETNAMES=YES` option indicates that the variable names are on the first row of data.

These options are in one way or another specified in the SAS Import Wizard. In the previous Wizard example, we skipped the option to output a code file. If you instruct SAS to save the code used to import the data set, it creates a file similar to `ImportExample.SAS`. You can include in the `PROC IMPORT` statement a number of other options described in the SAS documentation, but those are beyond the scope of this book.

DISCOVERING THE CONTENTS OF A SAS DATA SET

Data can come from a number of sources. A popular way to provide data, by e-mail or download, is in a SAS data set. (These data sets have an .SAS7BDAT file extension.) If you acquire a SAS data set from another source, you can find out about its contents in two ways:

- Copy the `SAS7BDAT`-type data file into a folder that is linked to a SAS library (such as `C:\SASDATA`). Use SAS Viewdata to view the contents of the data set.

- Use `PROC DATASETS` to list information about the variables in the data set.

We've already illustrated how to use Viewdata and `PROC PRINT` to see the actual contents of a data set. The `PROC DATASETS` technique does not show you the actual data. Instead, it provides details about the variables in the data set, including their names, formats, and labels. For example, the following SAS program (`CONTENTS.SAS`) displays information about the `SOMEDATA` data set in the `MYSASLIB` library:

HANDS-ON
EXAMPLE

In this example you will use a SAS code technique similar to that used in `IMPORTEXAMPLE.SAS` to import data from an Excel file.

1. Using the SAS code technique for importing Excel files, import the file `CARLIST.XLS` as a SAS data set (member) named `CARS3` (in the `MYSASLIB` library.)

2. After importing this data set, add the following code to display a list of the data:

```
PROC PRINT DATA=MYSASLIB.CARS3;RUN;
```

```
PROC DATASETS;
CONTENTS DATA= MYSASLIB.SOMEDATA;
RUN;
```

or

```
PROC DATASETS;
CONTENTS DATA= "C:\SASDATA\SOMEDATA";
RUN;
```

When you run this program, SAS produces a listing of the contents of the data set, including variable names and other information. It is a handy way to discover what information is in a particular SAS data set. This is illustrated in the following Hands-on Example.

HANDS-ON
EXAMPLE

In this example you will discover the contents of a SAS data file using PROC DATASETS.

1. In the Editor window, open the file CONTENTS.SAS. Run the program.

2. Examine the output. The first two sections of the output contain technical information, and the third section (listed below) contains a list of variables in the data set.

```
Alphabetic List of Variables and Attributes
 #   Variable   Type   Len   Label
 3   AGE        Num     8    Age on Jan 1, 2000
10   GENDER     Char    6
 2   GP         Char    1    Intervention Group
 1   ID         Num     8    ID Number
 9   SEX        Num     8
 8   STATUS     Num     8    Socioeconomic Status
 4   TIME1      Num     8    Baseline
 5   TIME2      Num     8    6 Months
 6   TIME3      Num     8    12 Months
 7   TIME4      Num     8    24 Months
```

Notice that this SAS data set description contains:

- ▪ Variable: Names are listed in alphabetical order.
- ▪ Type: The variable type— Num (numeric), Char (Character/Text), Date, and other SAS data types.
- ▪ Len: The number of characters or digits used to store the information.
- ▪ Label: A description of the variable (listed only if defined).

3. Change the DATA statement to read

   CONTENTS DATA= MYSASLIB._ALL_;

   Run the revised program. The _ALL_ keyword instructs SAS to display information about all SAS data sets in the MYSASLIB library.

SUMMARY

The tabular presentation that follows is presented as a summary of Chapters 2 and 3 pertaining to techniques used to read or import data into SAS.

Data source	Example	Comments
Data are within the SAS code.	**DATA** MYSASLIB; INPUT ID **1-4** AGE **5-7** ETC ...; DATALINES; 0001 23 ... ETC; 0002 34 ;	Use any INPUT statement type such as freeform, column, formatted input, etc. (Chapter 2).
Data are in an external text file.	**DATA** MYSASLIB; INFILE 'C:\SASDATA\EXAMPLE.DAT'; INPUT ID **1-3** GP $ **5** ...etc; **RUN**;	Use the INFILE statement, such as in example DINPUT. SAS (Chapter 2).

(Continued)

Data source	Example	Comments

Data are in a permanent SAS data set (with an .SAS7BDAT file extension).	`";PROC PRINT`
	`DATA=MYSASLIB.`
	`SOMEDATA;`
	`or`
	`DATA="C:\SASDATA\`
	`SOMEDATA";`
		Option 1: If your data are in a previously defined SAS library (such as MYSASLIB), use the two-part SAS name in the DATA statement.
		Option 2: Read data using the Windows file name.

Data are in another file type such as Excel.	From the SAS menu, select File ⇨ Import and use the Import Wizard to import the file into a working or permanent data set.	Or, use SAS code to import the data.

EXERCISES

3.1. Create a permanent SAS data set.

a. In the Editor window, open the file EX_3.1.SAS.

```
DATA WEIGHT;
INPUT TREATMENT LOSS @@;
DATALINES;
```

```
1 1.0 1 3.0 1 -1.0 1 1.5 1 0.5 1 3.5
2 4.5 2 6.0 2 3.5 2 7.5 2 7.0 2 6.0 2 5.5
3 1.5 3 -2.5 3 -0.5 3 1.0 3 .5
```

```
;
PROC PRINT;
RUN;
```

This program creates a temporary data set called WEIGHT (or WORK. WEIGHT). Use the SAS Explorer (WORK library) to verify that the data set was created.

b. Change the SAS program so that it creates a permanent SAS data set named MYSASLIB.WEIGHT in the C:\SASDATA folder *using the Windows folder name in the DATA statement*:

DATA "C:_____";

I. Verify that the data set was created by opening it in the SAS Viewer.

II. Close the SAS Viewer.

III. Use File ⇨ Print and select Entire Table to print a copy of this table.

c. Change the SAS program so that it creates a permanent SAS data set named
`MYSASLIB.WEIGHT` (in the previously created SAS library `MYSASLIB`)
using the two-level SAS data set name:

DATA _____ . _____

    I.   Verify that the data set was created by opening it in the SAS Viewer.

   II.   Close the SAS Viewer.

  III.   Use File/Print and select "Entire Table" to print a copy of this table.

d. Using the following code:

```
PROC DATASETS;
CONTENTS DATA= MYSASLIB.WEIGHT;
RUN;
```

produces a listing of the contents of the SAS data set `MYSASLIB.WEIGHT`.
Change the `DATA=` statement to

```
CONTENTS DATA=MYSASLIB._ALL_;
```

to display the contents of all data sets in the library.

3.2. **Going Deeper: Use code to import Excel data.**

a. Write the SAS code to import data from the Excel file `FAMILY.XLS` using
these criteria:

    I.   Create a SAS data set named `INCOME` in the `WORK` library using the
`OUT=` statement.

   II.   Use `DATAFILE=` to specify the location of the original Excel file on
your hard disk.

  III.   Use `DBMS=` to specify that the data source is Excel.

  IV.   Use `SHEET=` to designate `Data` as the name of the Excel table to
import.

   V.   Use the `GETNAMES=` option to indicate that the variable names are on
the first row of data.

b. Once the data are imported, view the contents of `WORK.INCOME` using
Viewdata. Close the Viewdata data grid.

c. Calculate descriptive statistics for the data using this code:

```
TITLE "PUT YOUR NAME HERE";
PROC MEANS DATA=INCOME;
RUN;
```

3.3. **Going Deeper: Create a SAS library.**

Suppose your SAS data sets are stored in the physical directory (folder)
named `C:\RESEARCH` on your hard drive.

a. If you want to create a shortcut library name in SAS named CLINICAL, what LIBNAME statement would specify your data's location? (Fill in the blanks.)

LIBNAME _____ 'C:_____';

b. If you want to use the data in a file named C:\RESEARCH\JAN2009. SAS7BDAT in your SAS program, fill in the blanks in the following DATA = statement:

LIBNAME CLINICAL 'C:\RESEARCH';
PROC MEANS DATA = _____._____;

c. Use the following information to create a LIBNAME statement:

Hard drive location is O:\CLINICAL

SAS library name is YOURNAME

LIBNAME _____ '_____';

d. If you have a SAS library named CLINICAL and you want to create a permanent data set named MAY2007 that is stored in the C:\RESEARCH folder on your hard drive, what is the name of the file used in SAS code?

_____._____

e. In step d of this exercise, what is the name of the SAS data file on your hard drive?

_____:\RESEARCH\MAY2007._____

CHAPTER

PREPARING DATA FOR ANALYSIS

LEARNING OBJECTIVES

- To be able to label variables with explanatory names
- To be able to create new variables
- To be able to use DROP and KEEP to select variables
- To be able to create a subset of a data set
- To be able to use PROC SORT
- To be able to merge data sets
- To be able to use the SET statement
- To be able to use PROC FORMAT

You've entered your data into SAS, but before you can use them in SAS you typically must make corrections, perform calculations, and otherwise prepare your data for analysis. This step is sometimes overlooked in classroom settings where you often use ready-to-analyze textbook data. When you gather your own data, or even when you acquire data from a database, the data may require some changes before you can use them in an analysis.

> All of the data manipulation statements discussed in this chapter appear in your program code within the DATA step, except for PROC FORMAT. That is, they appear after the DATA statement and before the first RUN or PROC statement. Thus, all of the results of the data manipulations performed by these statements become part of that active data set.

LABELING VARIABLES WITH EXPLANATORY NAMES

SAS labels are used to provide descriptive names for variables. Data sets often contain cryptic variable names such as ID, SBP, WT, and so on. For people familiar with the data set, these make perfect sense. However, if you want to produce output that is readable by others, creating explanatory labels for variables is good practice. In SAS, this can be accomplished by using the LABEL statement. The LABEL statement uses the format:

```
LABEL     VAR1 = 'A new label number 1'
          VAR2 = 'A new label number 2'     ;
```

You can use either single or double quotation marks in the LABEL statement, but you must match the type within each definition statement. When SAS prints out information for VAR1, it also includes the label, making the output more readable. The following program illustrates the use of labels (DLABEL.SAS):

```
DATA MYDATA;
INFILE 'C:\SASDATA\BPDATA.DAT'; * READ DATA FROM FILE;
INPUT ID $ 1 SBP 2-4 DBP 5-7 GENDER $ 8 AGE 9-10 WT 11-13;
LABEL  ID = 'Identification Number'
     SBP= 'Systolic Blood Pressure'
     DBP = 'Diastolic Blood Pressure'
     AGE = 'Age on Jan 1, 2000'
     WT = 'Weight' ;
PROC MEANS; VAR SBP DBP AGE WT;
RUN;
```

Notice that the LABEL statement is placed within the DATA step. Also, there is only one semicolon (;) in the LABEL statement, at the end.

The output listings below show how the LABEL statement adds information to the output. The first set of output shows PROC MEANS output *without* the LABEL statement. Notice that all variable names are listed just as they were created from the INPUT statement in the DATA statement.

Variable	N	Mean	Std Dev	Minimum	Maximum
SBP	5	127.0000000	8.3666003	120.0000000	140.0000000
DBP	5	82.0000000	10.9544512	70.0000000	100.0000000
AGE	5	35.8000000	30.2605354	15.0000000	89.0000000
WT	5	145.0000000	31.6227766	110.0000000	180.0000000

The next set of output from PROC MEANS is from the same data, and in this case the LABEL statement, as shown in the example code above, has been used. In this case more informative labels are included in the output.

Variable	Label	N	Mean	Std Dev	Minimum	Maximum
SBP	Systolic Blood Pressure	5	127.0000000	8.3666003	120.0000000	140.0000000
DBP	Diastolic Blood Pressure	5	82.0000000	10.9544512	70.0000000	100.0000000
AGE	Age on Jan 1, 2000	5	35.8000000	30.2605354	15.0000000	89.0000000
WT	Weight	5	145.0000000	31.6227766	110.0000000	180.0000000

Follow this Hands-on Example to include label definitions for a data set within the DATA step.

HANDS-ON
EXAMPLE

In this example you will create labels for variables and learn how to output the labels using PROC PRINT.

1. Open the file DLABEL2.SAS.

   ```
   DATA MYDATA;
   INPUT @1 FNAME $11. @12 LNAME $12. @24 BDATE DATE9.;
   FORMAT BDATE WORDDATE12.;
   LABEL   FNAME="First Name"; * Complete the labels;
   DATALINES;
   Bill       Smith       08JAN1952
   Jane       Jones       02FEB1953
   Clyde      York        23MAR1949
   ;
   PROC PRINT;
   RUN;
   ```

2. Add lines to create labels for LNAME (Last name) and BDATE (Birthdate). For example, the LABEL statement could be:

   ```
   LABEL FNAME="First Name"
   LNAME="Last Name"
   BDATE="Birth Date";
   ```

   Don't forget the semicolon (;) after the last label definition.

3. Run the program. Notice that the label information is *not* included in this output.

4. Most SAS PROCs output the label information automatically. However, for PROC PRINT you must add the option LABEL to the statement. Change the PROC PRINT statement in this program to read:

   ```
   PROC PRINT LABEL;
   ```

5. Run the program and observe how the labels are shown in the output. The output will look like this:

   ```
   Obs    First Name    Last Name    Birth Date
    1        Bill        Smith       Jan 8, 1952
    2        Jane        Jones       Feb 2, 1953
    3        Clyde       York        Mar 23, 1949
   ```

CREATING NEW VARIABLES

It is common to calculate new variables in a data set in preparation for analysis. For example, you may need to convert a temperature reading from Fahrenheit to Celsius, change a measure from centimeters to inches, or calculate a score from a series of values. One method for creating new variables in your data set is to calculate them within the DATA step. This section describes some of the techniques you can use.

You can create new variables within a SAS DATA statement by assigning a value to a new variable name or by calculating a new variable using a mathematical or logical expression. When the SAS program is run, data values for the new variables are assigned to each of the records in the currently active data set.

> If you have experience using Microsoft Excel, you know that when you calculate a new value it changes if you change any of the numbers that were used to calculate that value. The SAS calculations in the DATA step are not like those in Excel. They are one-time calculations that take place when you run the SAS program. If you want to re-calculate the expression you must re-run the SAS program.

Creating Numeric Variables in the DATA Step

Within the SAS DATA step you can calculate a new variable using current variables in your data set. These calculations use standard arithmetic operators as defined here:

+   Addition

-     Subtraction

*   Multiplication

/   Division

**   Exponentiation

Here are some examples:

```
SUM= X+Y;        Addition

DIF=X-Y;         Subtraction

TWICE=X*2;       Multiplication

HALF=X/2;        Division

CUBIC=X**3;      Exponentiation
```

The following Hands-on Example illustrates how you could calculate a new value for each record in your data set by using a simple arithmetic expression—in this case, by multiplying two variables (WIDTH and LENGTH) that are in the data set to create a new variable (AREA).

HANDS-ON
EXAMPLE

In this example you will calculate new variables from existing information in a SAS data set.

1. In the Editor window, open the file DCALC.SAS. This file calculates the square footage (AREA) in various rooms of a house, then adds up the total.

```
DATA ROOMSIZE;
INPUT ROOM $ WIDTH LENGTH;
AREA = LENGTH * WIDTH;
DATALINES;
LIVING     14 22
DINING     14 12
BREAKFAST 10 12
KITCHEN 12 16
BEDROOM1 18 12
BEDROOM2 12 14
BEDROOM3 13 16
BATH1      8 12
BATH2      7 10
BATH3      6 8
GARAGE 23 24
;
RUN;
PROC PRINT; SUM AREA;
RUN;
```

Notice the following statement within the data step:

```
AREA = LENGTH * WIDTH;
```

This statement creates a new variable named AREA that is a result of multiplying length by width.

2. Run the program and observe the output:

Obs	ROOM	WIDTH	LENGTH	AREA
1	LIVING	14	22	308
2	DINING	14	12	168
3	BREAKFAS	10	12	120
4	KITCHEN	12	16	192
5	BEDROOM1	18	12	216
6	BEDROOM2	12	14	168
7	BEDROOM3	13	16	208
8	BATH1	8	12	96
9	BATH2	7	10	70
10	BATH3	6	8	48
11	GARAGE	23	24	552
				2146

- The statement AREA = LENGTH * WIDTH; creates a new variable AREA in the data set named ROOMSIZE.

- The SUM AREA; statement in PROC PRINT causes SAS to report the sum of the AREA values. (More options for PROC PRINT will be presented in the next chapter.)

SAS allows you to perform more than just simple calculations. You can perform virtually any type of mathematical calculation needed. When creating more extensive calculations, you must pay attention to the order of evaluation used in expressions. This order is similar to that used in common algebraic practice and is also commonly used in other computer programs. The priority of evaluation is as follows:

( )   ***   /   +   -

That is, when SAS evaluates an expression, it first performs calculations in parentheses, then exponentiation, then multiplication and division, and finally addition and subtraction. For example,

ANSWER = A + B * C;

results in a *different answer* from

(Continued)

```
ANSWER = (A + B) * C;
```

The first example multiplies B * C, then adds to the product A. The second adds A + B then multiplies the resulting sum by C. If you are unsure about how an expression will be evaluated, use parentheses to force the evaluation to be as you intend. For example,

```
NEWVAL = (SCORE1-SCORE2)*INDEX**2;
```

gives the instruction to subtract SCORE2 from SCORE1 first, then multiply the result by INDEX^2.

You may find the following mnemonic from a previous math class helpful in remembering the order of operations: "Please Excuse My Dear Aunt Sally" (**P**arentheses **E**xponents **M**ultiplication **D**ivision **A**ddition **S**ubtraction).

Creating New Variables as Constant Values

Sometimes it is handy to define a new variable as a constant value. The reason for creating this type of variable is usually that you will use the value in a future calculation. For example, suppose you are about to calculate new values in your data set with a formula that uses the value of *pi* (π). A statement such as the following could appear within your DATA step (before you use the variable PI in another calculation):

```
PI = 3.1415927;   *Value to be used later;
```

For example, assuming RADIUS is a variable in your data set, you could define the following expression:

```
AREA = PI * RADIUS**2;
```

to calculate the area of a circle from the measure of its radius.

Variable names on the left side of each equation *are created as a result of the statement*. Variables used on the right side of any statement must have already been created or defined in an INPUT statement. If a variable on the right side of the statement is undefined or contains a missing value, the resulting value for the variable on the left side of the equation is missing (i.e., the value.).

Using SAS Functions

Even more sophisticated calculations can be created using SAS functions. These functions include arithmetic and text and date manipulation. The format for the use of SAS functions is

```
variable = function(argument1,argument2, etc.);
```

Functions can require one or more arguments. Some require no arguments. See Appendix B for more information.

For example, a few mathematical functions are:

S = ABS(X);	Absolute value
S = FACT(X);	Factorial
S = INT(X);	Decimal portion of a value (an integer)
S = LOG(X);	Natural log
S = SQRT(X);	Square root

Some of the other functions available in SAS are SUBSTR, LAG, COS, SIN, ARCS, LOG, LOG10, UNIFORM, NORMAL, SUM, and MEAN. (A list of commonly used SAS functions can be found in Appendix B.)

Functions can also be used as a part of a more extensive calculation. For example,

```
C = MEASURE + SQRT(A**2 + B**2)
```

would calculate the square of A, then the square of B, then add those two numbers, take the square root of that value, add that number to the value of MEASURE, and assign the result to the variable named C.

Functions may require no argument, one argument, or multiple arguments. A few multi-argument mathematical functions in SAS are:

S = MAX(x1,x2,x3,...)	Maximum value in the list of arguments
S = MIN(x1,x2,x3,...)	Minimum value in the list of arguments
S = SUM(x1,x2,x3,...)	Sum of nonmissing values in a list of arguments
S = MEDIAN(x1,x2,x3,...)	Median of a list of nonmissing values
S = ROUND(value, round)	Rounds value to nearest round off unit

These functions allow missing values in the list. Thus, the SUM function

```
TOTAL=SUM(TIME1,TIME2,TIME3,TIME4);
```

may be preferred over a statement such as

```
TOTAL= TIME1+TIME2+TIME3+TIME4;
```

In the second instance, if the value for TIME2 were missing for a subject, the value of TOTAL would be set at missing (.). However, in the assignment using the SUM function, the value of TOTAL would contain the sum of the other TIME values even if TIME2 were missing.

The round off unit in the ROUND function determines how the rounding will be performed. The default is 1. A round off value of 0.01 means to round to the nearest 100th, and a round off value of 5 means to round to the nearest 5. Here are a few examples:

ROUND(3.1415,.01)	Returns the value 3.14
ROUND(107,5)	Returns the value 105
ROUND(3.6234)	Returns the value 4

When arguments are a list of values, such as in MAX or MIN, you can specify the list as variables separated by commas, or as a range preceded by the word OF. For example, if these variables have the following values:

```
X1 = 1;   X2 = 2;   X3 = 13;   X4=10;
```

then

MAX(1,2,3,4,5)	Returns the value 5
MAX(X1,X2,X3,X4)	Returns the value 13
MAX(OF X1-X4)	Returns the value 13

Notice that the designation OF X1-X4 is interpreted by SAS as all values from X1 to X4 in the MAX() function example above. There is also an extensive list of functions available to allow you to manipulate text and date values. As an example of a date function, the INTCK function counts the number of intervals (INTerval Count) between two dates or times. The result is an integer value. The format for this function is

```
INTCK('interval',from,to)
```

The `from` and `to` variables are SAS date values. The `'interval'` argument can be one of the following lengths of time:

```
DAY

WEEKDAY

WEEK

TENDAY

SEMIMONTH

MONTH

QTR

SEMIYEAR

YEAR
```

Thus, the following function counts the number of years between the data variables BEGDATE and ENDDATE because the date interval indicated is `'YEAR'`.

```
INTCK('YEAR',BEGDATE,ENDDATE)
```

The following code counts the number of months between these two dates because the date interval indicated is `'MONTH'`.

```
INTCK('MONTH',BEGDATE,ENDDATE)
```

Another handy DATE function is the MDY function. This allows you to convert numbers into a SAS date value. For example,

```
BDATE = MDY(10,12,1989);
```

converts the date October 12, 1989, into a SAS date value. Dates must be in SAS date format in order for you to use other SAS date functions or to output dates using SAS format specifications. Or if in a data set you have these values

```
MTH=5;    DAY=9;    YR=2009;
```

the MDY function

```
VISITDATE = MDY(MTH,DAY,YR);
```

creates a SAS date variable named VISITDATE with the value May 9, 2009.

HANDS-ON
EXAMPLE

This example illustrates a method for calculating the difference between two dates (AGE) using the INTCK function. The procedure uses these steps:

A. Read in BDATE as a SAS date value using the INFORMAT MMYYDD8. specification in the INPUT statement.

B. Convert the target date 08/25/2007 into a variable named TARGET using the MDY function.

C. Use the INTCK function to count the number of years between each date (BDATE) in the data set and the TARGET date and assign this value to the variable AGE.

D. Assign the count of years to the variable named AGE.

Here are the steps:

1. In the Editor window, open the file DDATES.SAS.

```
DATA DATES;
INPUT @1 BDATE MMDDYY8.;
TARGET=MDY(08,25,2009);         * Uses MDY() function;
AGE=INTCK('YEAR',BDATE,TARGET); * Uses INTCK function;
DATALINES;
07101952
07041776
01011900

;
PROC PRINT;
FORMAT BDATE WEEKDATE. TARGET MMDDYY8.;
RUN;
```

2. Notice the statement

```
INPUT @1 BDATE MMDDYY8.;
```

This statement reads in a variable named BDATE as a SAS date value starting in column 1 (specified by the pointer @1) using the format MMDDYY8. The SAS date variable TARGET is created with the MDY function, using constant values for month, day, and year.

3. Run the program and observe the output:

```
Obs    BDATE                     TARGET      AGE
1      Thursday, July 10, 1952   08/25/09     57
2      Thursday, July 4, 1776    08/25/09    233
3      Monday, January 1, 1900   08/25/09    109
```

Notice that the program calculates AGE as the difference in years (the count of the "year" intervals) between the TARGET date and the date value for each record in the SAS data set.

4. Another function you can use to find the difference between two dates is YRDIF. Change the AGE=INTCK statement to the following:

```
AGE=YRDIF(BDATE,TARGET,'ACT/365');
```

This function finds the difference in two dates using the method of dividing the number of days by 365. Run the program. See Appendix B for more information about this and other functions.

For you history buffs: If you enter the date

```
09041752
```

(September 4, 1752) into the DDATES program in this example and run the program, it indicates that that date fell on a Monday (in the current Gregorian calendar). However, this date did not exist. When Britain adopted the Gregorian calendar, the day after September 2, 1752, was September 14, 1752. Thus, if SAS is used to calculate dates prior to September 2, 1752, care must be taken because SAS does not convert dates to the older Julian calendar designation.

Using IF-THEN-ELSE Conditional Statement Assignments

Another way to create a new variable in the DATA step is to use the IF-THEN-ELSE conditional statement construct. The syntax for this statement is:

```
IF expression THEN statement; ELSE statement;
```

For example:

```
IF SBP GE 140 THEN HIGHBP=1; ELSE HIGHBP=0;
```

This statement tells SAS to do the following: If SBP is greater than or equal to 140 (SBP GE 140), then set the variable named HIGHBP to the value 1; if SBP is less than 140 (IF SBP LT 140), set the value of the variable HIGHBP to 0. In effect, this creates a grouping variable for the data set using the variable HIGHBP with values 0 and 1. A list of common SAS comparison operators is given below:

= or EQ means equal to

<> or NE means not equal to

< or LT means less than

<= or LE means less than or equal to

^> or NG means not greater than

^= or NE means not equal to

> or GT means greater than

>= or GE means greater than or equal to

^< or NL means not less than

You can also put several conditions together in an IF statement such as

```
IF AGE GT 19 and GENDER="M" then GROUP=1;
```

or

```
IF TREATMENT EQ "A" OR GROUP=2 THEN CATEGORY="GREEN";
```

You can also stack IF-THEN-ELSE statements by using an ELSE IF clause, as in:

```
IF TRT="A" THEN GROUP=1;
ELSE IF TRT="B" OR TRT="C" THEN GROUP=2;
ELSE GROUP=3;
```

The preceding lines recode the variable (TRT) into a new variable (GROUP).

HANDS-ON
EXAMPLE

In this example you will use a conditional IF statement to create a new variable.

1. In the Editor window, open the file DCONDITION.SAS.

```
DATA MYDATA;
INPUT ID $ SBP DBP GENDER $ AGE WT;
IF SBP GE 140 then STATUS="HIGH"; else STATUS="OK";
DATALINES;
001 120 80 M 15 115
002 130 70 F 25 180
003 140 100 M 89 170
004 180 80 F 30 150
005 125 80 F 20 110

;
PROC PRINT;
RUN;
```

2. Notice the conditional IF statement. If systolic blood pressure (SBP) is greater than or equal to 140, the program assigns the value HIGH to the variable STATUS. Otherwise, it assigns the value OK to that variable.

3. Run the program and observe the results:

Obs	ID	SBP	DBP	GENDER	AGE	WT	STATUS
1	001	120	80	M	15	115	OK
2	002	130	70	F	25	180	OK
3	003	140	100	M	89	170	HIGH
4	004	180	80	F	30	150	HIGH
5	005	125	80	F	20	110	OK

Notice that the new variable STATUS is assigned either the value OK or HIGH depending on the value of SBP.

Using IF to Assign Missing Values

An IF statement is a common way to specify missing values in a SAS DATA step. For example,

```
IF AGE EQ -9 then AGE = . ;
```

indicates that if the value of AGE is equal to -9, the value of AGE is set to a missing value . (dot). Because there is no ELSE clause, the value of AGE is not changed when AGE is not equal to -9. To specify a missing character value, use two quotation marks. For example,

```
IF GENDER NE "M" and GENDER NE "F" then GENDER = "";
```

specifies a missing value for GENDER (two quotation marks in a row, " ") when it is neither M nor F.

A missing value code is commonly used when recoding values. For example, suppose you are recoding AGE into a new variable called TEEN. You could use the following code:

```
IF AGE GT 12 AND AGE LT 20 THEN TEEN=1;ELSE TEEN = 0;
IF AGE = . THEN TEEN = .;
```

The use of the IF AGE = . THEN TEEN = . ; statement guarantees that TEEN is set as missing for any observation for which AGE is missing. Otherwise, any observation where AGE is greater than 12 and less than 20 is coded as TEEN = 0;. Another way to accomplish this is with a more complex IF / ELSE statement:

```
IF AGE=. Then TEEN = .;
ELSE IF AGE GT 12 and AGE LT 20 then TEEN = 1;
ELSE TEEN = 0;
```

HANDS-ON
EXAMPLE

In this example you will use a conditional IF statement in the DATA step to create a new variable and define a missing value.

1. In the Editor window, open the file DMISSING.SAS.

```
DATA MYDATA;
INPUT ID $ SBP DBP GENDER $ AGE;
IF AGE GT 12 AND AGE LT 20 THEN TEEN=1;ELSE TEEN=0;
IF AGE=. THEN TEEN=.;
DATALINES;
001 120 80 M 15
002 130 70 F .
003 140 100 M 12
004 180 80 F 17
005 144 80 F 23
006 165 80 M 18
007 121 80 F 19
008 195 80 M 11
009 162 80 M 13
010 112 80 F 17
;
PROC PRINT;
RUN;
```

2. Notice the `IF` statements that define the new variable `TEEN`. They also set `TEEN` to missing (`.`) if `AGE` is missing. Run this program to see that the value of `TEEN` in the second observation is set to missing.

3. Use the second method described above to do the same task:

    ```
    IF AGE=. Then TEEN=.;
    ELSE IF AGE GT 12 and AGE LT 20 then TEEN=1;
    ELSE TEEN=0;
    ```

    Run the program. Are the results the same?

USING DROP AND KEEP TO SELECT VARIABLES

Sometimes you may have a data set containing variables you do not want to keep. The `DROP` and `KEEP` statements in the `DATA` step allow you to specify which variables to retain in a data set. The general form for these statements is:

```
DROP variables;
KEEP variables;
```

For example,

```
DATA MYDATA;
INPUT A B C D E F G;
DROP E F;
DATALINES;
...etc...
```

reads in all of the data but then drops the variables `E` and `F` so that these variables are no longer in the temporary SAS data set named `MYDATA`. The following Hands-on Example illustrates this technique.

HANDS-ON
EXAMPLE

In this example you will read in a data set but keep only a selection of the variables.

1. In the Editor window, open the file `DKEEP.SAS`.

    ```
    DATA MYDATA;
    INFILE 'C:\SASDATA\EXAMPLE.CSV' DLM=',' FIRSTOBS=2 OBS=26;
    ```

    (Continued)

```
INPUT  GROUP $ AGE TIME1 TIME2 TIME3 TIME4 SOCIO;
KEEP AGE TIME1 SOCIO;
PROC PRINT;
RUN;
```

This SAS program reads the first 25 records from a file with comma-separated values. In this type of data entry you must read in all variables. To eliminate variables you do not need, use the KEEP statement (or DROP statement).

2. Run the program. Even though the program reads in seven variables, the listing from the PROC PRINT statement includes only those variables you have specified in the KEEP statement.

3. Replace the KEEP statement with the statement

```
DROP GROUP AGE SOCIO;
```

Run the program and observe the results.

SUBSETTING DATA SETS

Data sets can be quite large. You may have a data set that contains some group of subjects (records) that you want to eliminate from your analysis. In that case, you can subset the data so it will contain only those records you need. For example, if your analysis concerns pregnancies, you may want to limit your data set to females.

One method of eliminating certain records from a data set is to use a subsetting IF statement in the DATA step. The syntax for this statement is:

```
IF expression;
```

where the expression is some conditional statement in terms of the variables in the data set. For example, to select records containing the value F (only females) from a data set, you could use this statement within a DATA step:

```
IF GENDER EQ 'F';
```

Note that you can use single or double quotation marks ("F" or 'F') in this statement.

This subsetting IF statement is like a gate. It allows only records that meet a certain criterion to enter into the data set. In this case, only those records whose GENDER value is recorded as F are retained in the data set.

The opposite effect can be created by including the statement THEN DELETE at the end of the statement:

```
IF expression THEN DELETE;
```

For example, to get rid of certain records (all males) in a data set, you could use the code

```
IF GENDER EQ 'M' THEN DELETE;
```

When data are read into a SAS data set using this procedure and a record contains M for GENDER, then that record is *not* retained in the SAS data set. If the only values for GENDER in the data set are F and M, then these two subsetting strategies will yield the same results.

> The statement DELETE *does not* indicate that these records are erased from the raw data file on disk. The records are eliminated from the SAS data set created in the DATA step.

You are not limited to using the IF statement on character variables. Here is an example that uses the IF statement on a numeric variable:

```
IF AGE GT 19;
```

You can also use combinations of conditions in any of these IF statements, such as

```
IF AGE GT 19 AND GENDER ="M";
```

HANDS-ON
EXAMPLE

In this example you use a subsetting IF to select only certain records for inclusion in the MYDATA SAS data set created in the DATA step.

1. In the Editor window, open the file DSUBSET1.SAS. In this example, subjects less than or equal to 10 years old are included in the data set named MYDATA.

```
DATA MYDATA;
INFILE 'C:\SASDATA\EXAMPLE.DAT';
INPUT  ID  $ 1-3 GP $ 5 AGE 6-9 TIME1 10-14 TIME2 15-19;
IF AGE LE 10;
PROC PRINT;
RUN;
```

Notice that the subsetting IF statement selects only records for which AGE is less than or equal to 10. (This does not change the contents of the file C:\SASDATA\EXAMPLE.DAT; it affects only the contents of the SAS data set MYDATA.)

2. Run this program and observe the results. The data listing includes only the 22 subjects whose age is less than or equal to 10.

USING THE SET STATEMENT TO READ AN EXISTING DATA SET

Often you have a "main" data set that is from some corporate, government, or organization source. If you don't want to change the original data set, you should work with a copy of it. The SET statement is what you need. The SET statement in a DATA step is used to transfer data from an existing SAS data set to a new one. When you use a SET statement, there is no need for an INPUT, INFILE, or DATALINES statement. The SET statement is often used when you want to:

■ create several other data sets through subsetting, but you want to keep the original SAS data set as well

■ create a new data set starting with the data in a current data set, but you want to preserve all data in the original data set

The general form of the SET statement is:

```
SET SASdataset;
```

For example:

```
DATA NEW;  SET OLD;
```

or

```
DATA NEW;  SET "C:\SASDATA\OLD";
```

In this example, the SAS data set named OLD already exists. All variables and observations in the existing SAS data set (OLD) are automatically passed through the input buffer to the new SAS data set (NEW) (unless otherwise directed with programming statements). Just as when any new data set is created, additional variables can be created with assignment statements within the SAS DATA step. For example:

1. A data set named ALL is created.

```
DATA ALL;
INPUT AGE GENDER $ FAT PROTEIN CARBO SODIUM;
DATALINES;
... etc ...
```

2. A second data set named MALES is created as a subset of the ALL data set. The SET statement is used to copy the data from ALL into a new data set named MALES, which uses a subsetting IF to retain only male subjects from the original SAS data set. The SAS code used to do this is:

```
DATA MALES;
SET ALL;
IF GENDER ='M';
```

Figure 4.1 illustrates this process.

3. Use another DATA, SET, and IF statement to create a similar FEMALE data set.

FIGURE 4.1. *Creating a new data set using the SET statement*

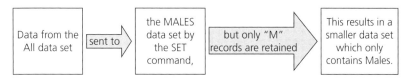

```
DATA FEMALES;
SET ALL;
IF GENDER ='F';
```

   or

```
DATA FEMALES;
SET ALL;
IF GENDER ='M' THEN DELETE;
```

The result is that you now have three active data sets available to you, named ALL, MALES, and FEMALES.

Once you've created multiple SAS data sets, you need a way to specify which SAS data set you want to use in a PROC statement. This is accomplished by including a DATA= option in your PROC statement. For example, to run a PROC MEANS on the MALES data set, use the statement

```
PROC MEANS DATA=MALES;
```

Similarly, for the FEMALE data set use

```
PROC MEANS DATA=FEMALES;
```

This is illustrated in the following Hands-on Example.

HANDS-ON
EXAMPLE

In this example you use the SET statement and subsetting IF to create subset data sets from a larger data set.

1. In the Editor window, open the file DSUBSET2.SAS.

```
DATA ALL;
INPUT AGE GENDER $ FAT PROTEIN CARBO SODIUM;
DATALINES;
```

(Continued)

```
25    M    40    40    109    1396
26    M    47    46    125    1731
38    M    42    40    104    1431
42    M    48    46    123    1711
65    M    41    41    112    1630
68    M    34    33    96     1192
20    F    39    29    118    1454
30    F    40    40    115    1532
60    F    39    40    123    1585
;
DATA MALES;
SET ALL;
IF GENDER ='M';
RUN;
```

Notice that this code already includes one subsetting IF statement in the DATA step to create a new data set named MALES.

2. At the end of the code, add these program lines to create a FEMALE data set using the appropriate SET and IF statements.

```
DATA FEMALES;
SET ALL;
IF GENDER ='F';
RUN;
```

3. Add lines that perform a PROC MEANS for MALES and a separate PROC MEANS for females. Remember to include a RUN statement at the end of the program. Here is the statement for MALES:

```
PROC PRINT DATA=MALES;RUN;
```

Similarly, add this line to the program to print the contents for the FEMALE data set:

```
PROC PRINT DATA=FEMALES;RUN;
```

USING PROC SORT

The SORT procedure can be used in the DATA step to rearrange the observations in a SAS data set or create a new SAS data set containing the rearranged observations. With PROC SORT, you can sort on multiple sort fields and sort in ascending or

TABLE 4.1. **SAS sorting sequence**

Sorting sequence for **character variables**	blank!"#$%&'()*+,-./0123456789:;<=>?@ ABCDEFGHIJKLMNOPQRSTUVWXYZ[\]^_ abcdefghijklmnopqrstuvwxyz(l)~
Sorting sequence for **numeric variables**	Missing values first, then numeric values
Default sorting sequence	Ascending (or indicate Descending)

descending order. The sorting sequence information for SAS data sets is shown in Table 4.1.

The syntax for PROC SORT is:

```
PROC SORT 'options'; BY variable(s);
```

Options for PROC SORT include

```
DATA=datasetname;
OUT= outputdatasetname;
```

For example,

```
PROC SORT DATA=MYDATA OUT=MYSORT; BY RECTIME;
```

creates a new sorted SAS data set named MYSORT (and the records in the original SAS data set MYDATA remain in their original order). If you *do not include* an OUT= statement, SAS sorts the current SAS data set. In the example above, if the OUT= statement is not included, the MYDATA data set is sorted.

The BY statement in the PROC SORT paragraph must contain one or more variables, and optionally the DESCENDING keyword. The BY DESCENDING statement tells SORT to arrange the values from highest to lowest instead of the default lowest to highest order. For example:

```
BY AGE;            * Sorts in ascending/alphabetical
                     order;
BY DESCENDING AGE; * Sorts in descending order;
```

You can also sort on several variables at a time. For example,

```
PROC SORT; BY GROUP SOCIO;
```

will cause the data set to be sorted on GROUP within SOCIO.

Uppercase characters (e.g., "A") come before lowercase characters (e.g., "a"). Thus, when sorting, Z comes before a. If variables such as GENDER are entered without consistency for upper- and lowercase (for example, M, F, m, and f) then your sort will not properly place the records into a Male and Female grouping.

HANDS-ON
EXAMPLE

In this example you sort data in ascending and descending order.

1. In the Editor window, open the file DSORT.SAS.

```
DATA MYDATA;
INPUT GROUP RECTIME;
DATALINES;
1       3.1
2       3.6
2       4.2
1       2.1
1       2.8
2       3.8
1       1.8
;
PROC SORT; BY RECTIME;
PROC PRINT;
Title 'Sorting Example - Ascending';
PROC SORT; BY DESCENDING RECTIME;
PROC PRINT;
Title 'Sorting Example - Descending';
RUN;
```

2. Run this program. (Because there is no OUT= statement, this program sorts the SAS MYDATA data set and does not create a new data set.) Output from the first PROC PRINT contains data sorted (ascending) by RECTIME, and output from the second contains data sorted (descending) by RECTIME, as shown in Table 4.2

TABLE 4.2.   **SAS output showing sort ascending and descending**

	Sorting Example - Ascending			Sorting Example - Descending	
OBS	GROUP	RECTIME	OBS	GROUP	RECTIME
1	1	1.8	1	2	4.2
2	1	2.1	2	2	3.8
3	1	2.8	3	2	3.6
4	1	3.1	4	1	3.1
5	2	3.6	5	1	2.8
6	2	3.8	6	1	2.1
7	2	4.2	7	1	1.8

APPENDING AND MERGING DATA SETS

Another useful SAS data manipulation capability is appending or merging data sets.

- Appending adds new *records* to an existing data set.
- Merging adds *variables* to a data set through the use of a key identifier that is present in both data sets (usually an identification code).

Appending Two Data Sets

Appending data sets combines records from two or more data sets. For example, suppose data are collected at two locations and you want to combine the data sets into one SAS data set for analysis. The data sets must have at least some of the same variables in common. Appending is accomplished by including multiple data set names in the SET statement. For example,

```
DATA NEW; SET OLD1 OLD2;
```

creates the data set NEW, which consists of the records in the OLD1 data set as well as the records from the OLD2 data set.

HANDS-ON
EXAMPLE

In this example you will append one SAS data set to another, creating a larger data set.

1. In the Editor window, open the file DAPPEND1.SAS.

```
DATA OLD1;
INPUT SUBJ $ AGE YRS_SMOKE;
DATALINES;
001 34 12
003 44 14
004 55 35
006 21 3

;
DATA OLD2;
INPUT SUBJ $ AGE YRS_SMOKE;
DATALINES;
011 33 11
012 25 19
023 65 45
032 71 55

;
RUN;
```

This program creates two data sets, one named OLD1 and the other named OLD2. It does not create any output. Run the program and verify by looking at the contents of the Log window that the data sets have been created. Observe these statements in the Log window:

```
NOTE: The data set WORK.OLD1 has 4 observations and 3
 variables.
NOTE: The data set WORK.OLD2 has 4 observations and 3
 variables.
```

2. Return to the Editor window and add the following statements to the end of this SAS program:

```
DATA NEW;SET OLD1 OLD2; RUN;
PROC PRINT DATA=NEW;RUN;
```

3. Run the SAS program and observe the results. The data from the `OLD2` data set is appended to the `OLD1` data set, and the combined data sets are stored in the `NEW` data set. The results (contents of the `NEW` data set) are listed using `PROC PRINT`.

4. In the Editor window, open the file `DAPPEND2.SAS`. Notice that in this version of the program, the `OLD2` data set contains an additional variable, `MARRIED`.

```
DATA OLD1;
... etc ...
DATA OLD2;
INPUT SUBJ $ AGE YRS_SMOKE MARRIED;
DATALINES;
011 33 11 1
012 25 19 0
023 65 45 1
032 71 55 1

;
RUN;
DATA NEW;SET OLD1 OLD2; RUN;
PROC PRINT DATA=NEW;RUN;
```

5. Run this SAS program and observe the results.
   Where there is no matching variable in an appended data set, the data are set to missing in the merged data set.

Merging Data Sets by a Key Identifier

Another way to combine data sets is to merge them by adding new variables from one data set to an existing data set. In order to accomplish this, you must have a matching identifier in each data set that can be used by SAS to match the records during the merge. For example, suppose you have data collected on patients taken on two separate occasions, and the data for each collection time are in separate data sets. If you want to combine the data so you can compare pre- and post-treatment values, the technique for merging the data sets using some key identifier (such as patient ID) is:

1. Sort each data set by the key identifier.

2. Within a `DATA` step, use the `MERGE` statement along with a `BY` statement to merge the data by the key identifier.

HANDS-ON
EXAMPLE

In this example you will merge data sets (interleave data) using a key identifier to match records. In this case, the new data set will contain more variables than either of the two original data sets.

1. In the Editor window, open the file DMERGE.SAS. The first data set created in this example is named PRE.

```
DATA PRE;
INPUT CASE PRETREAT;
DATALINES;
1 1.02
2 2.10
etc ...
```

A second data set in the program is named POST:

```
DATA POST;
INPUT CASE POSTREAT;
DATALINES;
1 1.94
2 1.63

etc ...
```

2. Note that each data set contains a variable named CASE. This is the key identifier that tells SAS which records to match when performing the merge. Before merging the data sets, you must sort them on the same identifier:

```
PROC SORT DATA=PRE; BY CASE;
PROC SORT DATA=POST; BY CASE;
```

(You must add the BY CASE; statement to the second PROC SORT statement.)

3. Complete the DATA statement in the program to perform the desired merge:

```
DATA PREPOST;                 * Create new data set;
  MERGE PRE POST; BY CASE;
  DIFF=POSTREAT - PRETREAT; * Calculate DIFF in new data set;
```

The MERGE statement merges the data sets. Also, because you are interested in the difference between the PRE and POST values, the DATA step includes the DIFF= calculation. (Notice that the DIFF calculation is appropriate here because the code is within a DATA step.)

4. The following lines produce a listing of the combined data:

```
ODS HTML;
TITLE 'Merge Example';
PROC PRINT DATA=PREPOST;
RUN;
ODS HTML CLOSE;
```

5. Run the completed program and observe the results shown in Figure 4.2.

FIGURE 4.2. *Example output from merged data sets*

Obs	CASE	PRETREAT	POSTREAT	DIFF
1	1	1.02	1.94	0.92
2	2	2.10	1.63	-0.47
3	3	1.88	2.73	0.85
4	4	2.20	2.18	-0.02
5	5	1.44	1.82	0.38
6	11	1.55	1.94	0.39
7	13	1.61	2.25	0.64
8	14	2.61	1.70	-0.91
9	15	1.56	1.78	0.22
10	16	0.99	1.52	0.53
11	22	1.53	1.97	0.44

GOING DEEPER: USING PROC FORMAT

In Chapter 3, we saw how you can use predefined SAS date formats to output dates in selected formats. For example, the format Worddate12. outputs dates in a Jan 10, 2009 format. The PROC FORMAT procedure allows you to create you own custom formats. These custom formats allow you to specify the information that will be displayed for selected values of a variable. Note that PROC FORMAT is *not* a part of the DATA step. However, it is related to how data are displayed in the output and is therefore related to the topics of this chapter.

Once a FORMAT has been created, it must then be applied within a SAS procedure to take effect. Thus the steps for using formatted values are:

1. Create a FORMAT definition in PROC FORMAT.

2. Apply the FORMAT to one or more variables in a PROC statement.

For example, suppose your SAS data set contains a variable named MARRIED coded as 0 and 1. To cause SAS to output the words Yes and No rather than 0 and 1, construct a format definition for MARRIED using the PROC FORMAT statement, as illustrated here:

```
PROC FORMAT;
     VALUE FMTMARRIED 0="No"
                      1="Yes";
RUN;
```

The following Hands-on Example illustrates how you would apply the FMTMARRIED format to a variable within a SAS procedure.

You can define as many format names as are required for your data set. Formats must be defined in your code before they are used; therefore, you will usually place the PROC FORMAT early in your program listing. Note that the formats you define in your program are active only during the current SAS job session.

Formats are not limited to numeric variables. For example, if your data were coded M and F for Male and Female, you could create the following format (for the text variable GENDER). Notice that formats for text variables begin with a dollar sign ($):

```
PROC FORMAT;
     VALUE $fmtGENDER 'F' = 'Female'
                      'M' = 'Male';
     PROC PRINT;
     FORMAT GENDER $fmtGENDER.;
     RUN;
```

This code causes PROC PRINT to use the formatted values Female and Male instead of M and F in the output. Note that the format name when specified in a FORMAT statement ends with a dot (.).

HANDS-ON EXAMPLE

In this example you create a format definition (FMTMARRIED) for a variable and apply that definition to the variable MARRIED in PROC PRINT.

1. In the Editor window, open the file DFORMAT1.SAS.

```
PROC FORMAT;
     VALUE FMTMARRIED 0="No"
                      1="Yes";
RUN;
PROC PRINT DATA="C:\SASDATA\SURVEY";
     VAR SUBJECT MARRIED;
     FORMAT MARRIED FMTMARRIED.;
RUN;
```

- ▪ The PROC FORMAT statement defines a format named FMTMARRIED.
- ▪ The FORMAT statement in PROC PRINT tells SAS to apply the FMTMARRIED format definition to the variable MARRIED.
- ▪ Notice that in a FORMAT statement, a SAS format specification ends with a dot (.).
- ▪ When SAS lists the data, as in a PROC PRINT, instead of listing data from the MARRIED variable as 0 or 1, it outputs the data as Yes or No.

2. Run the program and observe the output. Here is a listing of the (partial) output.

OBS	SUBJECT	MARRIED
1	1	Yes
2	2	Yes
3	3	No
4	4	No
5	5	Yes
6	6	Yes
... etc ...		

Notice that in the MARRIED column, the data are output as Yes and No rather than as 0 and 1.

(Continued)

3. Highlight and delete the entire line that begins with FORMAT MARRIED and re-run the program. Notice that in the output the data in the MARRIED column are listed as 1s and 0s because no format has been applied to the variable.

The steps used to create and use PROC FORMAT are as follows:

a. Define and name a format definition—the name of this format is FMTMARRIED.

```
PROC FORMAT;

    VALUE FMTMARRIED 0="No"
                     1="Yes";

RUN;
```

b. Apply that format definition to one or more variables.

```
PROC PRINT DATA=MYSASLIB.SURVEY;
        VAR SUBJECT MARRIED;
        FORMAT MARRIED FMTMARRIED.;

RUN;
```

The format name fmtGENDER is arbitrary. However, it is often a good idea to use the prefix fmt in any user-created format name to help you avoid getting format names mixed up with variable names.

Formats may also use ranges. For example, suppose you want to classify your AGE data using the designations child, teen, adult, and senior. You could do this with the following format:

```
PROC FORMAT;
    Value fmtAGE     LOW-12 = 'Child'
                     13,14,15,16,17,18,19 = 'Teen'
                     20-59 = 'Adult'
                     60-HIGH = 'Senior';
```

The term LOW means the lowest numeric value in the dataset; HIGH means the highest numeric value. You can also use the term OTHER to indicate any other data not specified by the other assignments. Also, you can use lists, as in the Teen specification. (Yes, it would have been simpler to use 13-19, but we did it this way for illustrative purposes.)

Multiple formats can be applied in a procedure using a single FORMAT statement. For example;

```
PROC PRINT;
    FORMAT GENDER fmtGENDER. AGE fmtAGE.;
RUN;
```

You can also assign the same format to several variables. If you have questionnaire data with variables names Q1, Q5, Q7 where each question is coded as 0 and 1 for answers Yes and No, respectively, and you have a format called fmtYN, you could use that FORMAT in a procedure as in the following example:

```
PROC PRINT;
    FORMAT Q1 Q5 Q7 fmtYN.;
RUN;
```

HANDS-ON
EXAMPLE

In this example you create formats using ranges.

1. In the Editor window, open the file DFORMAT2.SAS.

```
PROC FORMAT;
    VALUE FMTAGE    LOW-12 = 'Child'
                    13,14,15,16,17,18,19 = 'Teen'
                    20-59 = 'Adult'
                    60-HIGH = 'Senior';
    VALUE FMTSTAT   1='Lower Class'
                    2='Lower-Middle'
                    3='Middle Class'
                    4='Upper-Middle'
                    5='Upper';
DATA TEST;
SET "C:\SASDATA\SOMEDATA";
PROC PRINT DATA=TEST; VAR AGE STATUS GP;
FORMAT AGE FMTAGE. STATUS FMTSTAT.;
TITLE 'PROC FORMAT Example';
RUN;
```

(Continued)

2. Run the program and observe the output. Notice that values listed for AGE and STATUS are not the original values. Instead, the formatted values are listed.

3. Add the following format to the program:

```
VALUE $FMTGP 'A'='Southern Suburbs'
             'B'='Urban'
             'C'='Northern Suburbs';
```

4. Run the revised program and observe the output.

Occasionally, there is some confusion over the difference between labels and formats. Labels provide more explanatory names to variables and relate to the names of variables only (and not to data values). Formats affect how actual data values are listed in SAS output tables.

SUMMARY

This chapter discussed several techniques for preparing your data for analysis. All of the tasks described in the chapter are used in the DATA step except PROC FORMAT. In the next chapter we begin the discussion of SAS procedures that perform analyses on the the data.

EXERCISES

4.1. Sort data.

Modify the program (EX_4.1.SAS) to sort (alphabetically) first name within last (**last first**) by adding FIRST to the BY variables in the PROC SORT statement.

```
DATA MYDATA;
INPUT @1 LAST $20. @21 FIRST $20. @45 PHONE $12.;
Label LAST = 'Last Name'
      FIRST = 'First Name'
      PHONE = 'Phone Number';
DATALINES;
Reingold          Lucius                201-555-0987
Jones             Pam                   987-555-2948
Abby              Adams                 214-555-0987
Smith             Bev                   213-555-0987
Zoll              Tim Bob               303-555-2309
```

```
    Baker              Crusty                222-555-3212
    Smith              John                  234-555-0987
    Smith              Arnold                234-555-2345
    Jones              Jackie                456-987-8077
    ;
    *-------- Modify to sort by first name within last (by
    last first);
    PROC SORT; BY LAST;
    PROC PRINT LABEL;
    TITLE 'ABC Company';
    TITLE2 'Telephone Directory';
    RUN;
```

4.2. Create subset data sets.

Using the **CARS** permanent SAS dataset, write SAS code to do the following:

a. Create a subset (into a SAS data set named SMALL) consisting of all vehicles whose engine size is less than 2.0 liters. Based on this data set, find the average city and highway miles per gallon for these vehicles.

```
    DATA SMALL;SET "C:\SASDATA\CARS";
    IF ENGINESIZE LT 2;
```

b. Create a subset (into a SAS data set named HYBRID) of all hybrid vehicles in the 2005 dataset. For these vehicles:

    I.   List the BRAND and MODEL names.

    II.   Find the average city and highway miles per gallon.

c. Create a subset (into a SAS data set named AWDSUV) consisting of all vehicles that are both SUVs and have all-wheel drive. For these vehicles:

    I.   List the BRAND and MODEL names.

    II.   Use PROC MEANS to find the average city and highway miles per gallon.

d. Sort the data in AWDSUV by highway miles per gallon (smallest to largest). List the BRAND, MODEL, and highway miles per gallon for this sorted data set.

4.3. Use DROP or KEEP.

Using the SOMEDATA permanent SAS dataset, write SAS code to do the following:

a. Calculate the changes from baseline (i.e., six-month reading minus baseline, etc.) for six, twelve, and twenty-four months. Times are given as:

TIME1 is BASELINE

TIME2 is six months

TIME3 is twelve months

TIME4 is twenty-four months

To calculate the changes, use:

```
CHANGE6=TIME6-BASELINE;
CHANGE12=TIME12-BASELINE;
etc.
```

Use PROC MEANS to find the average and standard deviations for these new "change variables."

b. Create a SAS dataset that contains only the variables ID number, intervention group, age, and gender, and also includes only those subjects in the intervention group who were females. List the ID numbers for these subjects.

4.4. Use PROC FORMAT.

a. In the Editor window, open the file EX_4.4.SAS.

```
PROC FORMAT;
        VALUE fmtYN      0 = 'No'
                         1 = 'Yes';
DATA QUESTIONS;
INPUT Q1 Q2 Q3 Q4 Q5;
DATALINES;
1 0 1 1 0
0 1 1 1 0
0 0 0 1 1
1 1 1 1 1
1 1 1 0 1
;
PROC PRINT;
* PUT FORMAT STATEMENT HERE;
RUN;
```

b. Run the program and observe the output. The Q1-Q5 variables are reported as 0 and 1 values.

c. In the PROC PRINT paragraph, include the statement

```
FORMAT Q1-Q5 fmtYN.;
```

d. Run the program and observe the output. How does the output differ from the version without the FORMAT statement?

CHAPTER

5

PREPARING TO USE SAS PROCEDURES

LEARNING OBJECTIVES

- To be able to understand SAS support statements
- To be able to understand SAS PROC statement syntax
- To be able to use PROC PRINT
- To be able to use basic Output Delivery System (ODS)

In the research environment, one of the primary uses for SAS is to perform calculations for statistical data analysis. SAS provides a plethora of procedures, called PROCs, that allow the user to apply statistical procedures to data. This chapter describes general guidelines you need to know about SAS procedures in preparation for performing data analysis.

Figure 5.1 illustrates the steps involved in analyzing data using SAS. The preceding chapters have focused on the first step—getting data into SAS by creating a data

FIGURE 5.1. *Using SAS*

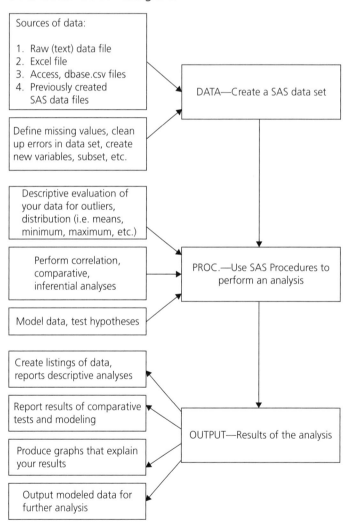

set. We'll now switch gears and focus on the next two steps: using SAS procedures to analyze data in a data set and producing results (output).

UNDERSTANDING SAS SUPPORT STATEMENTS

Before using specific SAS procedures for data analysis, you should understand several basic supporting SAS options and statements that are often used in conjunction with SAS data analysis procedures. This chapter introduces you to these options and statements.

Using the OPTIONS Statement

The OPTIONS statement will often be the first statement appearing in a SAS job, although it can appear anywhere in a SAS program. This statement temporarily changes the way SAS places information in the output listings. For example, when you run a SAS job, it puts several pieces of information at the top of each page, including the data and page number. The command

```
OPTIONS NODATE;
```

instructs SAS to not place date information at the top of each page. This option affects only the current SAS session; it is "forgotten" when you exit the SAS program. Several such options can be indicated in the OPTIONS statement. Following are some commonly used options.

LS = # (LINESIZE)
> This option specifies the maximum width of the printout. (Eighty is a typical page width for portrait mode and 128 is a typical width for landscape mode. The default depends on your SAS installation but is typically 116 in a Microsoft Windows environment.)

NOCENTER (or CENTER)
> This option produces left-justified output. The default option is to center the output.

NODATE (or DATE)
> This option specifies whether the date will be included in the printout. If left as the default (DATE), the current date will be printed at the top of each output page.

NONUMBER (or NUMBER)
> This option specifies whether a page number will be included on the printout. NUMBER is the default.

ORIENTATION=
> This option specifies the paper orientation of your output, either PORTRAIT or LANDSCAPE. For example, ORIENTATION=LANDSCAPE

PAGENO = #
> This option specifies the beginning page number for output. SAS keeps count of each page output from the time you begin the SAS program. Thus, within a SAS session, each time you run a new SAS program, SAS output begins with the next page number. You can use this command to reset the page number to 1 (or to any other number).

PS = # (PAGESIZE)
> This option specifies how many lines to print per page. You may adjust this according to how many lines your printer can print on a single sheet of paper. If you print output to a landscape layout instead of in portrait layout, for example, you may want to adjust the number of lines printed per page. The default PAGESIZE depends on your SAS installation but is typically 41 lines in a Windows environment.

As an example, to cause your SAS output to contain no date, to include 55 lines of text per page, and always to start on page 1, you would use the following OPTIONS statement:

```
OPTIONS NODATE PS=55 PAGENO=1;
```

Later in this chapter we'll introduce the Output Delivery System (ODS), which provides additional tools that you can use to enhance your SAS output. A related statement that specifies options for graphic output, GOPTIONS, is described in Chapter 14, "Creating Graphs."

Using TITLE and FOOTNOTE Statements

The TITLE statement instructs SAS to place a line of text at the top of each output page. Similarly, a FOOTNOTE statement places text lines at the bottom of each output page. Up to 9 title or footnote lines can be specified. For example:

```
TITLE 'title text ';
FOOTNOTE 'footnote text ';
```

or

```
TITLEn 'title text ';
FOOTNOTEn 'footnote text ';
```

where n is a number between 2 and 9. A TITLE or FOOTNOTE statement without a number specifies an initial TITLE or FOOTNOTE line. Subsequent TITLE or FOOTNOTE lines can be defined using TITLE2, TITLE3, and so on up to TITLE9;

and FOOTNOTE2, FOOTNOTE3, and so on up to FOOTNOTE9. (There are no blanks between TITLE or FOOTNOTE and the number.) For example:

```
TITLE 'The first line of the title ';
TITLE2 'The second line of the title ';
TITLE5 'Several lines skipped, then this title on the
   fifth line ';
FOOTNOTE 'This is a footnote ';
FOOTNOTE3 'This is a footnote, line 3 ';
```

You can use either single or double quotation marks when defining a title or footnote, but you must be consistent for each definition. Once you have specified a TITLE or FOOTNOTE, it is used in all subsequent SAS output (even in a new SAS program within the same session) until you redefine the TITLE or FOOTNOTE lines. You can cancel all TITLE (or FOOTNOTE) lines with the statement

```
TITLE;          or          FOOTNOTE;
```

A TITLEn or FOOTNOTEn statement eliminates all TITLE and FOOTNOTE definitions greater than or equal to n.

HANDS-ON
EXAMPLE

In this example, output is created using two SAS PROCs. A TITLE is defined for the first PROC and changed for the second.

1. In the Editor window, open the SAS program DTITLE.SAS.

```
DATA MYDATA;
INFILE 'C:\SASDATA\EXAMPLE.DAT';
INPUT  ID  1-3  GP  $  5  AGE  6-9  TIME1  10-14  TIME2  15-19
   TIME3 20-24;
RUN;
PROC PRINT;
TITLE 'Example SAS programs';
TITLE2 'These are data from the example file.';
TITLE4 'Using the EXAMPLE data set.';
FOOTNOTE 'This is a footnote';
PROC MEANS;
TITLE2 'This is output from PROC Means.';
RUN;
```

(Continued)

2. Run the program and observe the output. A sample page of the output is shown below. This program places the title "Example SAS programs" on all output pages. For the PROC PRINT procedure, the title on the second line is "These are data from the example file." For the PROC MEANS procedure, the new TITLE2 replaces the old TITLE2 and all higher titles (TITLE4) are canceled.

```
                    Example SAS Programs
            These are data from the example file.


                 Using the EXAMPLE data set.


    Obs     ID     GP     AGE     TIME1     TIME2     TIME3


     1      101    A      12       22.3      25.3      28.2
     2      102    A      11       22.8      27.5      33.3
     3      104    B      12       22.8      30.0      32.8
     4      110    A      12       18.5      26.0      29.0
     5      122    B       9       19.5      25.0      25.3
                          ... etc ...
    27      410    B      13       22.2      30.4      32.1
    28      412    C       9       19.0      22.5      24.9
    29      444    B      13       24.2      32.3      33.8
    30      445    A      12       22.1      31.3      31.6
    31      450    C      10       20.2      25.5      27.8
    32      461    B      13       21.3      27.1      31.4


                    This is a footnote
```

It is important to realize that TITLEs and FOOTNOTEs are remembered as long as you are in a SAS session. Therefore, if you create a title using one program, be sure to change or erase the TITLE when beginning a different analysis, such as starting a new procedure or performing analysis on a different set of data. Otherwise you'll end up having an incorrect TITLE and/or FOOTNOTE on your output. Because of this, some programmers always include a TITLE and FOOTNOTE statement at the beginning of a program to prevent leftover titles or footnotes from appearing in the output.

Including Comments in Your SAS Code

It is good programming practice to include explanatory comments in your code. This allows you to understand what you have done when you go back into your code the next day (or the next year).

Comment statements can be used almost anywhere in a SAS job to document the job. You can use any number of comment statements in a job. There are two ways to include comments in your code. In this first example, a comment begins with an asterisk (*) and ends with a semicolon.

```
*This is a message
It can be several lines long
But it always ends with an ;

*****************************************************
* Boxed messages stand out more, still end in a semicolon *
*****************************************************;
```

Another technique to use is to begin a comment with /* and end with */. This technique is useful when you want to include statements that contain a semicolon. For example, you can comment out several lines of code you do not want to use currently, but that you want to retain for possible future use or reference. Here are two examples of this comment technique:

```
/*This is a SAS comment*/

/* Use this comment technique to comment out lines of code
PROC PRINT;
PROC MEANS;
End of comment - the PROCS were ignored*/
```

> In your own programming, it is a good idea to begin every program with a note about what it does, when it was written, and who wrote it. It may not seem important at the moment, but six months or a year later the note can save you valuable time.

Using RUN to Execute Statements

The RUN statement causes previously entered SAS statements to be executed. For example:

```
PROC PRINT;
PROC MEANS;
RUN;
```

Include a RUN statement after major sections in your SAS code. A RUN statement *must* be the last statement in your Windows SAS program.

If you fail to include a RUN statement at the end of your SAS job (or if SAS runs into an error and never sees the RUN statement), the SAS processor may continue to run in the background. This can cause unpredictable problems. If this occurs, press Ctrl + Break. An option will appear allowing you to "Cancel Submitted Statements."

UNDERSTANDING PROC STATEMENT SYNTAX

Although there are scores of SAS PROCs, the syntax is consistent across all of them. Once you learn how SAS PROCs generally work, you should be able to use PROCs that are not covered in this book. This section discusses common syntax used in most analytical PROCs. **Options** and **statements** that are specific to a PROC are discussed in the context of that PROC. The general syntax of the SAS PROC statement is:

```
PROC name options;
    Statements/statementoptions;
...etc...
    Statements/statementoptions;
    RUN;
```

Notice the three parts to this statement. The first line, PROC name options;, contains the name of the procedure and possibly some procedure options. For example, a simple no-option use of a PROC is

```
PROC PRINT;
RUN;
```

Procedure options add information to the procedure. Two commonly used options are

```
DATA=
```
indicates the data set to use in the analysis

```
OUT=
```
creates an output data set containing results from the procedure

The most commonly used option within the PROC statement is the DATA= option. For example:

```
PROC PRINT DATA=MYDATA;
RUN;
```

The DATA= option tells SAS which data set to use in the analysis. If there has been only one data set previously created (within a session), there is no need for this statement. However, if you've created more than one data set during a particular SAS session, it's a good idea to include a DATA= option to specify which data set SAS is to use. SAS will use the most recently defined data set, unless you specify otherwise.

By default, SAS will use the most recently defined data set, unless you specify otherwise.

Another commonly used PROC name option is OUT=*datasetname*. This option is used to create a new SAS dataset from a procedure. (This option will be illustrated in upcoming examples.)

Procedure STATEMENTs are often required to indicate information about how an analysis is to be performed. For example, in the code

```
PROC PRINT;
VAR ID GROUP TIME1 TIME2;
RUN;
```

the VAR statement indicates that only the listed variables are to be used in the procedure. Statements can themselves have options. For example:

```
PROC FREQ;
    TABLES GROUP*SOCIO/CHISQ;
RUN;
```

In this example, the TABLES statement of the PROC FREQ (Frequencies) procedure (which is covered in detail in Chapter 7) instructs SAS to create a table based on data from the variables GROUP and SOCIO. The statement option /CHISQ tells SAS to calculate chi-square and other statistics on this table.

As described previously, the RUN statement causes SAS to execute all previous statements, or all statements since the most recent RUN statement.

Using common SAS syntax, you can build statements to perform many types of analyses. As each PROC is described in future chapters, additional options and statements will be described that are unique to that procedure. However, some statements can be used with (almost) every SAS procedure. These include the following:

VAR variable(s);
　　Instructs SAS to use only the variables in the list for the analysis.

BY variable(s);
　　Causes SAS to repeat the procedure for each different value of the named variable(s). (The data set must first be sorted by the variables listed in the BY statement.)

ID variable(s);
　　Instructs SAS to use the specified variable as an observation identifier in a listing of the data.

LABEL var='*label*';
　　Assigns a descriptive label to a variable.

```
WHERE (expression);
```
Instructs SAS to select only those observations for which the expression is true.

Using the VAR Statement in a SAS Procedure

The `VAR` statement specifies which variables in the selected SAS data set are to be used by the procedure. The syntax of the statement is:

```
VAR varlist;
```
An example is:

```
PROC MEANS; VAR HEIGHT WEIGHT AGE;
```

This statement tells SAS to perform `PROC MEANS` only on the three listed variables. If you have several variables in your data set, this is a way to limit your analysis only to those of interest.

> To save time and typing, you can use a list such as `Q1-Q50` (using a single dash) to indicate 50 different variable names (Q1, Q2, Q3, etc.) in a `VAR` statement where the variable names are from a consecutive numerical list. SAS also understands the variable list `ID -- SBP` (two dashes between variable names) to indicate all variables between `ID` and `SBP` (inclusive).

Using the BY Statement in a SAS Procedure

The `BY` statement is a powerful and handy method that allows you to quickly produce subset analyses from your data. To use the `BY` statement, you must have a grouping variable such as `GENDER`, `GROUP`, `RACE`, and so on. Then you must sort your data (using `PROC SORT`) by the variable on which you wish to subset. (Sorting was discussed in Chapter 4.) Finally, when you add the `BY` statement, SAS performs the analysis separately for the groups specified in the `BY` statement variable. The syntax for the `BY` statement is:

```
BY variable list;
```

> Sort a SAS data set using `PROC SORT` before you perform an analysis using the `BY` statement.

HANDS-ON
EXAMPLE

In this example you will calculate means BY group.

1. In the Editor window, open the file `DSORTMEANS.SAS`.

```
DATA MYDATA;
INFILE 'C:\SASDATA\EXAMPLE.DAT';
INPUT ID 1-3 GP $ 5 AGE 6-9 TIME1 10-14 TIME2 15-19 TIME3 20-24;
```

```
LABEL   ID= 'ID Number'
        GP='Intervention Group'
        AGE ='Age on Jan 1, 2000'
        TIME1='Baseline'
        TIME2='6 Months'
        TIME3='12 Months'
        TIME4='24 Months'
        STATUS='Socioeconomic Status';
PROC MEANS; VAR TIME1 TIME2;
PROC SORT ;BY GP;
PROC MEANS; VAR TIME1 TIME2;BY GP;
RUN;
```

2. Run the program. Observe that the first PROC MEANS produces the following output:

```
              The MEANS Procedure


Variable  Label      N      Mean     Std Dev    Minimum      Maximum
--------------------------------------------------------------------
TIME1     Baseline   50   21.2680000  1.7169551  17.0000000  24.2000000
TIME2     6 Months   50   27.4400000  2.6590623  21.3000000  32.3000000
--------------------------------------------------------------------
```

This output reports means for the entire data set (50 records).

3. Observe that when the BY statement is used (after the data are sorted), the means are calculated separately for each value of the grouping variable GP, which has two levels (A and B.)

```
------------------ Intervention Group=A ----------------------


Variable  Label      N      Mean     Std Dev    Minimum      Maximum
--------------------------------------------------------------------
TIME1     Baseline   11   20.9000000  2.0813457  17.0000000  23.0000000
TIME2     6 Months   11   27.0000000  2.9295051  21.3000000  31.3000000
--------------------------------------------------------------------


------------------ Intervention Group=B ----------------------


Variable  Label      N      Mean     Std Dev    Minimum      Maximum
--------------------------------------------------------------------
TIME1     Baseline   29   21.1862069  1.5853625  18.5000000  24.2000000
TIME2     6 Months   29   27.4344828  2.6357807  23.1000000  32.3000000
--------------------------------------------------------------------

... etc ...
```

(Continued)

Note also that the labels defined in the DATA step are used in the output.

4. Change the grouping variable used in the SORT and PROC statements to STATUS and re-run the program. Notice that the program creates five tables, one for each value of the variable STATUS.

USING THE ID STATEMENT IN A SAS PROCEDURE

The ID statement provides you with a way to increase the readability of your output. It allows you to specify a variable to be used as an observation (record, subject) identifier. For example, in a PROC PRINT procedure you can specify an ID statement that will be displayed at the far left of your listing.

HANDS-ON
EXAMPLE

In this example you will learn how to use the ID statement.

1. In the Editor window, open the file D_ID.SAS.

```
DATA WEIGHT;
INFORMAT MDATE MMDDYY10.;
FORMAT MDATE DATE9.;
INPUT MDATE RAT_ID $ WT_GRAMS TRT $ PINKEYE $;
DATALINES;
02/03/2009 001 093 A Y
02/04/2009 002 087 B N
02/04/2009 003 103 A Y
02/07/2009 005 099 A Y
02/08/2009 006 096 B N
02/11/2009 008 091 B Y
;
RUN;
PROC PRINT;
RUN;
```

This program lists information about results of an experiment involving six rats.

2. Run the program and observe the results. The first few lines of the output are:

```
Obs        MDATE     RAT_ID    WT_GRAMS    TRT    PINKEYE
 1      03FEB2009     001           93      A        Y
 2      04FEB2009     002           87      B        N
 . . . etc . . .
```

Notice that the RAT_ID is the second column of the data, and the data in the Obs column are the sequential record numbers from the data set.

3. Revise the PROC PRINT line to include the following statement, then re-run the program.

PROC PRINT;ID RAT_ID;

The output now places the RAT_ID variable in the leftmost column, replacing the generic Obs column.

```
RAT_ID         MDATE     WT_GRAMS    TRT    PINKEYE
  001       03FEB2009        93       A        Y
  002       04FEB2009        87       B        N
  003       04FEB2009       103       A        Y
  005       07FEB2009        99       A        Y
  006       08FEB2009        96       B        N
  008       11FEB2009        91       B        Y
```

The ID statement places a particular variable in the first column, usually to make it easier to identify your data records.

USING THE LABEL STATEMENT IN A SAS PROCEDURE

In Chapter 3 we learned how to use the LABEL statement within the DATA step to create labels for several variables. Another version of the LABEL statement allows you to create labels for variable names within a procedure. For example, suppose in the previous Hands-on Example you want the column for the variable TRT to read "Treatment." Include the statement

LABEL TRT='Treatment';

after the PROC PRINT statement. Also, include a LABEL option in the PROC PRINT statement to indicate that you want the printout to use defined labels.

```
PROC PRINT LABEL;
   ID RAT_ID;
   LABEL TRT='Treatment';
RUN;
```

In most other procedures you need to include only the LABEL statement without also using the LABEL option in the PROC statement.

HANDS-ON
EXAMPLE

In this example you will learn how to use the LABEL statement within a procedure.

1. Using the SAS file D_ID.SAS and assuming that you still have the ID statement in place from the previous Hands-on Example, add a LABEL statement to the PROC PRINT paragraph:

```
PROC PRINT LABEL;
    ID RAT_ID;
    LABEL TRT='Treatment';
RUN;
```

2. Run the revised program. Observe the new column label for TRT:

```
RAT_ID      MDATE    WT_GRAMS   Treatment    PINKEYE
  001     03FEB2009      93         A           Y
  002     04FEB2009      87         B           N
  003     04FEB2009     103         A           Y
  005     07FEB2009      99         A           Y
  006     08FEB2009      96         B           N
  008     11FEB2009      91         B           Y
```

3. Remove the LABEL option in the PROC MEANS statement and re-run the program. Observe the difference in the output (the TRT column).

4. Add a PROC MEANS with LABEL statement for WT_GRAMS:

```
PROC MEANS;
    LABEL WT_GRAMS="Weight in Grams";
RUN;
```

Run the revised program and observe the output. Notice that a LABEL is indicated for the WT_GRAMS variable, and that you were not required to use the LABEL option in the PROC MEANS statement.

```
Variable Label            N       Mean      Std Dev     Minimum       Maximum
-----------------------------------------------------------------------------
MDATE                     6     17934.17   3.0605010    17931.00      17939.00
WT-GRAMS  Weight in Grams  6    94.8333333  5.7416606   87.0000000   103.0000000
-----------------------------------------------------------------------------
```

USING THE WHERE STATEMENT IN A SAS PROCEDURE

The WHERE statement allows you to specify which output will be included in an analysis. This is different from the subsetting IF statements described in Chapter 3. In that chapter, the subsetting IF statement in the DATA step dictates which records are kept in a data set for subsequent analyses on that particular data set. The WHERE statement affects only the data used for a particular procedure. For example, in the ID example, suppose you want to output data only for treatment A in the PROC PRINT statement. Use the statement

```
WHERE TRT="A";
```

in the PROC PRINT (or any) procedure to limit the analysis to only those records that meet the criteria in the WHERE statement. Subsequent procedures on the data set will *not* be subject to the WHERE restriction unless it is invoked again for that procedure.

HANDS-ON EXAMPLE

In this example you will learn how to use the WHERE statement.

1. In the SAS file D_ID.SAS used in the previous Hands-on Example, modify the PROC PRINT statement to read:

```
PROC PRINT LABEL;
   ID RAT_ID;
   LABEL TRT='Treatment';
   WHERE TRT="A";
RUN;
```

2. Run the program and observe the output.

RAT_ID	MDATE	WT_GRAMS	Treatment	PINKEYE
001	03FEB2009	93	A	Y
003	04FEB2009	103	A	Y
005	07FEB2009	99	A	Y

Only the records that match the criteria specified by the WHERE statement are included in the output.

USING PROC PRINT

Although many examples have introduced you to PROC PRINT, a number of options for this procedure have not been discussed. As demonstrated, the PROC PRINT outputs a listing of the data values in a SAS dataset. Using these selected options in the

PROC PRINT statement, you can enhance that listing to create a more useful report. Some of the options listed below duplicate those already discussed but are included for the sake of completeness:

DATA=
> Specifies data set to use

DOUBLE
> Double-spaces the output

LABEL
> Uses variable labels as column headings

N <= label>
> Includes the number of observations in the listing

OBS=
> Allows you to specify a label for the Obs column

ROUND
> Rounds data before totaling

SUM *vars*
> Includes total for specified variables

The N option instructs SAS to print the number of observations and allows you to specify a label to be printed. The format for this is:

N='*label*' or n="*label*"

The OBS option allows you to specify a label at the top of the Obs column in the data listing. The syntax for this is:

OBS='*label*' or OBS="*label*"

The SUM option specifies that a sum of the values for the variables listed be reported. The syntax is:

SUM *variable list*;

The following SAS program (APRINT1.SAS) utilizes several of the PROC PRINT options and the SUM statement:

```
PROC PRINT DATA=MYSASLIB.SOMEDATA
    N= 'Number of Subjects is: '
    OBS='Subjects';
SUM TIME1 TIME2 TIME3 TIME4;
TITLE 'PROC PRINT Example';
RUN;
```

This code produces the following output:

```
Subjects  ID  GP  AGE  TIME1   TIME2   TIME3    TIME4   STATUS SEX GENDER
       1  101  A   12   22.3    25.3    28.2     30.6      5    0   Female
       2  102  A   11   22.8    27.5    33.3     35.8      5    0   Female
       3  104  B   12   22.8    30.0    32.8     31.0      4    0   Female
       4  110  A   12   18.5    26.0    29.0     27.9      5    1   Male
     etc.
      50  604  B   12   22.4    27.2    31.8     35.6      4    0   Female
                       ======  ======  ======   ======
                       1063.4  1372.0  1524.6   1541.9

                                Number of Subjects is: 50
```

Notice that the line in the SAS code

```
N = 'Number of Subjects is: '
```

produces the statement at the bottom of the printout reporting the number of subjects. Also, the option

```
Obs='Subjects';
```

causes the label above the record numbers to be Subjects. Finally, the statement

```
SUM TIME1 TIME2 TIME3 TIME4;
```

causes the totals for the four variables to be reported at the bottom of the report.

HANDS-ON
EXAMPLE

In this example you will learn how to use several options in the PROC PRINT procedure.

1. In the Editor window, open the file APRINT1.SAS.

2. Modify the program by adding

   PROC SORT DATA=MYSASLIB.SOMEDATA;BY GP;

   before the PROC PRINT.

3. Replace the SUM line with

   SUM TIME1 TIME2 TIME3 TIME4;BY GP;

4. Run the program. How does this change the output?

GOING DEEPER: INTRODUCING THE SAS OUTPUT DELIVERY SYSTEM (ODS)

The SAS Output Delivery System (ODS) is a feature that allows you to enhance your SAS output. Normally, SAS output appears in the Output window. This output listing is textual and there are few options for controlling the "look" of the listing.

With ODS, however, you can choose to create output in other formats, including HTML (HyperText Markup Language), RTF (Rich Text Format), and PDF (Portable Document Format). Output to these formats usually provides more professional-looking reports.

This section briefly introduces ODS; more information about ODS options is provided in Chapter 15. In the remainder of this book, many of the example programs will use ODS to create output.

For example, to output results using ODS-specified output format,

1. Turn on ODS (with a command such as ODS HTML;).

2. Perform one or more analyses that create output.

3. Turn off ODS (with a command such as ODS HTML CLOSE;).

   Previous examples in this chapter have used PROC PRINT to create a listing of the data. As you do the following Hands-on Example, compare the new ODS-generated output with the previous output.

HANDS-ON
EXAMPLE

In this example you will learn a basic use of the SAS Output Delivery System (ODS) for HTML.

1. In the Editor window, open the file DODS1.SAS.

   ```
   ODS HTML;
   PROC MEANS DATA="C:\SASDATA\SOMEDATA" MAXDEC=2 ;
   VAR AGE TIME1-TIME4;
   TITLE 'Example output to HTML';
   RUN;
   ODS HTML CLOSE;
   ```

2. Observe the output in the "Results Viewer" Window. See Figure 5.2.

FIGURE 5.2. *Example output*

Example output to HTML

The MEANS Procedure

Variable	Label	N	Mean	Std Dev	Minimum	Maximum
AGE	Age on Jan 1, 2000	50	10.46	2.43	4.00	15.00
TIME1	Baseline	50	21.27	1.72	17.00	24.20
TIME2	6 Months	50	27.44	2.66	21.30	32.30
TIME3	12 Months	50	30.49	3.03	22.70	35.90
TIME4	24 Months	50	30.84	3.53	21.20	36.10

Compare this ODS-generated `PROC PRINT` output with the output created by `PROC PRINT` in previous examples in this chapter. This ODS-generated output is in HTML format.

3. Another way to create professional-looking output is with the RTF option. In the program code, change all of the instances of HTML to RTF. Run the program.

4. When you run a SAS job with the ODS RTF option, you will be prompted to either Save or Open the results. For this example, select Save. Notice that the Save dialog box indicates that the output will be saved using Microsoft Word format (if you have Word installed on your computer) or to some other word processing format. Save the results to the file named `C:\SASDATA\MYOUTPUT.RTF`. SAS will automatically append the extension. RTF to the file name you specify.

5. Click the Output window to make it active and notice that the output was also sent to the standard output listing.

6. Open the saved document using your word processor. (WordPad will do if you do not have Microsoft Word or another word processor installed.) Observe that the output table created by ODS is an editable table in the word processor.

In most examples in this book, we use the HTML ODS output style because it is the simplest. After generating HTML output, you can also copy and paste it into almost any word processor.

SUMMARY

This chapter introduced you to the syntax of SAS procedures in preparation for using specific PROCs discussed in the remainder of the book. Understanding the basics of this SAS syntax will enable you to understand how to use PROCs.

EXERCISES

5.1. Add titles and footnotes to output.

Using the program code from FIRST.SAS:

a. Using the TITLE and FOOTNOTE statements, place five lines of titles at the beginning and two footnotes (i.e., footnote lines) at the end of the output.

b. Using the OPTION statement, tell SAS to leave the DATE off the output.

c. Run the program and observe the output.

5.2. Use the ID statement.

Working with the C:\SASDATA\CARS data set, use the ID statement in PROC PRINT to create a listing where the MODEL variable is listed in the first column of the output.

5.3. Use the LABEL statement.

a. Open the file DLABEL.SAS. Add a blank line between the PROC MEANS statement and the RUN Statement. Cut and paste the LABEL statement (from the word LABEL to the semicolon) from its current location to just before the final RUN statement (this places it in the PROC MEANS paragraph). Run the program.

b. Do the labels appear in the output?

c. After the final RUN statement in the program, add a new line:

```
PROC PRINT;RUN;
```

Re-run the program. Do the labels appear in the output? Why or why not?

d. Change the PROC PRINT statement to

```
PROC PRINT LABEL;RUN;
```

Re-run the program. Do the labels appear? Why or why not? If you don't remember, go back to the section titled "Using the LABEL Statement in a SAS Procedure" to find out.

5.4. Create ODS output.

a. Using the program file DODS1.SAS, change the ODS option to PDF, run the program, and observe the result.

b. Change the ODS specification to RTF and run the program. Save the results and open them in your word processor. Edit the table in your word processor by making the text in the top row red and the font size for the entire table set to 10. (In other words, you can edit this table using any method within your word processor.)

CHAPTER

6

EVALUATING
QUANTITATIVE DATA

LEARNING OBJECTIVES

- To be able to calculate basic descriptive statistics using PROC MEANS
- To be able to calculate basic and advanced descriptive statistics and analyze the characteristics of a set of data using PROC UNIVARIATE
- To be able to create histograms using PROC UNIVARIATE

The ancient Greek philosopher Socrates had a saying: "Know thyself." In statistics it's important to know thy data. You need to have knowledge of the distribution and character of your data before you can successfully perform other analyses. If your data are quantitative in nature (for example, a measure such as height or the volume of liquid in a bottle), the SAS procedures in this chapter can help you glean a lot of information from the numbers.

USING PROC MEANS

PROC MEANS is useful for evaluating quantitative data in your data set and for creating a simple summary report. Using this procedure, you can calculate simple statistics that include the mean and standard deviation, plus the minimum and maximum, all of which allows you to to see quickly whether data values fall within allowed limits for each variable. If a data value is smaller or larger than expected, check your data to determine if the value has been miscoded. PROC MEANS can be used for:

- Describing quantitative data (numerical data on which it makes sense to perform arithmetic calculations)
- Describing means by group
- Searching for possible outliers (unusually small or large values) or incorrectly coded values
- Creating a simple report showing summary statistics

The following section includes a list of commonly used options and statements illustrated in this chapter along with a few options that might be helpful when you use this procedure. For more information, refer to the SAS documentation.

PROC MEANS Statement Syntax and Options

The syntax of the PROC MEANS statement is:

    PROC MEANS <options> <statistics keywords>; <statements>;

The items listed in angle brackets (<>) are optional. The most commonly used options are:

DATA=	Specify data set to use
MAXDEC=n	Use n decimal places to print output
NOPRINT	Suppress output of descriptive statistics

Statistics keywords for PROC MEANS are:

N	Number of observations
NMISS	Number of missing observations
MEAN	Arithmetic average
STD	Standard deviation
MIN	Minimum (smallest)
MAX	Maximum (largest)
RANGE	Range
SUM	Sum of observations
VAR	Variance
USS	Uncorrected sum of squares
CSS	Corrected sum of squares
STDERR	Standard error
T	Student's t value for testing Ho: $\mu_d = 0$
PRT	P-value associated with t-test above
SUMWGT	Sum of the WEIGHT variable values
MEDIAN	50th percentile
P1	1st percentile
P5	5th percentile
P10	10th percentile
P90	90th percentile
P95	95th percentile
P99	99th percentile
Q1	1st quartile
Q3	3rd quartile
QRANGE	Quartile range

The items underlined are the default statistics reported by SAS if no statistics key-words are listed. The statement

```
PROC MEANS DATA=RESEARCH MEAN MEDIAN STD;RUN;
```

instructs SAS to calculate the mean, median, and standard deviation on the quantitative data in the `RESEARCH` data set.

Commonly Used Statements for PROC MEANS

`STATEMENTS` related to `PROC MEANS` appear after the semicolon in the initial `PROC MEANS` statement. Here are some commonly used `STATEMENTS` for `PROC MEANS`. For more information, consult the SAS documentation.

VAR *variable(s)*;
Identifies one or more variables to analyze.

BY *variable(s)*variable(s);
Specifies that the analysis is to be performed for each category of a specified variable. The data must first be sorted on that variable.

CLASS *variable(s)*variable(s);
Specifies variables that the procedure uses to group the data into classification levels.

OUTPUT
Specifies a SAS output data set that will contain statistics calculated in `PROC MEANS`. For example,

OUTPUT OUT=*SAS-data-set*;

To specify names of specific variables' output, use the format:

OUTPUT <OUT=*SAS-data-set*> *statistic-keyword-1=name(s)* <...*statistic-keyword-n-name(s)*> *<percentiles-specification>* ;

FREQ *variable* variable;
Specifies a variable that represents a count of observations.

The following examples illustrate the use of `PROC MEANS` options and statements:

```
* Simplest invocation - on all numeric variables *;
PROC MEANS;
```

```
*Specified statistics and variables *;
PROC MEANS N MEAN STD;
  VAR SODIUM CARBO;

* Subgroup descriptive statistics using BY statement*;
PROC SORT; BY SEX;
PROC MEANS; BY SEX;
  VAR FAT PROTEIN SODIUM;

* Subgroup descriptive statistics using CLASS statement*;
PROC MEANS; CLASS SEX;
  VAR FAT PROTEIN SODIUM;
```

HANDS-ON
EXAMPLE

In this example you will learn how to use some of the basic options in PROC MEANS. Suppose you have a data set of measurements (weight, height, and age) from several children. Perform the following tasks using PROC MEANS:

- Report simple descriptive statistics.
- Limit the output to two decimal places.
- Request a selected list of statistics.

1. In the Editor window, open the file AMEANS1.SAS.

```
DATA CHILDREN;
INPUT WEIGHT HEIGHT AGE;
DATALINES;
64 57 8
71 59 10
53 49 6
67 62 11
55 51 8
58 50 8
77 55 10
57 48 9
56 42 10
```

```
51 42 6
76 61 12
68 57 9
;
ODS HTML; * NOTICE INVOCATION OF ODS OUTPUT;
PROC MEANS;
TITLE 'PROC MEANS, simplest use';
RUN;
PROC MEANS MAXDEC=2;VAR WEIGHT HEIGHT;
TITLE 'PROC MEANS, limit decimals, specify variables';
RUN;
PROC MEANS MAXDEC=2 N MEAN STDERR MEDIAN;VAR WEIGHT HEIGHT;
TITLE 'PROC MEANS, specify statistics to report';
RUN;
ODS HTML CLOSE; *ODS OUTPUT CLOSED;
```

2. Run the program and observe the output. Table 6.1 shows the HTML/ODS output for the program. Notice:

- In the first output table, statistics are reported to seven decimal points in the first PROC MEANS output and are limited to two decimal points for the other procedures, as controlled by the MAXDEC=2 option.

- In the second table, descriptive statistics are reported only for the two variables specified in the VAR statement.

- In the third table, only the statistics selected in the PROC statement are reported.

TABLE 6.1. **Output for PROC MEANS**

Variable	N	Mean	Std Dev	Minimum	Maximum
WEIGHT	12	62.7500000	8.9861004	51.0000000	77.0000000
HEIGHT	12	52.7500000	6.8240884	42.0000000	62.0000000
AGE	12	8.9166667	1.8319554	6.0000000	12.0000000

Variable	N	Mean	Std Dev	Minimum	Maximum
WEIGHT	12	62.75	8.99	51.00	77.00
HEIGHT	12	52.75	6.82	42.00	62.00

Variable	N	Mean	Std Error	Median
WEIGHT	12	62.75	2.59	61.00
HEIGHT	12	52.75	1.97	53.00

Using PROC MEANS with BY Group and CLASS Statements

It is common to compare means across the levels of some grouping factor that, for example, specifies treatment times. The following Hands-on Example shows you how to use PROC MEANS to calculate weight gain in chickens by type of feed. This example uses two methods for producing the desired calculations:

- Results reported for each group in separate tables using the BY group option
- Results reported for each group in a single table using the CLASS option

HANDS-ON EXAMPLE

In this example you will learn how to display basic statistics by groups using two techniques.

1. In the Editor window, open the file AMEANS2.SAS.

```
DATA FERTILIZER;
INPUT FEEDTYPE WEIGHTGAIN;
DATALINES;
1 46.20
1 55.60
1 53.30
1 44.80
1 55.40
1 56.00
1 48.90
2 51.30
2 52.40
2 54.60
2 52.20
2 64.30
2 55.00
;
ODS HTML;
PROC SORT DATA=FERTILIZER;BY FEEDTYPE;
PROC MEANS; VAR WEIGHTGAIN; BY FEEDTYPE;
TITLE 'Summary statistics by group';
RUN;
PROC MEANS; VAR WEIGHTGAIN; CLASS FEEDTYPE;
TITLE 'Summary statistics USING CLASS';
RUN;
ODS HTML CLOSE;
```

2. Examine the SAS code. Notice that the data must be sorted before you can use a `BY` group option in a `PROC MEANS` statement. In the second `PROC MEANS`, where you are using the `CLASS` option, sorting is not necessary (even if the data are not already sorted).

3. Run the program. Examine the output from the first `PROC MEANS`, which uses the `BY` option (Table 6.2). The output contains two separate tables, one for each value of `FEEDTYPE`.

TABLE 6.2. **PROC MEANS output using the BY option**

FEEDTYPE=1

Analysis Variable : WEIGHTGAIN				
N	Mean	Std Dev	Minimum	Maximum
7	51.4571429	4.7475808	44.8000000	56.0000000

FEEDTYPE=2

Analysis Variable : WEIGHTGAIN				
N	Mean	Std Dev	Minimum	Maximum
6	54.9666667	4.7944412	51.3000000	64.3000000

4. Examine the output shown in Table 6.3 for the second `PROC MEANS` statement. In this instance, which uses the `CLASS` option, the output for both variables appears in a single table, broken down by `FEEDTYPE`.

TABLE 6.3. **PROC MEANS output using the CLASS option**

	N		Analysis Variable : WEIGHTGAIN			
FEEDTYPE	Obs	N	Mean	Std Dev	Minimum	Maximum
1	7	7	51.4571429	4.7475808	44.8000000	56.0000000
2	6	6	54.9666667	4.7944412	51.3000000	64.3000000

5. Modify the program to output the following statistics:

```
N MEAN MEDIAN MIN MAX
```

and use `MAXDEC=2` to limit number of decimals in output. Run the edited program and observe the output.

USING PROC UNIVARIATE

The previous section described how to use the `PROC MEANS` statement to calculate basic statistics for a quantitative variable. `PROC UNIVARIATE` provides a wider variety of statistics and graphs and is better suited to helping you discover important information about the distribution of each variable, such as whether:

- the data are approximately normally distributed

- there are outliers in the data (if so, where?)

- data distributions for variables differ by group

With this information in hand, you can make informed decisions about how best to present and analyze your data. The syntax of the `PROC UNIVARIATE` statement is:

```
PROC UNIVARIATE <options>; <statements>
```

Common options for `PROC UNIVARIATE` include:

`DATA=`
Specify data set to use

`CIBASIC`
Request confidence limits for the mean, standard deviation, and variance based on normally distributed data

`ALPHA=`
Specify the level for the confidence limits

`MU0=`
Specify the value of the location parameter for the one-sample t-test, sign test, and signed rank test (MU stands for the Greek letter μ, which symbolizes the population mean)

`NORMAL`
Request tests for normality

`PLOTS`
Request stem-and-leaf, box, and probability plots

`NOPRINT`
Suppress the output of descriptive statistics (primarily used in conjunction with the `OUTPUT` statement)

`TRIMMED=`
Trim the top and bottom proportion of the data before calculating the mean; this can be used to eliminate outliers from the calculation (for example, `TRIMMED=0.1`)

The following are commonly used statements for PROC UNIVARIATE. Several of these will be illustrated in upcoming examples.

VAR *variable(s)*;
Identifies one or more variables to analyze

BY *variable(s)*;
Specifies that the analysis is to be performed for each category of a specified variable; the data must first be sorted on that variable

CLASS *variable(s)*;
For use when creating a histogram; specifies one or two variables that the procedure uses to group the data into classification levels

OUTPUT
Identifies output data set and statistics to include in the data set; the syntax for this statement is

OUTPUT <OUT=*SAS-data-set*> *statistic-keyword-1=name(s)* <*...statistic-keyword-n=name(s)*> <*percentiles-specification*>;

HISTOGRAM
Produces a histogram of one or more specified variables; the syntax is

HISTOGRAM <*variable(s)*> </ *option(s)*>;

A simple program that creates a histogram using the variable AGE in the SOMEDATA data set is:

```
PROC UNIVARIATE DATA="C:\SASDATA\SOMEDATA";
   VAR AGE;
   HISTOGRAM AGE;
   RUN;
```

The following options for the HISTOGRAM statement provide a number of ways you can enhance the basic histogram. These statements appear in the */options* part of the HISTOGRAM statement.

NORMAL
This option specifies that a normal (bell-shaped) curve is to be superimposed on the histogram. This option itself has options that appear in parentheses. For example:

HISTOGRAM AGE/NORMAL (COLOR=RED W=5)

specifies that the normal curve will be red with a width of 5. These are the only two options for the normal curve discussed in this book.

MIDPOINTS

This option allows you to specify the intervals for the histogram bars.

`MIDPOINTS = min to max by units`

for example:

`MIDPOINTS =0 to 40 by 2`

specifies that the horizontal axis will have a minimum of 0, a maximum of 40, and increment of two units. The midpoints of the intervals would be 0, 2, 4, etc. to 40.

VSCALE

This option specifies the scale of the vertical axis.

`VSCALE=type-scale (count, proportion, or percent)`

For example:

`VSCALE=COUNT`

specifies that the scale of the vertical axis will be the number of observations per bin (count). You can alternately request that the scale be proportion or percent.

WAXIS

This option specifes the width of the histogram bars.

`WAXIS= width-scale (1 is the default)`

For example:

`WAXIS= 3`

specifies that the axis-width be three units wide.

WBARLINE

This option specifies the width of the line around the bar.

`WBARLINE= width-scale (1 is the default)`

For example:

`WBARLINE= 3`

specifies that the lines around the histogram bars be three units wide.

COLOR OPTIONS: The following color options specify color for various parts of the histogram:

Use the following statements to specify **color options** in the */options* section of the HISTOGRAM statement. A listing of SAS colors can be found in Appendix A.

CAXIS=*color*
> specifies the color of axes

CBARLINE=*color*
> specifies the color of the line around the bars

CFILL=*color*
> specifies the color of the bars

CFRAME=*color*
> specifies the background color within the frame

CTEXT=*color*
> specifies the color of tick mark values and labels

> For example:

> HISTOGRAM AGE/CBARLINE=GREEN;

> specifies that the lines around the histogram bars will be green.

BAR CHARACTERISTICS: Use the following statements to specify bar characteristics in the /*options* section of the HISTOGRAM statement. A listing of SAS pattern codes can be found in Appendix A.

BARWIDTH=*n*
> specifies barwidth where *n* is the percent of the screen

PFILL=*patterncode*
> indicates which fill pattern to use in the histogram bars

> For example:

HISTOGRAM AGE/PFILL=R4;
> specifies that right 45-degree stripes will fill the boxes. The 4 specifies the width of the stripes.
> See also CBARLINE and WBARLINE above.

INSET
> This option specifies one or more keywords that identify the information to display in the inset. The syntax is

> **INSET** <*keyword(s)* DATA=SAS-data-set> </ *option(s)*>;

These options for the HISTOGRAM statement are illustrated in upcoming examples in the Going Deeper section.

Whereas PROC MEANS is useful for calculating descriptive statistics for many variables at a time, PROC UNIVARIATE is best for the case in which you want to analyze only one or a few variables in depth, because the procedure creates a lot of output. The following Hands-on Example illustrates commonly used options and statements.

HANDS-ON EXAMPLE

In this example you will learn how to use `PROC UNIVARIATE`.

1. In the Editor window, open the file `AUNI1.SAS`.

```
DATA EXAMPLE;
INPUT AGE @@;
DATALINES;
12 11 12 12 9 11 8 8 7 11 12 14 9 10 7 13
6 11 12 4 11 9 13 6 9 7 13 9 13 12 10 13
11 8 11 15 12 14 10 10 13 13 10 8 12 7 13
11 9 12
;
ODS HTML;
PROC UNIVARIATE DATA=EXAMPLE;
    VAR AGE;
RUN;
ODS HTML CLOSE;
```

2. Run this program and observe that this procedure produces a large amount of output and that the output in the Results Viewer is in HTML format.

Understanding PROC UNIVARIATE Output

The output from the Hands-on Example is shown in several tables, and we describe the contents in each table below.

Moments output: The first table (Moments; Table 6.4) provides a list of descriptive statistics for the variable AGE.

N is the sample size.

Sum Weights is the same as the sample size unless a `WEIGHT` statement is used to identify a separate variable that contains counts for each observation.

Mean is the arithmetic mean (also known as the average).

Sum Observations is the total (sum) of all the data values.

Std Deviation is the standard deviation.

Variance is a measure of the spread of the distribution (and is the square of the standard deviation).

Skewness is a measure of the symmetry of the data. For normally distributed data, skewness should be close to 0. A positive value indicates that the skew is to the right (long right tail), and a negative value indicates a skew to the left (long left tail).

Kurtosis measures the shape of the distribution (0 indicates normality) where a positive value indicates a distribution that is more peaked with heavier tails than a normal distribution and a negative value indicates a flatter distribution with lighter tails.

Uncorrected SS is the sum of the squared data values.

Corrected SS is the sum of the squared deviations from the mean, a quantity that is used in the calculation of the standard deviation and other statistics.

Coef Variation is the coefficient of variation, which is a unitless measure of variability. It is usually expressed as a percentage and is helpful in comparing the variability between two measures that may have differing units of measurement.

Std Err Mean is the standard error of the mean. This is calculated as the standard deviation divided by $\sqrt{N}$, and it provides a measure of the variability of the sample mean. That is, if we were to take similar samples over and over again, the standard error of the mean would approximate the standard deviation of the sample means.

TABLE 6.4. **Moments output for PROC UNIVARIATE**

Moments			
N	50	Sum Weights	50
Mean	10.46	Sum Observations	523
Std Deviation	2.42613323	Variance	5.88612245
Skewness	-0.5119219	Kurtosis	-0.2610615
Uncorrected SS	5759	Corrected SS	288.42
Coeff Variation	23.1943903	Std Error Mean	0.34310705

Basic Statistical Measures: The second table from PROC UNIVARIATE (Table 6.5) provides several measures of the central tendency and spread of the data. Some values are repeated from the previous table. Terms from this table not already defined are:

Median is the centermost value of the ranked data.

Mode is the most frequent value in the data.

Range is the maximum value minus the minimum value, which is a measure of the spread of the data.

Interquartile Range (IQR) is the difference between the 25th and 75th percentiles of the data and is a measure of spread of the data.

Tests for Location: The tests for location shown in Table 6.6 are used to determine whether the mean (or central tendency) of the data is significantly different from 0 (or another hypothesized value). These tests are discussed more thoroughly in upcoming chapters and are only briefly described here.

TABLE 6.5. **Basic statistical measures from PROC UNIVARIATE**

Basic Statistical Measures			
Location		Variability	
Mean	10.46000	Std Deviation	2.42613
Median	11.00000	Variance	5.88612
Mode	12.00000	Range	11.00000
		Interquartile Range	3.00000

TABLE 6.6. **Tests for location from PROC UNIVARIATE**

Tests for Location: Mu0=0					
Test		Statistic		p Value	
Student's t	t	30.48611	Pr > |t|	<.0001
Sign	M	25	Pr >= |M|	<.0001
Signed Rank	S	637.5	Pr >= |S|	<.0001

Student's *t*-test is a single sample *t*-test of the null hypothesis that the mean of the data is equal to the hypothesized value (in this case 0 by default). When $p < 0.05$, you would typically reject this hypothesis.

Sign Test is a test of the null hypothesis that the probability of positive values (often these values are differences) is the same as for negative values.

Signed Rank Test is a nonparametric test often used instead of the Student's *t*-test when the data are not normally distributed and the sample sizes are small.

Quantiles: Table 6.7 provides a listing of commonly used quantiles of the data including the median (listed as the 50th quantile). To interpret the values in the quantile table, note that the *k*th quantile is the value below which *k%* of the values in the data fall. ("Definition 5" in the table refers to the specific method used to calculate the quantiles using an empirical distribution with averaging. See Frigge, Hoaglin, and Iglewicz, 1989).

Extreme Observations: The Extreme Observations table (Table 6.8) provides a listing of the largest and smallest values in the data set. This is useful for locating

TABLE 6.7.   **Quantiles from PROC UNIVARIATE**

Quantiles (Definition 5)	
Quantile	**Estimate**
100% Max	15
99%	15
95%	14
90%	13
75% Q3	12
50% Median	11
25% Q1	9
10%	7
5%	6
1%	4
0% Min	4

TABLE 6.8.   **Extreme values output from PROC UNIVARIATE**

Extreme Observations			
Lowest		Highest	
Value	Obs	Value	Obs
4	20	13	42
6	24	13	47
6	17	14	12
7	46	14	38
7	26	15	36

outliers in your data. Notice that with each extreme value listed in the table the observation number is also provided. This helps you to be able to go back to locate these extreme observations in your data set.

Using PROC UNIVARIATE to Assess the Normality of the Data

When you select certain options in the PROC UNIVARIATE statement, SAS produces information helpful in assessing the normality of your data. This is important information because a number of statistical tests are based on an assumption of normality. For example:

```
PROC UNIVARIATE NORMAL PLOT DATA=EXAMPLE; VAR AGE;
    HISTOGRAM AGE/NORMAL;
```

The NORMAL and PLOT options produce the following output:

- tests for normality
- stem-and-leaf plot
- box plot
- normal probability plot

The HISTOGRAM statement with the NORMAL option produces a

- histogram
- superimposed normal distribution curve

HANDS-ON
EXAMPLE

In this example you will learn how to request options to assess normality using PROC UNIVARIATE.

1. In the Editor window, open the file AUNI2.SAS.

```
DATA EXAMPLE;
INPUT AGE @@;
DATALINES;
12 11 12 12 9 11 8 8 7 11 12 14 9 10 7 13
6 11 12 4 11 9 13 6 9 7 13 9 13 12 10 13
11 8 11 15 12 14 10 10 13 13 10 8 12 7 13
11 9 12

;
ODS HTML;
PROC UNIVARIATE NORMAL PLOT DATA=EXAMPLE; VAR AGE;
HISTOGRAM AGE/NORMAL ;
TITLE 'PROC UNIVARIATE EXAMPLE';
RUN;
ODS HTML CLOSE;
```

2. Run this program and observe the output, as described below. Based on these normality tests, there is some indication that the variable AGE may not be normally distributed. PROC UNIVARIATE provides several graphical methods also useful in assessing normality. Three of these (older and somewhat rudimentary) graphs are shown in Figure 6.1.

(Continued)

FIGURE 6.1. *Plots to assess normality from PROC UNIVARIATE*

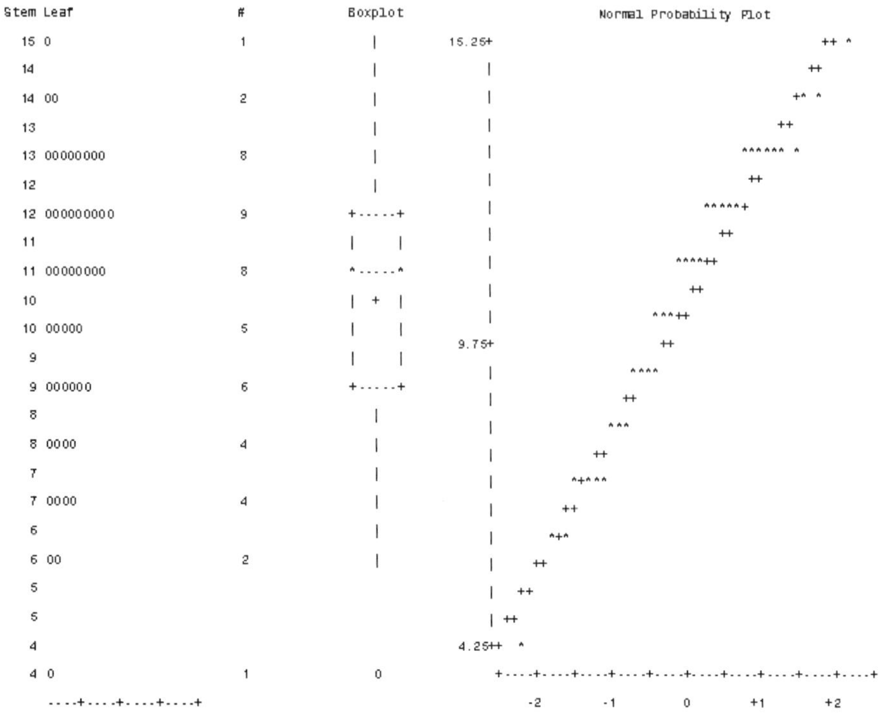

Tests for Normality: Tests for normality are one way to assess whether the data appear normally distributed. Four tests for normality are provided: Shapiro-Wilk, Kolmogorov-Smirnov, Cramer–von Mises, and Anderson-Darling as shown in Table 6.9.

TABLE 6.9. Test for normality from PROC UNIVARIATE

Tests for Normality				
Test	Statistic		p Value	
Shapiro-Wilk	W	0.958283	Pr < W	0.0753
Kolmogorov-Smirnov	D	0.148067	Pr > D	<0.0100
Cramer-von Mises	W-Sq	0.145762	Pr > W-Sq	0.0259
Anderson-Darling	A-Sq	0.834989	Pr > A-Sq	0.0301

The *p*-values in Table 6.9 are for testing the null hypothesis that the AGE variable is normally distributed. Notice that in this case these tests differ in conclusion (assuming a criterion of 0.05 is strictly followed). The Shapiro-Wilk test does not reject normality ($p > 0.05$) while the others reject this hypothesis.

> The four tests for normality represent differing statistical approaches for answering the same question. Frankly, many statisticians believe that these tests are helpful tools but should not be used as the only basis for assessing normality. Also, some references indicate that these tests are helpful only when the size of the data set is less than 50.

- The **stem-and-leaf plot** (on the left of Figure 6.1) is a pseudo-histogram that enumerates each value as a leaf off of a stem that represents the root value of each observation. Thus, you can see that the data contained one value of 15, two values of 14, and so on. The shape of this plot shows a tendency for the data to be skewed to the left (that is, a longer than expected tail in the small values of the distribution). If the stem-and-leaf plot is fairly bell-shaped and symmetrical, this suggests that the data are normally distributed. (See information about histograms in the section "Creating a Histogram Using PROC UNIVARIATE," which follows.)

- The **box-and-whiskers plot** (or boxplot) is a graphical representation of the quartiles of the data with 50 percent (the middle) of the data represented by the box and the whiskers representing 25 percent of the data on each side. The dashed center line represents the median (50th percentile) and the "+" indicates the mean. The "0" that stands alone at the bottom of the box-and-whiskers plot in Figure 6.1 indicates an extreme value or outlier. If the data are normally distributed, the box-and-whiskers plot is approximately symmetric with similar values for the mean and median.)

- The **normal probability plot** shown in Figure 6.1 provides a graphic that (if the data are normally distributed) is a plot of points (shown as asterisks) that lie in a tight random scatter around the reference (diagonal) line (shown as plus signs).

> The default distribution tested by PROC UNIVARIATE is the normal distribution. You can also specify tests for other distributions, but that will not be covered in this book. For more information, look up information on the PROBPLOT statement in the SAS documentation.

The statement to create a higher quality normal Q-Q (probability) plot in the PROC UNIVARIATE paragraph is

```
QQPLOT variablename;
```

See the Exercises at the end of the chapter.

Creating a Histogram Using PROC UNIVARIATE

A histogram is a commonly used plot for visually examining the distribution of a set of data. You can produce a histogram in PROC UNIVARIATE with the following statement:

```
HISTOGRAM AGE/NORMAL;
```

The statement HISTOGRAM AGE produces a histogram for the variable AGE. The NORMAL option produces a superimposed normal curve. The command above produces the plot in Figure 6.2.

The superimposed normal curve on the histogram allows you not only to assess whether the data are approximately normally distributed but also to visualize the apparent departure from normality. If the data are normally distributed, you will expect the peak of the histogram bars to approximately coincide with the peak of the normal curve. In this case, the data again appear to be skewed to the left.

These options provide several methods for you to assess the normality of your data. No plot or test by itself is definitive. They should be taken as a whole.

GOING DEEPER: ADVANCED PROC UNIVARIATE OPTIONS

With a few additional commands using PROC UNIVARIATE, it is relatively easy to create a series of histograms that allows you to compare subgroups of your data. In

FIGURE 6.2. *Histogram with normal curve superimposed*

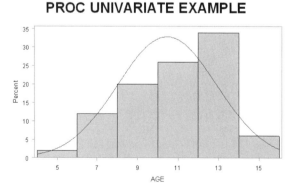

this Going Deeper section we show how to display the distributions of a variable at each of several levels of a grouping variable using data in a simulated dataset. The following Hands-on Example illustrates how you could create histograms for systolic blood pressure by RACE using PROC UNIVARIATE.

HANDS-ON
EXAMPLE

In this example you will learn how to create multiple histograms using a grouping (CLASS) variable.

1. In the Editor window, open the file AUNI3.SAS. The variables in the WOUND data set include AGE, GENDER, RACE_CAT, ISS (Injury Severity Score), DISSTATUS (Discharge Status), WOUND (Wound type), SBP, and TEMP_C (Temperature in Celsius).

```
ODS HTML;
PROC UNIVARIATE DATA="C:\SASDATA\WOUND" NOPRINT;
   CLASS RACE_CAT;
   LABEL RACE_CAT="RACE";
   VAR SBP;
   HISTOGRAM /NORMAL (COLOR=GREEN W=5) NROWS=3;
RUN;
ODS HTML CLOSE;
```

The new statements used in this example include:

■ The NOPRINT statement suppresses most output except the graph because we're interested only in producing the graph.

■ The CLASS RACE statement indicates that the data are to be examined for each category (classification) of the RACE variable.

■ LABEL creates an output label for RACE_CAT as RACE.

■ ROWS=3 indicates that three graphs (three rows) will appear on each output page. Because there are three RACE groups, all graphs will appear together. Similarly, you can use NCOLS=3 to place all three graphs on the same page in three columns.

(Continued)

- The COLOR=GREEN and W=5 statements in parentheses refer to the NORMAL option and tell SAS to display the fitted normal curve with a green line and with a width of 5.

- The DATA= statement accesses the data from the file WOUND.SAS7BDAT. You could also use the statement DATA=MYSASLIB.WOUND to access the data if the MYSASLIB library is defined.

2. Run the program and observe the output in the Results Viewer (see Figure 6.3). Notice that the three histograms are for the variable SBP separately for three values of RACE_CATEGORY. In this case, there is visual agreement that SBP is similarly distributed for all races, and the assumption of normality for each race appears plausible.

FIGURE 6.3. *Multiple histograms from PROC UNIVARIATE*

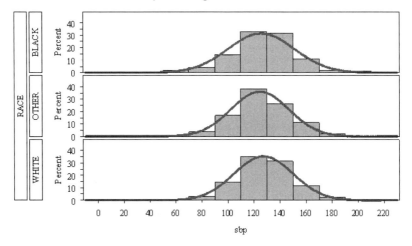

Other options that can make these histograms more useful include

NCOLS=*n*
> Specifies the number of graphs to fit side by side on a page

PFILL= *specifications*
> Specifies the type of fill pattern to use for the histogram

INSET *specifications*
> Allows you to place statistics in the graph. These are illustrated in the next Hands-on Example.

HANDS-ON
EXAMPLE

In this example you will learn how to apply several formatting options to a histogram created using PROC UNIVARIATE.

1. In the Editor window, open the file AUNI4.SAS.

```
PROC FORMAT;
VALUE FMTWOUND 0="NONPENETRATE"
               1="PENETRATE";
RUN;
TITLE 'HISTOGRAMS of SBP by GENDER and WOUND TYPE';
ODS HTML;
PROC UNIVARIATE DATA="C:\SASDATA\WOUND" NOPRINT;
  CLASS WOUND GENDER;
  VAR SBP;
  HISTOGRAM / NROWS=2 NCOLS=2 CFILL=BLUE PFILL=M3N45;
  INSET N='N:' (4.0) MIN='MIN:' (4.1) MAX='MAX:' (4.1)
              / NOFRAME POSITION=NE HEIGHT=2;
  FORMAT WOUND FMTWOUND.;
RUN;
ODS HTML CLOSE;
```

2. Observe the statements in this program. In this example you are telling SAS to display histograms by two grouping variables, WOUND and GENDER:

PROC FORMAT

This procedure creates a format for the WOUND variable to describe the coded 0,1 variables. Using this format allows you to label the categories of groups in the graph with words (PENETRATE and NONPENETRATE) rather than with the 0, 1 data codes. (See Chapter 3 for more information on PROC FORMAT.)

CLASS statement

In this example two grouping variables are indicated in the CLASS statement. For example, CLASS WOUND GENDER;

(Continued)

HISTOGRAM

The options within the HISTOGRAM statement define how the graph will appear. The statements NROWS=2 NCOLS=2 produce two histograms per row (for WOUND, the first item in the CLASS statement) and two histograms per column (for GENDER or the second item in the CLASS statement).

CFILL

The bar colors are specified by the CFILL (color fill) statement: CFILL=BLUE. Some of the colors available in SAS (there are thousands to choose from) are listed in Appendix A.

PFILL

The pattern for the bars is specified by the PFILL (pattern fill) statement: PFILL=M3N45. You can select from a number of available patterns. The default pattern is solid. Additional patterns are listed in Appendix A.

INSET option

This option defines an inset or key to the graph. The following example illustrates several of the options:

```
INSET N='N:' (4.0) MIN='MIN:' (4.1) MAX='MAX:' (4.1)
                / NOFRAME POSITION=NE HEIGHT=2;
```

The statement

```
N='N:' (4.0) MIN='MIN:' (4.1) MAX='MAX:' (4.1)
```

defines which statistics will be included in the inset. In this case N (the sample size) will be designated with N: and will be displayed using the SAS output format 4.0 (designated in the code in parentheses). (See Table 2.4 for examples of SAS formats.) The MIN and MAX are similarly defined.

The remaining options

```
/ NOFRAME POSITION=NE HEIGHT=2;
```

specify that

- No frame will be printed around the inset
- Its position will be in the NE (northeast) corner of the graph
- The height of the characters will be set at 2 units.

3. Run this SAS code and observe the output, shown in Figure 6.4.

FIGURE 6.4. *PROC UNIVARIATE histogram output using two groups*

HISTOGRAMS of SBP by GENDER and WOUND TYPE

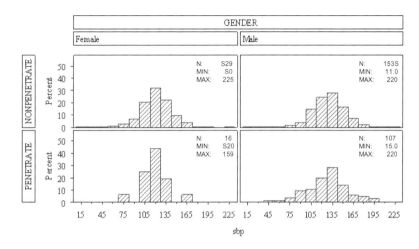

4. Change the program using these items:

   a. Make the histogram color green.

   b. Add the option `MEAN='MEAN:'` (4.1) to the `INSET` option. For example:

   `N='N:' (4.0) MIN='MIN:' (4.1) MAX='MAX:' (4.1) MEAN='MEAN:' (4.1)`

   c. After `HISTOGRAM/,` add the option

   `NORMAL (COLOR=BROWN W=3)`

   to superimpose a normal plot on each histogram.

   d. Run the revised program and observe the results.

SUMMARY

In this chapter you learned how to use `PROC MEANS` and `PROC UNIVARIATE` to calculate basic statistics and graphics for describing the characteristics of a set of data.

EXERCISES

6.1. Create histograms.

Use the WOUND data set (C:\SASDATA\WOUND) as in this chapter's Hands-on Examples and create the following histograms:

a. Create a matrix of histograms with RACE_CATEGORY (three categories) using the pattern M3XO and CFILL=RED.

b. Place the key on the upper left corner (NW).

c. Add MEAN='MEAN:' (4.1) to the list of statistics reported.

d. Put your name in a TITLE2 statement.

e. Redo the plot using solid blue bars.

f. Most of the examples in the book use the ODS HTML option to capture SAS output. For this exercise, capture the output using ODS RTF (word processing) and print the results.

6.2. Produce normal probability plots using PROC UNIVARIATE.

Using the WOUND data set from Exercise 6.1, use PROC UNIVARIATE with the statement

```
PROBPLOT SBP/NORMAL (COLOR=BLUE W=5) NROWS=3;
```

to produce a normal probability plot by RACE_CATEGORY.

6.3. Assess normality using a Q-Q Plot.

Open the file AUNI1.SAS. After VAR AGE; and before the RUN; command, enter the statement

```
QQPLOT AGE;
```

to request a Q-Q plot, which can be used to assess normality. Run the program. If the data are normal, the plot will show a tight cluster of points around a straight line. Do you think this plot suggests the data are normally distributed?

6.4. Display multiple histograms.

Open the file AUNI5.SAS and complete the code to create two columns and two rows of histograms from the CARS data set showing a comparison of city MPG for vehicles that are SUVs or not and for vehicles that have automatic transmissions or not. Missing information in the code is indicated as ???.

a. Complete the PROC FORMAT statement to define values for the 0/1 codes for the SUB and AUTOMATIC variables where 1 means "SUV" for the SUV variables and 0 means "Standard" for the AUTOMATIC variable.

b. Because there are two values for each CLASS variable, indicate NROWS=2 and NCOLS=2.

c. Indicate that the format for the MEAN should be (4.1).

d. Place the inset in the northeast corner of the graph.

e. In the FORMAT statement, indicate the name of the defined format for the AUTOMATIC variable as FMTAUTO. (Don't forget the dot at the end of the definition.)

```
PROC FORMAT;
VALUE FMTSUV 0="NOT SUV"
             1="???";
VALUE FMTAUTO 0="???"
              1="Automatic";
RUN;
TITLE 'HISTOGRAMS of CITY MPG by SUV and AUTOMATIC';
ODS HTML;
 PROC UNIVARIATE DATA="C:\SASDATA\CARS" NOPRINT;
  CLASS AUTOMATIC SUV;
  VAR CITYMPG;
  HISTOGRAM / NROWS=??? NCOLS=??? CFILL=BLUE
  PFILL=M3N45;
  INSET N='N:' (4.0) MIN='MIN:' (4.1) MAX='MAX:'
    (4.1) MEAN='MEAN' (???)
                / NOFRAME POSITION=??? HEIGHT=2;
  FORMAT AUTOMATIC ??? SUV FMTSUV.;
RUN;
ODS HTML CLOSE;
```

Run the program. Your results should look like the histograms in Figure 6.5.

FIGURE 6.5. *Multiple Histograms from the CAR dataset*

HISTOGRAMS of CITY MPG by SUV and AUTOMATIC

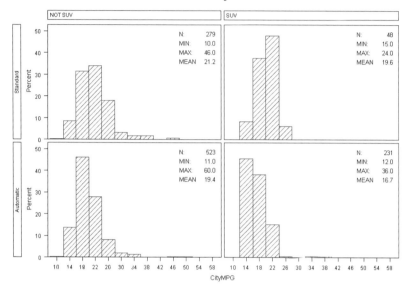

CHAPTER

7

ANALYZING COUNTS AND TABLES

LEARNING OBJECTIVES

- To be able to use PROC FREQ to create one-way frequency tables
- To be able to use PROC FREQ to create two-way (cross-tabulation) tables
- To be able to use two-by-two contingency tables to calculate relative risk measures
- To be able to use Cohen's Kappa to calculate inter-rater reliability

Data that are collected as counts require a specific type of treatment. It doesn't make sense to calculate means and standard deviations on this type of data. Instead, categorical data (also called qualitative data) are often analyzed using frequency and cross-tabulation tables. The primary procedure within SAS for this type of analysis is PROC FREQ.

USING PROC FREQ

PROC FREQ is a multi-purpose SAS procedure for analyzing count data. It can be used to obtain frequency counts for one or more single variables or to create two-way tables (cross-tabulations) from two variables. PROC FREQ can also be used to perform statistical tests on count data. The syntax for PROC FREQ and commonly used options and statements that are discussed in this chapter is:

> **PROC FREQ** *<options(s)>*; *<statements>>* TABLES requests *</options>* ;;

Commonly used options in PROC FREQ are:

DATA=
> Specifies which data set to use

ORDER=
> Specifies the order in which results are listed in the output table

PAGE
> Specifies that only one table will appear per page

COMPRESS
> Begins next table on the same page when possible

Statements commonly used with PROC FREQ are:

BY *variable(s)*
> Creates tables for each BY group

EXACT
> Produces exact test for selected statistics

OUTPUT=
> Creates an output data set containing statistics from an analysis

WEIGHT *variable*
> Identifies a weight variable that contains summarized counts

The TABLES statement is required for all of the examples in this chapter. Its format is:

> **TABLES** *<variable-combinations/options>*;

TABLE 7.1. **Sample TABLE statements**

Description	Tables statement
Specify counts for a single variable	TABLE A;
Specify a crosstabulation between two variables	TABLE A*B;
Specify several cross-tabulation tables	TABLE A*B B*C X*Y; Also, TABLE A*(B C D); is the same as TABLE A*B A*C A*D;
Use a range of variables in a TABLE statement	TABLE (A -- C)*X; is the same as TABLE A*X B*X C*X;

where *variable-combinations* specifies frequency or cross-tabulation tables. For examples, see Table 7.1.

Options for the TABLE statement follow a slash (/). For example,

```
TABLES A*B / CHISQ;
```

requests that the chi-square and related statistics be reported for the cross-tabulation A*B.

Commonly used TABLE options following a / include:

AGREE
   Request KAPPA statistic (inter-rater reliability). To include significance tests, add the following statement:

TEST *option*
   Use KAPPA option with AGREE statement to get tests for Kappa. Use the WTKAP option to specify test for weighted Kappa. For example:

```
TABLES A*B / /AGREE; TEST KAPPA;
```

CHISQ
   Requests chi-square and related tests

RELRISK
   Requests relative risk calculations

`FISHER`
  Requests Fisher's Exact test for tables greater than 2×2

`SPARSE`
  Requests all possible combinations of variable levels even when a particular combination never occurs

`MISSING`
  Requests that missing values be treated as nonmissing

`CELLCHI2`
  Displays the contribution to chi-square for each cell

`NOCOL`
  Suppresses column percentages for each cell

`NOCUM`
  Suppresses cumulative frequencies and cumulative percentages in one-way frequency tables and in list format

`NOFREQ`
  Suppresses frequency count for each cell

`NOPERCENT`
  Suppresses row percentage and column percentage in cross-tabulation tables, or percentages and cumulative percentages in one-way frequency tables and in list format

`NOPRINT`
  Suppresses tables but displays statistics

`NOROW`
  Suppresses row percentage for each cell

For example, in a simple use of `PROC FREQ`, to obtain counts of the number of subjects observed in each category of group (`GP`), use the following:

```
PROC FREQ; TABLES GP; RUN;
```

To produce a cross-tabulation table of `GENDER` by treatment `GP`, use:

```
PROC FREQ; TABLES GENDER*GP;RUN;
```

The variables specified in the `TABLES` statement can be either text or numeric. To request statistics for a table, include the option `/CHISQ` at the end of the `TABLES` statement. For example:

```
PROC FREQ; TABLES GENDER*GP/CHISQ;
```

The following sections describe in more detail how to use PROC FREQ to create and analyze tables of counts.

ANALYZING ONE-WAY FREQUENCY TABLES

When count data are collected, you can use PROC FREQ to produce tables of the counts by category as well as to perform statistical analyses on the counts. This section describes how to create tables of counts by category and how to perform a goodness-of-fit test.

The number and type of tables produced by the PROC FREQ procedure are specified with a TABLES statement. When single variables are used in the TABLES statement, PROC FREQ produces a frequency table. The following Hands-on Example illustrates how to create a frequency table for a single variable.

> Recall that sample data sets are in the C:\SASDATA folder and the SOMEDATA data set contains a sample data set of 50 records. In the following Hands-on Example, note that the DATA= statement could also be DATA=MYSASLIB.SOMEDATA if you have the MYSASDATA library defined.

HANDS-ON
EXAMPLE

In this example you will learn how to use PROC FREQ to display frequency information for a qualitative (categorical) data variable.

1. In the Editor window, open the file AFREQ1.SAS.

```
ODS HTML;
PROC FREQ DATA="C:\SASDATA\SOMEDATA";
    TABLES STATUS;
TITLE 'Simple Example of PROC FREQ';
RUN;
PROC FREQ DATA="C:\SASDATA\SOMEDATA" ORDER=FREQ;
 TABLES STATUS;
TITLE 'Example of PROC FREQ Using ORDER= Option';
RUN;
ODS HTML CLOSE;
```

(Continued)

This SAS code includes two PROC FREQ statements. In the first example, a table is requested for the variable STATUS. The second example is similar, but an additional option, ORDER=FREQ, is used to request that the table be sorted by the descending order of the frequency count.

Following are some of the PROC FREQ ORDER= options.

DATA
Orders values by their order in the data set

FORMATTED
Orders values by ascending values determined by a FORMAT statement (see PROC FORMAT in Chapter 4)

FREQ
Orders values by descending frequency count

ORDER
Orders values by order in data set

2. Run this program and observe the output (Table 7.2) from the first PROC FREQ.

TABLE 7.2. Simple output for PROC FREQ

Socioeconomic Status				
STATUS	Frequency	Percent	Cumulative Frequency	Cumulative Percent
1	3	6.00	3	6.00
2	7	14.00	10	20.00
3	6	12.00	16	32.00
4	8	16.00	24	48.00
5	26	52.00	50	100.00

The "Frequency" column gives the count of the number of times the STATUS variable takes on the value in the STATUS column. The "Percent" column is the percent of total (50). The "Cumulative Frequency" and "Percent" columns report an increasing count and percent for values of STATUS. You use this type of analysis to learn about the distribution of the categories in your data set. For example, in these data, more than half of the subjects fall into the STATUS=5 category. If you had planned to have approximately the same number of observations in each category, this table would indicate that that criterion had not been met.

3. Observe the output from the program, which used the `PROC FREQ` state-
    ment, but this time with the `ORDER=FREQ` option. See Table 7.3.

    ```
    PROC FREQ ORDER=FREQ;
    TABLES STATUS;
    ```

TABLE 7.3. **PROC FREQ output using the ORDER FREQ option**

Socioeconomic Status				
STATUS	Frequency	Percent	Cumulative Frequency	Cumulative Percent
5	26	52.00	26	52.00
4	8	16.00	34	68.00
2	7	14.00	41	82.00
3	6	12.00	47	94.00
1	3	6.00	50	100.00

Using the `ORDER=FREQ` option helps you quickly identify which categories
have the most and fewest counts.

HANDS-ON
EXAMPLE

This example illustrates the `ORDER=FORMATTED` option for `PROC FREQ`. In this
case, you use a custom format created in a `PROC FORMAT` command to define
the order that you want used in your output table.

1. In the Editor window, open the file `AFREQ2.SAS`.

    ```
    PROC FORMAT;
    VALUE $FMTRACE "AA"="African American"
                   "H"="Hispanic"
                   "OTH"="Other"
                   "C"="White";
    RUN;
    ODS HTML;
    PROC FREQ ORDER=FORMATTED DATA="C:\SASDATA\SURVEY";
    ```

(Continued)

```
        TABLES RACE;
        TITLE 'Example of PROC FREQ using OPTION=Formatted';
        FORMAT RACE $FMTRACE.;
RUN;
ODS HTML CLOSE;
```

This program uses the ORDER=FORMATTED option. To use this option, you must have a format defined for the specified variable. In this case, a format named $FMTRACE was created in a PROC FORMAT statement. (See Chapter 4.) In the PROC FREQ statement, the option

ORDER=FORMATTED

specifies that the table is to be sorted in ascending order by the formatted values for RACE based on the $FMTRACE format (which contains alphabetized format values for the categories). To complete the statement, you must include the statement

FORMAT RACE $FMTRACE.;

which applies the $FMTRACE format to the RACE variable.

2. Run this program and observe the results, shown in Table 7.4.

TABLE 7.4. Output from PROC FREQ using the ORDER= FORMATTED option

RACE				
RACE	Frequency	Percent	Cumulative Frequency	Cumulative Percent
African American	37	46.84	37	46.84
Hispanic	30	37.97	67	84.81
Other	4	5.06	71	89.87
White	8	10.13	79	100.00

3. To emphasize the effect of this format statement, place an asterisk at the beginning of the SAS statement containing the FORMAT statement:

```
*     FORMAT RACE $FMTRACE.;
```

This turns the statement into a comment. Re-run the program and observe how the table has changed. Because no format is associated with RACE, the order used is the alphabetic order of the category values AA, C, H, and OTH.

CREATING ONE-WAY FREQUENCY TABLES FROM SUMMARIZED DATA

Suppose your data have already been summarized into counts. In this case you can use the WEIGHT statement to indicate that the data are counts.

HANDS-ON
EXAMPLE

This example illustrates how to summarize counts from a data set into a frequency table.

1. In the Editor window, open the program AFREQ3.SAS.

```
DATA COINS;
     INPUT @1 CATEGORY $9. @11 NUMBER 3.;
DATALINES;
CENTS     152
CENTS     100
NICKELS    49
DIMES      59
QUARTERS   21
HALF       44
DOLLARS    21
;
ODS HTML;
PROC FREQ; WEIGHT NUMBER;
  TITLE3 'READ IN SUMMARIZED DATA';
  TABLES CATEGORY;
RUN;
ODS HTML CLOSE;
```

Notice that the data are already in counts. The statement

```
WEIGHT NUMBER;
```

tells PROC FREQ that the data for the variable NUMBER are counts. Even though there are two records for CENTS, the program is able to combine the WEIGHT (counts) into a single CENTS category (252 CENTS).

(Coutinued)

2. Run the program and observe the output, as shown in Table 7.5.

3. To tell SAS to reorder this table in the *order in which you specified the categories* in the data set (which makes more sense in this example), use the `ORDER=DATA` option in the `PROC FREQ` statement:

```
PROC FREQ ORDER=DATA;
```

Re-run the analysis and observe the new frequency table.

TABLE 7.5.   Proc FREQ output for summarized counts

CATEGORY	Frequency	Percent	Cumulative Frequency	Cumulative Percent
CENTS	252	56.50	252	56.50
DIMES	59	13.23	311	69.73
DOLLARS	21	4.71	332	74.44
HALF	44	9.87	376	84.30
NICKELS	49	10.99	425	95.29
QUARTERS	21	4.71	446	100.00

Testing Goodness-of-Fit in a One-Way Table

A goodness-of-fit test of a single population is a test to determine if the distribution of observed frequencies in the sample data closely matches the expected number of occurrences under a hypothetical distribution for the population. The observations are assumed to be independent, and each data value can be counted in one and only one category. It is also assumed that the number of observations is fixed. The hypotheses being tested are:

H_0: The population follows the hypothesized distribution.

H_a: The population does not follow the hypothesized distribution.

A chi-square statistic is calculated, and a decision can be made based on the p-value associated with that statistic. A low p-value indicates that the data do not follow the hypothesized, or theoretical, distribution. If the p-value is sufficiently low (usually less than 0.05), you will reject the null hypothesis. The syntax to perform a goodness-of-fit test is:

```
PROC FREQ; TABLES variable / CHISQ TESTP=(list of ratios);
```

As an example, we will use data from an experiment conducted by the nineteenth-century monk Gregor Mendel. According to a genetic theory, crossbred pea plants show a 9:3:3:1 ratio of yellow smooth, yellow wrinkled, green smooth, and green wrinkled offspring. Out of 250 plants, under the theoretical ratio (distribution) of 9:3:3:1, you would expect about

$(9/16) \times 250 = 140.625$ yellow smooth peas (56.25%)

$(3/16) \times 250 = 46.875$ yellow wrinkled peas (18.75%)

$(3/16) \times 250 = 46.875$ green smooth peas (18.75%)

$(1/16) \times 250 = 15.625$ green wrinkled peas (6.25%)

After growing 250 of these pea plants, Mendel observed the following:

152 have yellow smooth peas

39 have yellow wrinkled peas

53 have green smooth peas

6 have green wrinkled peas

Do these offspring support the hypothesized ratios? The following Hands-on Example illustrates the use of SAS FREQ to run a goodness-of-fit test to assess whether the observed phenotypic frequencies seem to support the theory.

HANDS-ON
EXAMPLE

This example illustrates how to perform a goodness-of-fit-test.

1. In the Editor window, open the program AFREQ4.SAS.

```
DATA GENE;
      INPUT @1 COLOR $13. @15 NUMBER 3.;
DATALINES;
YELLOWSMOOTH   152
YELLOWWRINKLE   39
GREENSMOOTH     53
GREENWRINKLE     6

;
* HYPOTHESIZING A 9:3:3:1 RATIO;
ODS HTML;
PROC FREQ ORDER=DATA; WEIGHT NUMBER;
```

(Continued)

```
TITLE3 'GOODNESS OF FIT ANALYSIS';

TABLES COLOR / NOCUM CHISQ TESTP=(0.5625 0.1875 0.1875
0.0625);
RUN;
ODS HTML CLOSE;
```

Notice the following components of this SAS program:

- The data are summarized as indicated by the WEIGHT NUMBER statement in PROC FREQ.

- The ORDER=DATA option causes the output frequencies to be ordered as they were input into the data set.

- Frequencies are based on the variable COLOR.

- The /CHISQ and TESTP= statements request the goodness-of-fit test. The test ratios are based on the percent progeny expected from each of the four categories.

- The NOCUM option instructs SAS to not include the "Cumulative Frequency" column in the table.

Note that you must use the ORDER=DATA option to ensure that the hypothesized ratios listed in the TESTP= statement match up correctly with the categories in the table.

2. Run the program and observe the output, as shown in Table 7.6.

TABLE 7.6. **Goodness-of-fit test using PROC FREQ**

COLOR	Frequency	Percent	Test Percent
YELLOWSMOOTH	152	60.80	56.25
YELLOWWRINKLE	39	15.60	18.75
GREENSMOOTH	53	21.20	18.75
GREENWRINKLE	6	2.40	6.25

Chi-Square Test for Specified Proportions	
Chi-Square	8.9724
DF	3
Pr > ChiSq	0.0297

It is a good idea to make sure the "Test Percent" column matches the hypothesized percentages for the categories of the tested variable.

Notice that in this case, the *p*-value for the chi-square test is less than 0.05, which leads us to reject the null hypothesis and conclude there is evidence to conclude that the peas do not come from a population having the 9:3:3:1 phenotypic ratios.

ANALYZING TWO-WAY TABLES

To create a cross-tabulation table using PROC FREQ for relating two variables, use the TABLES statement with both variables listed and separated by an asterisk (*), (for example, A * B). A cross-tabulation table is formed by counting the number of occurrences in a sample across two grouping variables. The number of columns in a table is usually denoted by c and the number of rows by r. Thus, a table is said to have $r \times c$ "r by c cells." For example, in a dominant-hand (left-right) by hair color table (with 5 hair colors used), the table would be referred to as a 2×5 table. The hypotheses associated with **a test of independence** are:

H_0: The variables are independent (no association between them).

H_a: The variables are not independent.

Thus, in the "eye color/hair color" example, the null hypothesis is that there is no association between dominant hand and hair color (each hand dominance category has the same distribution of hair color). The alternative hypothesis is that left- and right-handed people have different distributions of hair color—perhaps left-handed people are more likely to be brown-haired.

Another test that can be performed on a crosstabulation table is a **test of homogeneity**. In this case, the table is built of independent samples from two or more populations, and the null hypothesis is that the populations have the same distribution (they are homogeneous). In this case the hypotheses are:

H_0: The populations are homogeneous.

H_a: The populations are not homogeneous.

Rows (or columns) represent data from different populations (e.g., treated and not treated), and the other variable represents categorized data observed on the population.

The chi-square test of independence or homogeneity is reported by PROC FREQ (the tests are mathematically equivalent) by the use of the /CHISQ option in the TABLES statement. For example,

```
PROC FREQ; TABLES GENDER*GP/CHISQ;
```

will create a two-way cross-tabulation table and statistics associated with the table. Also included in the output are the likelihood ratio chi-square, Mantel-Haenszel chi-square, phi, contingency coefficient, and Cramer's V. For a 2×2 table, a Fisher's Exact test is also performed.

HANDS-ON EXAMPLE

Data for this example come from a study performed by Karl Pearson in 1909 involving the relationship between criminal behavior and drinking alcoholic beverages. The category "Coining" refers to counterfeiting. For the DRINKER variable, 1 means yes and 0 means no.

1. In the Editor window, open the program AFREQ5.SAS.

```
DATA DRINKERS;
INPUT CRIME DRINKER COUNT;
DATALINES;
Arson       1       50
Arson       0       43
Rape        1       88
Rape        0       62
Violence    1       155
Violence    0       110
Stealing    1       379
Stealing    0       300
Coining     1       18
Coining     0       14
Fraud       1       63
Fraud       0       144
;
ODS HTML;
PROC FREQ DATA=DRINKERS;WEIGHT COUNT;
     TABLES DRINKER*CRIME/CHISQ;
TITLE 'Chi Square Analysis of a Contingency Table';
RUN;
ODS HTML CLOSE;
```

2. Run the program and observe the cross-tabulation table shown in Table 7.7. The four numbers in each cell are the overall frequency, the overall percent,

the row percent, and the column percent. The cells in the margins show total frequencies and percentages for columns and rows.

TABLE 7.7.   **Cross-tabulation from PROC FREQ**

Table of CRIME by DRINKER			
CRIME	**DRINKER**		
Frequency Percent Row Pct Col Pct	**0**	**1**	**Total**
Arson	43 3.02 46.24 6.39	50 3.51 53.76 6.64	93 6.52
Coining	14 0.98 43.75 2.08	18 1.26 56.25 2.39	32 2.24
Fraud	144 10.10 69.57 21.40	63 4.42 30.43 8.37	207 14.52
Rape	62 4.35 41.33 9.21	88 6.17 58.67 11.69	150 10.52
Stealing	300 21.04 44.18 44.58	379 26.58 55.82 50.33	679 47.62
Violence	110 7.71 41.51 16.34	155 10.87 58.49 20.58	265 18.58
Total	673 47.19	753 52.81	1426 100.00

3. Observe the statistics table shown in Table 7.8. The chi-square value is 48.7 and $p<0.001$. Thus, you reject the null hypothesis of no association (independence) and conclude that there is evidence of a relationship between drinking status and type of crime committed.

TABLE 7.8.   **Statistics for drinking and crime cross-tabulation**

Statistic	DF	Value	Prob
Chi-Square	5	49.7306	<.0001
Likelihood Ratio Chi-Square	5	50.5173	<.0001
Mantel-Haenszel Chi-Square	1	13.0253	0.0003
Phi Coefficient		0.1867	
Contingency Coefficient		0.1836	
Cramer's V		0.1867	

(Continued)

Note that the likelihood ratio statistic given in Table 7.8 is an alternative to the chi-square. While the results are usually similar, most practitioners prefer to report the chi-square statistic. The other statistics reported in this table are for special settings and are not discussed here.

4. To discover the nature of the relationship suggested by the significant chi-square test, alter the program by changing the TABLES statement to the following:

```
TABLES CRIME*DRINKER/CHISQ EXPECTED NOROW NOCOL NOPERCENT;
```

EXPECTED specifies that expected values are to be included in the table, and NOROW, NOCOL, and NOPERCENT tell SAS to exclude these values from the table. The results are shown in Table 7.9.

Run the revised program and notice that while most of the expected values are close to the observed values, those for Fraud are very different from what was expected. This information leads to the conclusion that those involved in Fraud as a crime are less likely to drink alcoholic beverages than those involved in other crimes.

TABLE 7.9. **Expected values for drinking and crime data**

Table of CRIME by DRINKER			
CRIME	DRINKER		
Frequency Expected	0	1	Total
Arson	43 / 43.891	50 / 49.109	93
Coining	14 / 15.102	18 / 16.898	32
Fraud	144 / 97.694	63 / 109.31	207
Rape	62 / 70.792	88 / 79.208	150
Stealing	300 / 320.45	379 / 358.55	679
Violence	110 / 125.07	155 / 139.93	265
Total	673	753	1426

Creating a Contingency Table from Raw Data, the 2 × 2 Case

If your data are stored as individual observations in a SAS data set, you can use the PROC FREQ procedure to create a table of counts and analyze the results. The following Hands-on Example illustrates this.

HANDS-ON EXAMPLE

In this example we consider a data set collected for the purpose of studying the relationship between two commercial floor cleaners and the presence or absence of the appearance of a skin rash on the hands of the users. The data for 40 subjects are in a SAS data set named `RASH.SAS7BDAT`. A few of the records are shown in Figure 7.1. The floor cleaner brands are coded `1` or `2`, and the presence of a rash is coded `Y` or `N`.

FIGURE 7.1. *Example data records from the RASH dataset*

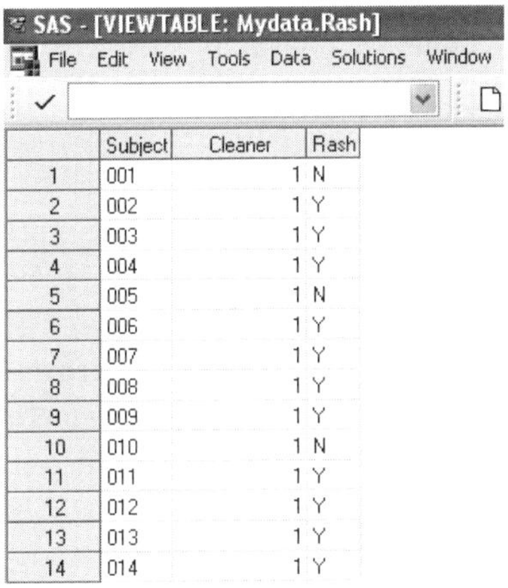

	Subject	Cleaner	Rash
1	001	1	N
2	002	1	Y
3	003	1	Y
4	004	1	Y
5	005	1	N
6	006	1	Y
7	007	1	Y
8	008	1	Y
9	009	1	Y
10	010	1	N
11	011	1	Y
12	012	1	Y
13	013	1	Y
14	014	1	Y

1. In the Editor window, open the program `AFREQ6.SAS`.

```
ODS HTML;
PROC FREQ DATA="C:\SASDATA\RASH";
   TABLES CLEANER*RASH /CHISQ;
   TITLE 'CHI-SQUARE ANALYSIS FOR A 2X2 TABLE';
RUN;
ODS HTML CLOSE;
```

2. Run the program and observe the output. The cross-tabulation table is shown in Table 7.10, which contains the cell count for each combination of cleaner type and observed rash.

(Continued)

TABLE 7.10.   **Cross-tabulation of cleaner by rash**

Table of Cleaner by Rash				
Cleaner(Cleaner)		Rash(Rash)		
Frequency Percent Row Pct Col Pct		N	Y	Total
	1	7 17.50 35.00 30.43	13 32.50 65.00 76.47	20 50.00
	2	16 40.00 80.00 69.57	4 10.00 20.00 23.53	20 50.00
Total		23 57.50	17 42.50	40 100.00

3. Observe the statistics tables as shown in Table 7.11. Statistics for a 2 × 2 cross-tabulation are reported in two tables. The first table is similar to the one reported for the crime data, while the second reports the results of a Fisher's Exact test. In this case the chi-square statistic, 8.29, $p=0.004$, indicates an association between CLEANER and RASH (rejects the null hypothesis that the proportion of rash for the two cleaners is the same). The Continuity Adj. Chi-Square (sometimes called Yates's Chi-Square) is an adjustment that some statisticians use to improve the chi-square approximation in the case of a 2 × 2 table. It is most often reported when the counts in the cells are small. The second table of statistics reports the Fisher's Exact test. This test is based on all possible 2 × 2 tables that have the same marginal counts as those observed. This test is often reported instead of the chi-square when counts in the table are small. Typically, the two-sided p value $Pr <= F$ value is the correct value to report except in specialized cases. For this example, the Fisher's p-value is $p =0.0095$.

TABLE 7.11.   **Statistics tables for a 2 × 2 analysis**

Statistic	DF	Value	Prob
Chi-Square	1	8.2864	0.0040
Likelihood Ratio Chi-Square	1	8.6344	0.0033
Continuity Adj. Chi-Square	1	6.5473	0.0105
Mantel-Haenszel Chi-Square	1	8.0793	0.0045
Phi Coefficient		-0.4551	
Contingency Coefficient		0.4143	
Cramer's V		-0.4551	

Fisher's Exact Test	
Cell (1,1) Frequency (F)	7
Left-sided Pr <= F	0.0048
Right-sided Pr >= F	0.9995
Table Probability (P)	0.0042
Two-sided Pr <= P	0.0095

GOING DEEPER: CALCULATING RELATIVE RISK MEASURES

Two-by-two contingency tables are often used when examining a measure of risk. In a medical setting, these tables are often constructed when one variable represents the presence or absence of a disease and the other is some risk factor. A measure of this risk in a retrospective (case-control) study is called the odds ratio (OR). In a case-control study, a researcher takes a sample of subjects and looks back in time for exposure (or non-exposure). If the data are collected prospectively, where subjects are selected by presence or absence of a risk and then observed over time to see if they develop an outcome, the measure of risk is called relative risk (RR).

In either case, a risk measure (OR or RR) equal to 1 indicates no risk. A risk measure different from 1 represents a risk. Assuming the outcome studied is undesirable, a risk measure greater than 1 indicates that exposure is harmful and a risk measure less than 1 implies that exposure is a benefit.

In PROC FREQ, the option to calculate the values for OR is RELRISK and appears as an option to the TABLES statement as shown here:

```
TABLES CLEANER*RASH /RELRISK;
```

The following Hands-on Example illustrates how to calculate OR for the cleaner/rash data described previously.

HANDS-ON EXAMPLE

This example uses the RASH data in the previous Hands-on Example. Here we assume that the data were collected in a retrospective (case-control) study.

1. Using the program from the previous example (AFREQ6.SAS), change the TABLES statement to read

    ```
    TABLES CLEANER*RASH /RELRISK;
    ```

2. Run the revised program and observe the output as shown in Table 7.12. In this table, the OR=0.13 specifies the odds of Row1/Row2—that is, for cleaner 1 versus cleaner 2. Because OR is less than 1, this is interpreted to mean that the odds of a person's having a rash who is using cleaner 1 is less than they are when the person is using cleaner 2.

    It is helpful to note that the inverse of this OR (1/0.1346=7.49) indicates that the odds of a person using cleaner 2 getting a rash is 7.49 times greater

    (Continued)

than that of a person using cleaner 1. A method to alter this program to report the odds of cleaner 2 versus cleaner 1 is given in the chapter exercises.

TABLE 7.12. **Relative risk measures for the floor cleaner data**

Estimates of the Relative Risk (Row1/Row2)			
Type of Study	**Value**	**95% Confidence Limits**	
Case-Control (Odds Ratio)	0.1346	0.0322	0.5625
Cohort (Col1 Risk)	0.4375	0.2316	0.8265
Cohort (Col2 Risk)	3.2500	1.2776	8.2673

GOING DEEPER: INTER-RATER RELIABILITY (KAPPA)

A method for assessing the degree of agreement between two raters is Cohen's kappa coefficient. For example, this test is useful for analyzing the consistency of two raters who evaluate subjects on the basis of a categorical measurement.

Using an example from Fleiss (1981, p. 213), suppose you have 100 subjects rated by two raters on a psychological scale that consists of three categories. The data are given in Table 7.13.

TABLE 7.13. **Data for inter-rater reliability analysis**

		RATER A			
		Psyc.	Neuro.	Organic	
		1	2	3	
	Psych 1	75	1	4	80
Rater B	Neuro 2	5	4	1	10
	Organic 3	0	0	10	10
		80	5	15	100

HANDS-ON
EXAMPLE

This example illustrates how to calculate the kappa statistic in an inter-rater reliability analysis.

1. In the Editor window, open the file `AKAPPA.SAS`.

```
DATA KAPPA;
INPUT RATER1 RATER2 WT;
DATALINES;
1  1    75
1  2    1
1  3    4
2  1    5
2  2    4
2  3    1
3  1    0
3  2    0
3  3    10

ODS HTML;
PROC FREQ;
   WEIGHT WT;
   TABLE  RATER1*RATER2 / AGREE ; TEST KAPPA;
   TITLE 'KAPPA EXAMPLE FROM FLEISS';
RUN;
ODS HTML CLOSE;
```

This SAS command is similar to that used for a chi-square analysis except with an `/AGREE` option to request the kappa statistic and a `TEST KAPPA` option to request a kappa analysis.

2. Run this program and observe the tables of output, shown in Table 7.14. The first table is a cross-tabulation of the observed counts. The "Test of Symmetry" table provides a Bowker's test of marginal homogeneity. (If $r=c=2$, then this is the same as McNemar's test.) A nonsignificant result (which is usually what you want) indicates that there is no evidence that the two raters have differing tendencies to select categories. In this case the results are marginally nonsignificant ($p=.053$).

(Continued)

TABLE 7.14. **Results for Kappa analysis**

Table of RATER1 by RATER2				
RATER1	**RATER2**			
Frequency Percent Row Pct Col Pct	**1**	**2**	**3**	**Total**
1	75 75.00 93.75 93.75	1 1.00 1.25 20.00	4 4.00 5.00 26.67	80 80.00
2	5 5.00 50.00 6.25	4 4.00 40.00 80.00	1 1.00 10.00 6.67	10 10.00
3	0 0.00 0.00 0.00	0 0.00 0.00 0.00	10 10.00 100.00 66.67	10 10.00
Total	80 80.00	5 5.00	15 15.00	100 100.00

Test of Symmetry	
Statistic (S)	7.6667
DF	3
Pr > S	0.0534

Simple Kappa Coefficient	
Kappa	0.6765
ASE	0.0877
95% Lower Conf Limit	0.5046
95% Upper Conf Limit	0.8484

Test of H0: Kappa = 0	
ASE under H0	0.0762
Z	8.8791
One-sided Pr > Z	<.0001
Two-sided Pr > |Z|	<.0001

Weighted Kappa Coefficient	
Weighted Kappa	0.7222
ASE	0.0843
95% Lower Conf Limit	0.5570
95% Upper Conf Limit	0.8874

The "Simple Kappa Coefficient" table reports the kappa statistic and related measures. In this case kappa=0.6765. ASE is the Asymptotic

Standard Error. A 95 percent confidence interval is also reported. A large value of kappa (many would say 0.7 or higher) indicates a moderate to substantial level of agreement. This is based on a widely referenced interpretation of kappa suggested by Landis and Koch (1977) and shown in Table 7.15.

The test of hypothesis "Test of H0:" table in Table 7.14 provides a test that kappa is 0. In this case, the test indicates you would reject the hypothesis that kappa = 0 ($p<0.0001$).

As described in the next section, the information in the last table in the output, "Weighted Kappa Coefficient," is *not* the appropriate statistic to report for these data because the rater categories are not ordinal.

TABLE 7.15. Interpretation of kappa statistic

AN INTERPRETATION OF KAPPA	
Kappa	Interpretation
<0	No agreement
0.0–0.20	Poor agreement
0.21–0.40	Fair agreement
0.41–0.60	Moderate agreement
0.61–0.80	Substantial agreement
0.81–1.00	Almost perfect agreement

Calculating Weighted Kappa

For the case in which rated categories are ordinal, it is appropriate to use the weighted kappa statistic because it is designed to give partial credit to ratings that are close to but not on the diagonal.

For example, in a test of recognition of potentially dangerous airline passengers, suppose a procedure is devised that classifies passengers into three categories: 1=No threat/Pass, 2=Concern/Recheck, and 3=Potential threat/Detain. To assess the reliability of this measure, two security officers are trained in the procedure, and then they observe 99 passengers on videotape. Each officer rates the individuals, resulting in the data set named SECURITY.

The resulting partial data set is shown in Table 7.16. Note that the categories are ordinal, so weighted kappa is an appropriate analysis.

TABLE 7.16. **Partial SECURITY data**

RATER1	RATER2
1	1
1	1
1	1
1	1
1	3
3	2
2	2
etc.	etc.

HANDS-ON
EXAMPLE

This example illustrates how to calculate the kappa statistic in an inter-rater reliability analysis when categories are ordinal. Unlike the first example, in which the data are summarized in the data set, in this example the data are listed by subject, and the PROC FREQ procedure creates the appropriate cross-tabulation of counts for the analysis.

1. In the Editor window, open the file AKAPPA2.SAS.

   ```
   ODS HTML;
   PROC FREQ data="C:\SASDATA\SECURITY";
      TABLE  RATER1*RATER2 / AGREE ; TEST WTKAP;
      TITLE 'Security Data';
   RUN;
   ODS HTML CLOSE;
   ```

2. Run the program and observe the cross-tabulation table shown in Table 7.17.

3. The AGREE option specifies the kappa statistic, and the TEST WTKAP produces tests for the weighted statistic. The results are shown in Table 7.18.

TABLE 7.17.   Cross-tabulation of security data

Table of RATER1 by RATER2				
RATER1(RATER1)	RATER2(RATER2)			
Frequency Percent Row Pct Col Pct	1	2	3	Total
1	58 58.59 93.55 90.63	3 3.03 4.84 10.71	1 1.01 1.61 14.29	62 62.63
2	5 5.05 16.13 7.81	24 24.24 77.42 85.71	2 2.02 6.45 28.57	31 31.31
3	1 1.01 16.67 1.56	1 1.01 16.67 3.57	4 4.04 66.67 57.14	6 6.06
Total	64 64.65	28 28.28	7 7.07	99 100.00

TABLE 7.18.   Kappa statistics for security data

Test of Symmetry	
Statistic (S)	0.8333
DF	3
Pr > S	0.8415

Simple Kappa Coefficient	
Kappa	0.7386
ASE	0.0654
95% Lower Conf Limit	0.6104
95% Upper Conf Limit	0.8667

Weighted Kappa Coefficient	
Weighted Kappa	0.7413
ASE	0.0674
95% Lower Conf Limit	0.6092
95% Upper Conf Limit	0.8735

Test of H0: Weighted Kappa = 0	
ASE under H0	0.0845
Z	8.7682
One-sided Pr > Z	<.0001
Two-sided Pr > |Z|	<.0001

(Continued)

The test of symmetry is nonsignificant ($p=0.84$) and suggests there is no evidence that the two raters have differing tendencies to select categories. Note that both the simple and weighted kappa statistics and confidence limits are calculated by SAS. Because the data are ordinal, the appropriate statistic for this analysis is the weighted kappa. The test of hypothesis "Test of H0:" table indicates that you would reject the hypothesis that kappa=0 ($p<0.0001$).

The weighted kappa=0.74 statistic can be interpreted as suggesting a "substantial agreement" between the two raters using the criteria of Landis and Koch. The researcher involved in this experiment must determine, in relation to the importance of the decision involving the lives of passengers, if this result indicates sufficient agreement to adopt the classification method.

SUMMARY

This chapter discussed the capabilities of PROC FREQ for creating one- and two-way frequency tables, analyzing contingency tables, calculating relative risk measures, and measuring inter-rater reliability (using KAPPA).

EXERCISES

7.1. Perform a goodness-of-fit analysis.

Suppose you conducted a marketing survey in a city where you hypothesize that people frequent restaurants at lunchtime in the following proportions: Mexican food (40 percent), home cooking (20 percent), Italian food (20 percent), and Chinese food (20 percent). The results of a random sample from the population are given below in which subjects were asked to specify the type of restaurant at which they most recently ate lunch.

Mexican: 66

Home cooking: 25

Italian: 33

Chinese: 38

The DATA statement to read in this information is in EX_7.1.SAS:

```
DATA FOOD;
     INPUT @1 CATEGORY $13. @14 NUMBER 3.;
DATALINES;
```

```
Mexican       66
Home cooking 25
Italian       33
Chinese       38
```

;

Using this as a starting point, perform a goodness-of-fit test using PROC FREQ. Hint: Use the coins Hands-on Example discussed earlier in this chapter as a template for the analysis. Use the statements:

PROC FREQ ORDER=DATA; WEIGHT NUMBER;

and

TESTP=(.4,.2,.2,.2);

in your SAS program to perform the appropriate goodness-of-fit test.

7.2. Perform a contingency table analysis.

Historical data used to research the question of whether smoking causes cancer yields the following table.

Smoking Habit/Cancer	Cancer	No Cancer	Total
None to Slight	56	956	1012
Moderate to Excessive	269	1646	1915
Total	325	2602	2927

a. Using the cleaner/rash SAS program example as a template for your SAS program code (AFREQ6.SAS), perform a chi-square test on these data using PROC FREQ and state your conclusions.

b. What is the hypothesis tested in this example?

7.3 Going Deeper: Calculate risk.

a. Using the data in Exercise 7.2, calculate the risk of a person who is a moderate or excessive smoker having cancer.

b. Using the relative risk Hands-on Example as an example, run the program and observe that the OR = 0.1346 represents the risk of getting a rash when using cleaner1 vs cleaner2. To change the table to calculate the risk of Cleaner 2 versus Cleaner 1, you must change the order of the cleaner categories. By default, SAS orders them in numerical order (1 and 2). To change this order, create a formatted value for CLEANER and use the ORDER=FORMATTED option to put the categories in the desired order. To do this, enter this code at the top of the program:

```
PROC FORMAT;
VALUE $FMTYN "Y"="1 YES"
              "N"="2 NO";
RUN;
```

Also, change the PROC FREQ statement to read

```
PROC FREQ DATA="C:\SASDATA\RASH" ORDER=FORMATTED;
```

and add a FORMAT statement after the TITLE statement and before RUN.

```
FORMAT RASH $FMTYN.;
```

Run the revised program. The order of CLEANER should be changed according to the formatted values, and the OR reported is the reciprocal of 0.1346, or 7.49.

7.4. Going Deeper: Calculate kappa.

Suppose a researcher is examining the reliability of a method for X-rays displayed on photographic film. Two raters examine a series of images and classify the severity of a bone break using a 1, 2, 3 system with 1 indicating a minor break and 3 indicating a severe break. The data are as follows.

		Rater 1		
		1	2	3
Rater 2	1	43	7	1
	2	9	24	5
	3	4	8	19

a. Which is the appropriate Kappa statistic to use for this analysis (Kappa or weighted Kappa)?

b. Write a SAS program to read the data and calculate the appropriate Kappa statistic.

c. What is the value of the Kappa statistic?

According to the Landis and Koch criteria, how would you characterize the strength of this result?

CHAPTER

8

COMPARING MEANS USING *T*-TESTS

LEARNING OBJECTIVES

- To understand the use of the one-sample *t*-test using PROC UNIVARIATE and PROC TTEST
- To understand the use of the two-sample *t*-test using PROC TTEST
- To understand the use of the paired *t*-test using PROC MEANS and PROC TTEST

Experiments whose outcome measures are quantitative variables are often analyzed by comparing means. The Student's *t*-test is the most commonly used statistical test for comparing two means or for comparing an observed mean with a known value. If more than two groups are observed, an analysis of variance (ANOVA) is used to compare means across groups (discussed in Chapter 9).

PERFORMING A ONE-SAMPLE *T*-TEST

A one-sample *t*-test is often used to compare an observed mean with a known or "gold standard" value. For example, in a quality control setting, you may be interested in comparing a sample of data to an expected outcome, such as the observed calories of liquid in cans of baby formula against the claim on the label. The purpose of the one-sample *t*-test, in this case, is to determine if there is enough evidence to dispute the claim. In general, for a one-sample *t*-test you obtain a random sample from some population and then compare the observed sample mean to some known value. The typical hypotheses for a one-sample *t*-test are:

$H_0:\mu = \mu_0$: The population mean is equal to a hypothesized value, μ_0

$H_a:\mu \neq \mu_0$: The population mean is not equal to μ_0

The key assumption underlying the one-sample *t*-test is that the population from which the random sample is selected is normal. If the data are non-normal, then non-parametric tests such as the sign test and the signed rank test are available (see Chapter 12). However, because of the central limit theorem, whenever N is sufficiently large, the distribution of the sample mean is approximately normal even when the population is non-normal. A variety of rules of thumb have been recommended to help you determine whether to go ahead and trust the results of a one-sample *t*-test even when your data are non-normal. The following are general guidelines (see Moore and McCabe, 2006).

- Small sample size ($N < 15$): You should not use the one-sample *t*-test if the data are clearly skewed or if outliers are present.

- Moderate sample size ($N > 15$ at least 15): The one-sample *t*-test can be safely used except when there are severe outliers.

- Large sample size ($N > 40$): The one-sample *t*-test can be safely used without regard to skewness or outliers.

Running the One-Sample *t*-test in SAS

In SAS there are (at least) two ways to perform a one-sample *t*-test. Using PROC UNIVARIATE, you can specify the value of μ_0 for the test reported in the "Tests for Location" table shown in Table 8.1 using the option MU0=*value*. For example,

```
PROC UNIVARIATE MU0=4;VAR LENGTH ;RUN;
```

would request a one-sample *t*-test based on the null hypothesis that $\mu_0 = 4$.

A second method in SAS for performing this one-sample *t*-test is to use the PROC TTEST procedure. For this procedure, the example SAS code is

```
PROC TTEST H0=4;VAR LENGTH; RUN;
```

HANDS-ON
EXAMPLE

In this example you will learn how to perform a one-sample *t*-test using SAS commands. A certain medical implant component is reported to be 4 cm in length by its manufacturer. Precision of the component length is of the utmost importance. To test the reliability of the manufacturer's claim, a random sample of 15 of the components is collected, and the following lengths (in cm) are recorded.

1. In the Editor window, open the file ATTEST1.SAS.

```
DATA ONESAMPLE;
INPUT LENGTH @@;
DATALINES;
4    3.95 4.01 3.95 4
3.98 3.97 3.97 4.01 3.98
3.99 4.01 4.02 4.02 3.98
;
ODS HTML;
ODS GRAPHICS ON;
Title 'One-sample t-test, using PROC UNIVARIATE';
PROC UNIVARIATE MU0=4;VAR LENGTH ;RUN;
Title 'One-sample t-test using PROC TTEST';
PROC TTEST H0=4;var LENGTH;
RUN;
ODS GRAPHICS OFF;
ODS HTML CLOSE;
```

Notice that the *t*-test is performed twice: once using PROC UNIVARIATE and again using PROC TTEST.

2. Run this program and observe the "Test for Location" table from PROC UNIVARIATE shown in Table 8.1. The row titled "Student's *t*" includes the information for the test $t = -1.79$ and $p = 0.0958$. This *p*-value indicates

(Continued)

that you would not reject $H_0:\mu = 4$ at the $\alpha = 0.05$ level of significance. PROC UNIVARIATE also reports that the sample mean is 3.989 and the sample standard deviation is 0.023 (not shown here). Two nonparametric tests are also performed: the sign and signed rank tests. These tests are discussed in Chapter 12. Because the sample size is small, normality is an issue that needs to be addressed. The results of these tests show that we make the same decision (i.e., to not reject the null hypothesis) whether or not normality is assumed. A more direct assessment of the normality of the data is discussed in step 5.

3. Observe the results from PROC TTEST, shown in Table 8.2. Note that the *t*-statistic is the same as with PROC UNIVARIATE, and the sample mean and standard deviation are 3.989 and 0.023, respectively, as before. This table also reports the Degrees of Freedom (DF). The results of this analysis are that $t(14) = -1.79$ and $p = 0.0958$. The "$t(14)$" includes DF, which should be included when you report these results. The TTEST output also gives you a 95 percent confidence interval of the mean under the 95% CL Mean heading (3.977,4.002). Both the *p*-value and the fact that the confidence interval contains the hypothesized value 4 indicate that $H_0:\mu = 4$ would not be rejected at the 0.05 level of significance.

TABLE 8.1. *t*-test results using PROC UNIVARIATE

Tests for Location: Mu0=4				
Test		Statistic	p Value	
Student's t	t	-1.78567	Pr > |t|	0.0958
Sign	M	-1.5	Pr >= |M|	0.5811
Signed Rank	S	-24	Pr >= |S|	0.0925

TABLE 8.2. *t*-test results using PROC TTEST

N	Mean	Std Dev	Std Err	Minimum	Maximum
15	3.9893	0.0231	0.00597	3.9500	4.0200

Mean	95% CL Mean		Std Dev	95% CL Std Dev	
3.9893	3.9765	4.0021	0.0231	0.0169	0.0365

DF	t Value	Pr > |t|
14	-1.79	0.0958

FIGURE 8.1. *Plots produced by PROC TTEST*

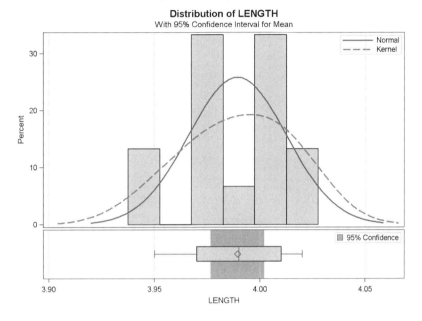

4. Although the statistical test did not reject the null hypothesis, the researcher should also consider the minimum and maximum values in the table to determine if, in a clinical setting, either of these lengths would present a detrimental clinical issue.

5. Observe the plots in Figure 8.1. These were produced using the ODS GRAPHICS ON/GRAPHICS OFF commands in the code. Special graphics output such as the plots that follow are sometimes produced by SAS procedures, but you will not see them unless you place the command

ODS GRAPHICS ON;

before the procedure(s) and

ODS GRAPHICS OFF;

after the procedure(s). Whenever you are in doubt about what type of graphics are available or what graphics may have been implemented in a new version of SAS, it is a good idea to run your code with ODS GRAPHICS ON/OFF.

The graph in Figure 8.1 was first implemented in SAS version 9.2, and it displays a wealth of information. A histogram of the variable LENGTH is

(*Continued*)

given along with two curves. The solid curve is a normal curve based on the mean (3.989) and standard deviation (0.023) estimated from the data. The dashed curve is a kernel density estimator, which is a smoothed version of the histogram. If dramatic skewness were evident in the data, then the skewness would also be displayed in the kernel density estimator.

These plots provide information about the normality assumption. There does not appear to be a dramatic departure from normality because the kernel density estimator is fairly bell-shaped. At the bottom of the plot is a box-plot that plots the minimum, 25th, 50th, and 75th percentiles along with the maximum of the data. The boxplot is fairly symmetrical in shape with some tendency for the left whisker to be longer than the right one.

SAS always reports two-tailed *p*-values for this statistical test. If you are interested only in rejecting the null hypothesis if the population mean differs from the hypothesized value in a particular direction of interest, you may want to use a one-tailed (sometimes called a one-sided) test. For example, if you want to reject the null hypothesis only if there is sufficient evidence that the mean is smaller than the hypothesized value, the hypotheses become:

$H_0: \mu = \mu_0$: The population mean is equal to a hypothesized value, μ_0.
$H_a: \mu < \mu_0$: The population mean is less than μ_0.

SAS always reports a two-tailed *p*-value, so you need to modify the reported *p*-value to fit a one-tailed test by dividing it by 2 if your results are consistent with the direction specified in the alternative hypothesis. These comments also apply to the two-sample and paired *t*-tests discussed in this chapter.

PERFORMING A TWO-SAMPLE *T*-TEST

The SAS PROC TTEST procedure is used to test for the equality of means for a two-sample (independent group) *t*-test. For example, you might want to compare males and females regarding their reaction to a certain drug. The purpose of the two-sample *t*-test is to determine whether your data provide you with enough evidence to conclude that there is a difference in mean reaction levels. In general, for a two-sample *t*-test you obtain independent random samples of size N_1 and N_2 from the two populations of interest, and then you compare the observed sample means. The typical hypotheses for a two-sample *t*-test are

$H_0: \mu_1 = \mu_2$: The population means of the two groups are equal.

$H_a: \mu_1 \neq \mu_2$: The population means are not equal.

which are tested with a *t*-test. As in the case of the one-sample *t*-test, SAS provides *p*-values for this two-tailed test. If you have a one-tailed alternative, the *p*-values will need to be modified as mentioned in the section on one-sample *t*-tests. Key assumptions underlying the two-sample *t*-test are that the random samples are independent and that the populations are normally distributed with equal variances. If the data are non-normal, then nonparametric tests such as the Mann-Whitney U are available (see Chapter 12).

The following are guidelines regarding normality and equal variance assumptions:

> **Normality:** As in the one-sample case, rules of thumb are available to help you determine whether to go ahead and trust the results of a two-sample *t*-test even when your data are non-normal. The sample size guidelines given earlier in this chapter for the one-sample test can be used in the two-sample case by replacing N with $N_1 + N_2$ (see Moore and McCabe, 2006).

> **Equal variances:** There are two *t*-tests reported by SAS in this setting: one based on the assumption that the variances of the two groups are equal (and thus using a pooled estimate of the common variance) and one (Satterthwaite) not making that assumption. Both methods make the same assumptions about normality. There is no universal agreement concerning which *t*-test to use.

A conservative approach suggested by some statisticians (see Moore and McCabe, 2006; Watkins, Schaeffer, and Cobb, 2004) is to always use the version of the *t*-test (Satterthwaite) that does not assume equal variances. The classical approach to deciding which version of the *t*-test to use is to formally test the equal variance assumption using an *F*-test that SAS gives in the *t*-test output. The typical decision criterion using this approach is that if the *p*-value for the *F*-test test is less than α (say 0.05), then you conclude that the variances are unequal and use the Satterthwaite *t*-test. If the *p*-value for the *F*-test is greater than α, you use the *t*-test based on a pooled estimate of the variances. At least one of the reasons for the recommendation to always use the Satterthwaite test is that studies have shown that the *F*-test for assessing whether the variances are equal is unreliable.

If your observations are related across "group" as paired or repeated measurements, this is an *incorrect* version of the *t*-test. For that case, see the section on the paired *t*-test that follows.

Running the Two-Sample *t*-test in SAS

The syntax for the TTEST procedure is

```
PROC TTEST <options>; CLASS variable; <statements>;
```

Some of the common options for PROC TTEST are the following:

DATA = datasetname
   Specifies what data set to use.

COCHRAN
    Specifies that the Cochran and Cox probability approximation is to be used for unequal variances.

H0=value
    Specifies the hypothesized value under H_0 (null hypothesis) in a one-sample *t*-test.

Commonly used statements for `PROC TTEST` include:

CLASS statement
    The `CLASS` statement is required, and it specifies the grouping variable for the analysis. The data for this grouping variable must contain two and only two values. An example `PROC TTEST` command is

> **PROC TTEST;**
> CLASS GROUP;
> VAR SCORE;

    In this example, GROUP contains two values, say 1 or 2. A *t*-test will be performed on the variable SCORE.

BY *variable list;*

    Causes *t*-tests to be run separately for groups specified by the BY statement.

VAR; *variable list*

    Specifies which variables will be used in the analysis.

HANDS-ON
EXAMPLE

In this example, a biologist experimenting with plant growth designs an experiment in which 15 seeds are randomly assigned to one of two fertilizers and the height of the resulting plant is measured after two weeks. She wants to know if one of the fertilizers provides more vertical growth than the other.

1. In the Editor window, open the file ATTEST2.SAS.

```
DATA TTEST;
INPUT BRAND $ HEIGHT;
DATALINES;
   A    20.00
   A    23.00
   A    32.00
```

```
    A    24.00
    A    25.00
    A    28.00
    A    27.50
    B    25.00
    B    46.00
    B    56.00
    B    45.00
    B    46.00
    B    51.00
    B    34.00
    B    47.50
;
ODS HTML;
ODS GRAPHICS ON;
PROC TTEST;
     CLASS BRAND; VAR HEIGHT;
     Title 'Independent Group t-Test Example';
RUN;
ODS GRAPHICS OFF;
ODS HTML CLOSE;
QUIT;
```

2. Run this program and observe the output for PROC TTEST, shown in Table 8.3.

   ■ There is a lot of output, so you have to be careful about what you are reading. Notice that there are actually four tables. The first table gives you the sample mean, standard deviation, standard error of the mean, and the minimum and maximum for each value of BRAND (A and B). The last line includes similar information for the mean difference.

   ■ The second table gives the mean and standard deviations again along with 95 percent confidence intervals for the means and standard deviations in each group along with 95 percent confidence intervals for the difference in the group means using a pooled estimate of the variance (if you believe the variances are equal) and based on the Satterthwaite method that does not make an assumption of equal variances.

   ■ The third table gives the results of the two *t*-tests. If the variances are assumed to be equal, then the top (or pooled) method is used, and the

   (Continued)

TABLE 8.3. Two-sample *t*-test output from PROC TTEST

BRAND	N	Mean	Std Dev	Std Err	Minimum	Maximum
A	7	25.6429	3.9021	1.4748	20.0000	32.0000
B	8	43.8125	9.8196	3.4717	25.0000	56.0000
Diff (1-2)		-18.1696	7.6778	3.9736		

BRAND	Method	Mean	95% CL Mean		Std Dev	95% CL Std Dev	
A		25.6429	22.0340	29.2517	3.9021	2.5145	8.5926
B		43.8125	35.6031	52.0219	9.8196	6.4925	19.9855
Diff (1-2)	Pooled	-18.1696	-26.7541	-9.5852	7.6778	5.5660	12.3692
Diff (1-2)	Satterthwaite	-18.1696	-26.6479	-9.6914			

Method	Variances	DF	t Value	Pr > |t|
Pooled	Equal	13	-4.57	0.0005
Satterthwaite	Unequal	9.3974	-4.82	0.0008

Equality of Variances				
Method	Num DF	Den DF	F Value	Pr > F
Folded F	7	6	6.33	0.0388

p-value for the test is 0.0005. If the variances are not assumed to be equal, then the second (or Satterthwaite) method is appropriate and the *p*-value for the test is 0.0008. Note that the Satterthwaite version generally reports fractional degrees of freedom. In this case, that value is 9.4. Note also that the decision regarding which *t*-test to use is not crucial here because both suggest rejecting the null hypothesis. This will often be the situation.

- The fourth table gives the results of the *F*-test for deciding whether the variances can be considered equal. The *p*-value for this test is 0.0388, so at the 0.05 level we would conclude that the variances are not equal, and it appears that the variance for BRAND B is larger than that for BRAND A. Thus the classical approach would lead us to use the Satterthwaite *t*-test.

3. Observe the graphical information shown in Figure 8.2. This figure is similar to Figure 8.1, but it shows histograms, normal curves, kernel density

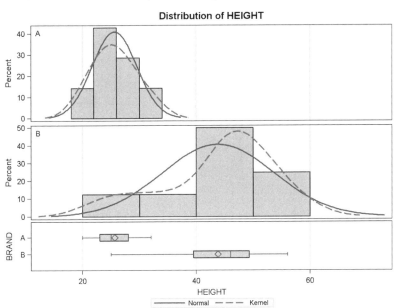

FIGURE 8.2. *Plots produced by PROC TTEST*

estimators, and boxplots for HEIGHT separately for BRAND A and BRAND B. In both cases normality looks like a fairly good assumption, but there seems to be evidence that the variance for BRAND B is larger than that for A. The observation about the variances is consistent with the conclusions of the *F*-test shown in Table 8.3.

Using PROC BOXPLOT

A complementary graphical procedure that can be used to compare means visually is PROC BOXPLOT. Although boxplots are produced using the ODS GRAPHICS option in this example, you might want a plot that includes only the side-by-side boxplots. You can use PROC BOXPLOT to create this type of graph. (See Chapter 14.)

PERFORMING A PAIRED *T*-TEST

To compare two paired groups (such as in a before–after situation) wherein both observations are taken from the same or matched subjects, use PROC TTEST with the PAIRED statement. Suppose your data contain the variables WBEFORE and WAFTER (before and after weight on a diet) for eight subjects. The hypotheses for this test are:

$H_0: \mu_{\text{Loss}} = 0$: The population average weight loss is zero.

$H_a: \mu_{\text{Loss}} \neq 0$: The population average weight loss is not zero.

HANDS-ON EXAMPLE

In this example you will learn how to perform a paired *t*-test using `PROC TTEST`.

1. In the Editor window, open the file named `ATTEST3.SAS`.

```
DATA WEIGHT;
INPUT WBEFORE WAFTER;
DATALINES;
200 185
175 154
188 176
198 193
197 198
310 275
245 224
202 188
;
ODS HTML;
PROC TTEST;
PAIRED WBEFORE*WAFTER;
TITLE 'Paired t-test example';
RUN;
ODS HTML CLOSE;
```

2. Run the program and observe the output in Table 8.4. The mean of the difference is 15.25. The *t*-statistic used to test the null hypothesis is 3.94, and the *p*-value for this paired *t*-test is $p = 0.0056$, which provides evidence to reject the null hypothesis. The output also provides a 95 percent confidence interval on the difference (7.23, 22.26), which indicates that the population's mean weight loss could plausibly have been as little as 7.23 pounds and as much as 22.26 pounds. In either case, it appears that the mean weight loss is greater than zero. A one-sided test might have been used here because the goal of the study (before any data were collected) was to produce a positive weight loss.

3. Observe the graphics displayed in Figure 8.3. These plots are based on the differenced data. The histogram, kernel density estimator, and the boxplot all suggest that the differences are reasonably normally distributed. Thus,

TABLE 8.4.   **Paired *t*-test output**

Difference: WBEFORE - WAFTER

N	Mean	Std Dev	Std Err	Minimum	Maximum
8	15.2500	10.9381	3.8672	-1.0000	35.0000

Mean	95% CL Mean		Std Dev	95% CL Std Dev	
15.2500	6.1055	24.3945	10.9381	7.2320	22.2621

DF	t Value	Pr > |t|
7	3.94	0.0056

even though the sample size is quite small, it seems reasonable to use the paired *t*-test. The PAIRED option produces several other plots in SAS version 9.2 that are not shown here.

FIGURE 8.3.   *Plots produced by PROC TTEST using the PAIRED option*

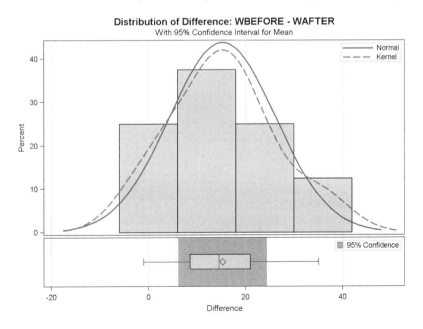

Distribution of Difference: WBEFORE - WAFTER
With 95% Confidence Interval for Mean

The paired *t*-test is actually a one-sample *t*-test computed on the differenced data. That is, if we computed a new variable `DIF=WBEFORE-WAFTER` and ran a one-sample *t*-test on the variable `DIF`, we would get identical results. The normality assumption in this case applies to the differenced data.

SUMMARY

This chapter illustrated how to perform tests on one or two means using `PROC MEANS`. In particular, the chapter emphasized the fact that it is important to keep in mind the distinction between an independent groups comparison and a repeated (paired) observations comparison.

EXERCISES

8.1. Perform a *t*-test.

Suppose you are interested in knowing if comprehension of certain medical instructions is dependent on the time of day when the instructions are given. In a school setting, you randomize members of a twelfth-grade class into two groups. In the morning at 8:30, Group A is shown a video describing how to use an infant forehead thermometer. The same video is shown to Group B at 3:00 on the same day. The next day all students are given a test over the material. The following scores were observed.

Group A Subjects	Test Score	Group B Subjects	Test Score
1	88	1	87
2	89	2	69
3	79	3	78
4	100	4	79
5	98	5	83
6	89	6	90
7	94	7	85
8	95		

a. Is this analysis an independent or paired comparison?

b. Enter these data into a SAS data set and perform the appropriate *t*-test. Here is some code to get you started:

```
DATA TEMP;
   INPUT GROUP $ SCORE;
   DATALINES;
```

```
A 88
A 89
...etc...
;
PROC TTEST DATA=TEMP;
CLASS _____; VAR _____;
...etc...
RUN;
```

c. What is your conclusion?

8.2. Perform a *t*-test on pre- and post-data.

To test if a memory technique was effective, a researcher provided five people with a list of ten objects for forty-five seconds then tested them to see how many they remembered (pretest). He then taught them a memory technique and then presented them with a list of ten different (although similar) objects and administered a similar test (posttest). The results follow.

Subject	Pretest	Posttest
AD	6	10
GE	7	7
KL	9	10
MM	4	7
OU	7	9

a. Assuming that the test data are approximately normally distributed, what analysis is appropriate to test the hypothesis that training subjects on a memory technique would improve their ability to remember a list of ten objects?

b. Using code similar to that in the paired *t*-test Hands-on Example, write a SAS program to perform the appropriate test for this analysis. Here is some code to get you started:

```
DATA MEMORY;
INPUT PRETEST _____;
DATALINES;
6 10
...etc...
;
PROC TTEST DATA=MEMORY;
...etc...
RUN;
```

c. What are your conclusions?

CHAPTER

9

ANALYSIS OF VARIANCE

LEARNING OBJECTIVES

- To be able to compare three or more means using one-way ANOVA with multiple comparisons
- To be able to perform a repeated measures (dependent samples) analysis of variance with multiple comparisons
- To be able to graph mean comparisons

This chapter illustrates how to perform an analysis of variance (ANOVA) for several common designs. These procedures are used to compare means across groups or to compare three or more repeated measures (dependent samples). SAS provides three major procedures for performing analysis of variance: PROC ANOVA, PROC GLM, and PROC MIXED. We will discuss the use of the first two of these in this chapter and then will discuss PROC MIXED in Chapter 13. PROC ANOVA is a basic procedure that is useful for one-way ANOVA or for multi-way factorial designs with fixed factors and an equal number of observations per cell.

In this chapter we use PROC ANOVA in our analysis of a one-way ANOVA. PROC GLM is a SAS procedure that is similar to but more advanced than PROC ANOVA. (GLM stands for General Linear Model.) We use PROC GLM for the one-way repeated measures analysis because it involves techniques not supported by PROC ANOVA. In Chapter 13 we will illustrate the use of PROC MIXED (the newest of the three SAS ANOVA procedures) to analyze a model with both fixed and random factors and for a repeated measures design with a grouping factor. The Going Deeper section describes how to create appropriate graphs for the analyses discussed in this chapter.

COMPARING THREE OR MORE MEANS USING ONE-WAY ANALYSIS OF VARIANCE

A one-way analysis of variance is an extension of the independent group t-test where there are more than two groups. Assumptions for this test are similar to those for the t-test: Data within groups are normally distributed with equal variances across groups. Another key assumption is that of independent samples. That is, not only do the observations within a group represent a random sample, but there is no matching or pairing of observations among groups. This is analogous to the independent samples requirement in the two-sample t-test. As with the t-test, the ANOVA is robust against moderate departures from the assumptions of normality and equal variance (especially for larger sample sizes). However, the assumption of independence is critical. The hypotheses for the comparison of independent groups are (k is the number of groups):

H_0: $\mu_1 = \mu_2 = \lambda = \mu_k$: Means of all the groups are equal.

H_a: $\mu_i \neq \mu_j$ for some $i \neq j$: At least two means are not equal.

The test statistic reported is an F test with k-1 and N-k degrees of freedom, where N is the number of subjects. A low p-value for the F-test is evidence for rejecting the null hypothesis. In other words, there is evidence that at least one pair of means is not equal. These tests can be performed in SAS using PROC ANOVA. The syntax for the statement is:

```
PROC ANOVA <options>;
    CLASS variable;
    MODEL dependentvar = independentvars;
    MEANS independentvars / typecomparison <meansoptions>;
```

Some of the common options for PROC ANOVA are:

DATA = *datasetname*
Specifies the data set to use

ORDER=*option*
Options are DATA, FORMATTED, FREQ, and INTERNAL

Some of the commonly used statements for PROC ANOVA are:

CLASS *variable*
This statement is required and specifies the grouping variable for the analysis.

MODEL statement
This statement specifies the dependent and independent variables for the analysis. More specifically, it takes the form

MODEL *dependentvariable=independentvariable;*

The dependent variable is the quantitative variable of interest (your outcome variable), and the independent variable (one independent variable in the simple ANOVA case) is the grouping variable for the analysis (the variable listed in the CLASS statement). For example, if you have measured weight and want to determine if there is a weight difference by group, your model statement would be

MODEL WEIGHT=GROUP;

> You will see the MODEL statement in a number of SAS procedures. In general, the information on the left side of the equal sign is the dependent variable or the variable you are trying to predict, and the variable or variables on the right side of the equal sign are independent (predictor) variables.

Using the MEANS Statement

When you perform a one-way analysis of variance, typically there is a two-step procedure: (1) test $H_0: \mu_1 = \mu_2 = \lambda = \mu_k$ to determine whether any significant differences exist and (2) if H_0 is rejected then run subsequent multiple comparison tests to determine which differences are significantly different. Pairwise comparison of means can be performed using one of several multiple comparison tests specified using the MEANS statement, which has the following format:

MEANS *independentvar / typecomparison <meansoptions>;*

where the comparison types are selected from the following (not an exhaustive list of SAS options):

BON
> Bonferroni *t*-tests of differences

DUNCAN
> Duncan's multiple range test

SCHEFFE
> Scheffe multiple comparison procedure

SNK
> Student Newman Keuls multiple range test

LSD
> Fisher's Least Significant Difference test

TUKEY
> Tukey's studentized range test

DUNNETT ('x')
> Dunnett's test—compare to a single control, where 'x' is the category value of the control group

MEANS options are

ALPHA=*pvalue*
> Specifies the significance level for comparisons (default: 0.05)

CLDIFF
> Requests that confidence limits be included in the output

For example, suppose you are comparing the time to relief of three headache medicines—brands 1, 2, and 3. The time-to-relief data are reported in minutes. For this experiment, fifteen subjects were randomly placed on one of the three medications. Which medicine (if any) is the most effective? The data for this example are as follows:

Brand 1	Brand 2	Brand 3
24.5	28.4	26.1
23.5	34.2	28.3
26.4	29.5	24.3
27.1	32.2	26.2
29.9	30.1	27.8

HANDS-ON EXAMPLE

This example illustrates how to compare the means of three or more independent groups using SAS ANOVA. We also illustrate here a technique for performing multiple comparisons.

1. In the Editor window, open the file AANOVA2.SAS.

```
DATA ACHE;
INPUT BRAND RELIEF;
CARDS;
1 24.5
1 23.5
1 26.4
1 27.1
1 29.9
2 28.4
2 34.2
2 29.5
2 32.2
2 30.1
3 26.1
3 28.3
3 24.3
3 26.2
3 27.8
;
ODS HTML;
PROC ANOVA DATA=ACHE;
    CLASS BRAND;
    MODEL RELIEF=BRAND;
    MEANS BRAND/TUKEY;
TITLE 'COMPARE RELIEF ACROSS MEDICINES - ANOVA EXAMPLE';
RUN;
ODS HTML CLOSE;
```

Examine the PROC ANOVA statement:

■ BRAND is the CLASS or grouping variable (containing three levels).

■ The MODEL statement indicates that RELIEF is the dependent variable, whose means across groups are to be compared. The grouping factor is BRAND.

■ The MEANS statement requests a multiple comparison test for BRAND using the Tukey method.

■ Note how the data are set up in the DATA step, with one subject per line, where the grouping variable BRAND indicates to SAS the group membership for each subject.

2. Run this analysis and observe the results. The analysis of variance (partial) results are shown in Table 9.1.

   The first analysis of variance table is a test of the full model, which in this case is the same as the test of the BRAND effect shown in the second table because only one factor is in the model. This is a test of the hypothesis that all means are equal. The small p-value ($p = 0.009$) provides evidence for rejecting the null hypothesis that the means are equal.

   If the p-value for the model is not significant ($p > 0.05$), end your analysis here and conclude that you cannot reject the null hypothesis that all means are equal. If, as in this case, the p-value is small, you can perform multiple comparisons to determine which means are different.

3. Observe the multiple comparison results, shown in Table 9.2.

TABLE 9.1. ANOVA results

Source	DF	Sum of Squares	Mean Square	F Value	Pr > F
Model	2	66.7720000	33.3860000	7.14	0.0091
Error	12	56.1280000	4.6773333		
Corrected Total	14	122.9000000			

Source	DF	Anova SS	Mean Square	F Value	Pr > F
BRAND	2	66.77200000	33.38600000	7.14	0.0091

(Continued)

TABLE 9.2. **Tukey multiple comparisons results**

Means with the same letter are not significantly different.			
Tukey Grouping	Mean	N	BRAND
A	30.880	5	2
B	26.540	5	3
B			
B	26.280	5	1

This table graphically displays any significant mean differences using Tukey's multiple comparison test. Groups that *are not* significantly different from each other are included in the same Tukey Grouping. From Table 9.2 we see that there are two groupings, A and B. Notice that BRAND 2 is in a group by itself. This indicates that the mean for BRAND 2 (30.88) is significantly higher than (different from) the means of BRAND 1 (26.28) and BRAND 3 (26.54). Because BRAND 1 and BRAND 3 are in the same grouping, there is no significant difference between these two brands. Because a shorter time to relief is desirable, the conclusion would be that BRANDs 1 and 3 are preferable to BRAND 2.

4. Another method for displaying the Tukey results is provided when you include the option CLDIFF in the MEANS statement. Change the MEANS statement to read:

```
MEANS BRAND/TUKEY CLDIFF;
```

Re-run the program and observe in Table 9.3 the Tukey comparison table showing simultaneous confidence limits on the difference between means.

TABLE 9.3. **Simultaneous confidence limits**

Comparisons significant at the 0.05 level are indicated by ***.				
BRAND Comparison	Difference Between Means	Simultaneous 95% Confidence Limits		
2 - 3	4.340	0.691	7.989	***
2 - 1	4.600	0.951	8.249	***
3 - 2	-4.340	-7.989	-0.691	***
3 - 1	0.260	-3.389	3.909	
1 - 2	-4.600	-8.249	-0.951	***
1 - 3	-0.260	-3.909	3.389	

The asterisks (***) in the multiple comparisons table indicate paired comparisons that are significant at the 0.05 level. In this case, all comparisons except means 1 versus 3 are different. This indicates that mean time to relief for BRAND 3 is not significantly different from that of BRAND 1, but that the mean time to relief for BRAND 2 is significantly different from those for BRAND 1 and BRAND 3. The Simultaneous 95 percent Confidence Limits provide an estimate of how small or large the difference between the means is likely to be. You can use this information to assess the (clinical) importance of the difference. For example, the difference between BRANDs 2 and 3 could plausibly be as small as 0.69 and as large as 7.99. If such differences are determined to be of clinical significance, then the conclusions are the same as those obtained from Table 9.2—that is, BRANDs 1 and 3 are preferable to BRAND 2.

By changing ANOVA to GLM in this SAS code and re-running the program, you will see essentially the same results. So, GLM could have been used for this one-way ANOVA problem. Some people choose to always use GLM where GLM or ANOVA would have applied. In the GLM output you will see results in tables labeled TYPE I and TYPE III sums of squares. In this example, the results in the two tables will be the same. In some more complex settings—for example, multi-way ANOVA designs with an unequal number of observations per cell—the TYPE I and TYPE III sums of squares will differ. In this case, the typical recommendation is to use the TYPE III sums of squares (see Elliott and Woodward, 1986).

COMPARING THREE OR MORE REPEATED MEASURES

Repeated measures are observations taken from the same or related subjects over time or in differing circumstances. Examples include weight loss or reaction to a drug over time. When there are two repeated measures, the analysis of the data becomes a paired *t*-test (as discussed in Chapter 8). When there are three or more repeated measures, the analysis is a repeated measures analysis of variance.

Assumptions for the repeated measures ANOVA are that the dependent variable is normally distributed and that the variances across the repeated measures are equal. As in the one-way ANOVA case, the test is robust against moderate departures from the normality and equal variance assumptions. As in the independent groups ANOVA procedure, you will usually perform the analysis in two steps. First, an analysis of variance will determine if there is a difference in means across time. If a difference is found, then multiple comparisons can be performed to determine where the differences lie.

The hypotheses being tested with a repeated measures ANOVA are:

H_0 There is no difference among the groups (repeated measures).

H_a There is a difference among the groups.

For this analysis, the PROC GLM procedure will be used because the complexity of this procedure is not supported in PROC ANOVA. The abbreviated syntax for PROC GLM is similar to that for PROC ANOVA:

```
PROC GLM <options>;
        CLASS variable;
        MODEL dependentvar = independentvars/options;
        MEANS independentvars / typecomparison
        <meansoptions>;
```

The CLASS, MODEL, and MEANS statements are essentially the same as for PROC ANOVA. These are not all of the options available in PROC GLM, but this list is sufficient for performing the analysis in this section. Also note that GLM gives TYPE I and TYPE III sums of squares. In the Hands-on Example that follows, these will be the same. However, in more complex settings they may differ, in which case the typical advice is to use the TYPE III sums of squares.

> This analysis is also called a within-subjects or treatment-by-subject design. Some call it a "Single-factor" experiment having repeated measures on the same element.

The data in the following Hands-on Example are repeated measures of reaction times (OBS) of five persons after being treated with four drugs in randomized order. (These types of data may come from a crossover experimental design.) The data are as follows where it is important to understand that, for example, the first row of results (i.e., 31, 29, 17, and 35) consists of results observed on Subject 1. The data must be entered into SAS in such a way that this relationship is identified. You will note that in the SAS code to follow, each reading on the dependent variable (OBS) is identified with respect to its corresponding SUBJ and DRUG.

Subj	Drug1	Drug2	Drug3	Drug4
1	31	29	17	35
2	15	17	11	23
3	25	21	19	31
4	35	35	21	45
5	27	27	15	31

HANDS-ON
EXAMPLE

This example illustrates how to compare three or more repeated measures (dependent samples) and perform pairwise comparisons using the DUNCAN procedure.

1. In the Editor window, open the file AGLM1.SAS.

```
DATA STUDY;
INPUT SUBJ DRUG OBS;
DATALINES;
1    1    31
1    2    29
1    3    17
1    4    35
2    1    15
...etc
5    3    15
5    4    31

;
run;
ODS HTML; ODS GRAPHICS ON;
PROC GLM DATA=STUDY;
     CLASS SUBJ DRUG;
     MODEL OBS= SUBJ DRUG;
     MEANS DRUG/DUNCAN;
     TITLE 'Repeated Measures ANOVA';
RUN;
ODS HTML CLOSE;
ODS GRAPHICS OFF;
```

2. Run the program and observe the results. Several tables are included in the output. Table 9.4 shows the overall analysis of variance table and the "Type III SS" table. The test in the first table is an overall test to determine whether there are any significant differences across subjects or drugs. If this test is not significant, you can end your analysis and conclude that there is insufficient evidence to show a difference among subjects or drugs. In this case $p < 0.0001$, so you continue to the Type III results table.

(Continued)

TABLE 9.4. Analysis of variance results

Source	DF	Sum of Squares	Mean Square	F Value	Pr > F
Model	7	1331.800000	190.257143	25.03	<.0001
Error	12	91.200000	7.600000		
Corrected Total	19	1423.000000			

Source	DF	Type III SS	Mean Square	F Value	Pr > F
SUBJ	4	648.0000000	162.0000000	21.32	<.0001
DRUG	3	683.8000000	227.9333333	29.99	<.0001

In the Type III results table, the DRUG row reports a p-value of $p < 0.0001$. This is the test of the null hypothesis of interest, which is that there is no difference among the drugs. Because $p < 0.05$, you reject the null hypothesis and conclude that there is a difference among the drugs. Although SUBJ is included as a factor in the model statement, you will generally not be interested in a subject (SUBJ) effect.

3. The multiple comparison test results are shown in Table 9.5. This table is similar to the one discussed in the one-way ANOVA example shown in Table 9.2 except that in this example we have used the Duncan multiple range test rather than the Tukey test for multiple comparisons. The Duncan multiple range test for DRUG indicates that the time to relief for drug 3 is significantly lower than that for all other drugs. There is no statistical difference between drugs 2 and 1; drug 4 has the highest time to relief for all drugs tested, while the time to relief for drug 3 is significantly lower than that for other drugs. Thus, on this basis, drug 3 would be the preferred drug.

4. Change the DUNCAN option to SNK (Student Newman Keuls multiple range test). Re-run the program and see if the multiple comparison results have changed.

TABLE 9.5. Duncan's multiple comparison results

Means with the same letter are not significantly different.			
Duncan Grouping	Mean	N	DRUG
A	33.000	5	4
B	26.600	5	1
B			
B	25.800	5	2
C	16.600	5	3

GOING DEEPER: GRAPHING MEAN COMPARISONS

A graphical comparison allows you to compare the groups visually. If the *p*-value is low in a *t*-test or ANOVA analysis, a visual analysis of the means can be used to illustrate the separation among the means. If the *p*-value is not significant, a graphical comparison will often show a fair amount of overlap among the groups. We use two types of graphs, dot plots and boxplots, to illustrate this comparison and to examine assumptions.

HANDS-ON
EXAMPLE

This example illustrates the plotting of means by group to accompany an ANOVA or *t*-test. This program uses the same ACHE data set that was used in AANOVA2. SAS in the Hands-on Example in the section "Using the MEANS Statement" earlier in this chapter. In this example we illustrate the additional plots provided by ODS GRAPHICS along with an application of the GPLOT command.

1. In the Editor window, open the file AANOVA3.SAS.

```
ODS HTML;
ODS GRAPHICS ON;
TITLE 'GRAPHICAL ANOVA RESULTS - HEADACHE ANALYSIS';
PROC ANOVA DATA=ACHE;
    CLASS BRAND;
    MODEL RELIEF=BRAND;
    MEANS BRAND/TUKEY;
TITLE 'COMPARE RELIEF ACROSS MEDICINES - ANOVA EXAMPLE';
RUN;
PROC GPLOT DATA=ACHE;
    PLOT RELIEF*BRAND;
RUN;
QUIT;
ODS GRAPHICS OFF;
ODS HTML CLOSE;
```

Observe the two changes from AANOVA2.SAS:

■ We have used the ODS GRAPHICS command, which produces side-by-side box-and-whiskers plots of RELIEF with BRAND, as the grouping variable as a part of the one-way ANOVA output from PROC ANOVA.

(Continued)

■ GPLOT produces a graphical plot (scatterplot, which in this case results in side-by-side dot plots) with BRAND as the *x*-axis (horizontal axis) and RELIEF as the *y*-axis (vertical axis).

2. Using ODS GRAPHICS ON/ODS GRAPHICS OFF produces the box-and-whiskers plots seen in Figure 9.1. PROC GPLOT illustrates the time to relief as a series of points (by default shown as crosses) indicating individual observations for each BRAND in Figure 9.2. In both of these graphs you can see that times to relief for brands 1 and 3 are comparable and that the time to relief for brand 2 is higher than the others'.

   These graphs are plotted using default values. Advanced plotting techniques that can help you make these graphs more suited for presentation are discussed in Chapter 14.

   Note that side-by-side box-and-whiskers plots like those in Figure 9.1 could also have been created without using PROC ANOVA with the commands:

   ```
   PROC BOXPLOT DATA=ACHE;
      PLOT RELIEF*BRAND;
   ```

3. As a preview of some of the graphic enhancement options shown in Chapter 14, open the SAS program file AANOV4A.SAS and observe the SYMBOL1 and AXIS1 statements. The SYMBOLn statement defines the symbol to be plotted (as a dot), and the AXIS1 statement (along with the /HAXIS=AXIS1 option) instructs SAS to offset the horizontal axis so that

FIGURE 9.1. *Side-by-side boxplots produced by ODS GRAPHICS*

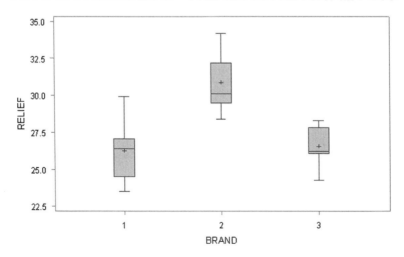

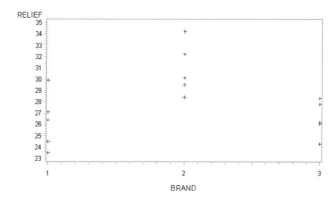

FIGURE 9.2. *Side-by-side dot plots produced by GPLOT*

ANOVA RESULTS - HEADACHE ANALYSIS

groups 1 and 3 are not as close to the sides of the graph. Run this program and compare the output to Figure 9.2.

```
ODS HTML;
TITLE 'ANOVA RESULTS - HEADACHE ANALYSIS';
SYMBOL1 V=DOT;
AXIS1 OFFSET=(5);
PROC GPLOT DATA=ACHE;
     PLOT RELIEF*BRAND/HAXIS=AXIS1;
RUN;
QUIT;
ODS HTML CLOSE;
```

SUMMARY

This chapter illustrated SAS procedures for comparing three or more means in both an independent group setting and for repeated measures. In both cases, the chapter included examples illustrating how to perform post hoc multiple comparisons analysis.

EXERCISES

9.1. Perform multiple comparisons.

a. Modify the PROC ANOVA program (AANOVA2.SAS) by replacing the Tukey comparison code to perform the Scheffe, LSD, and Dunnett's tests. Use these statements:

```
MEANS BRAND/SCHEFFE;
```

```
MEANS BRAND/LSD;
MEANS BRAND/DUNNETT ('1');
```

   Compare results.

b. Replace PROC ANOVA with PROC GLM in this program and re-run it. Notice that the answers are the same. PROC GLM is a more advanced procedure that can do the same analysis as PROC ANOVA as well as more complex analyses.

9.2. Run a one-way ANOVA.

   A researcher is considering three training videos on how to operate a medical device. To determine which training video is the most effective, he randomly selects students from a class and organizes them into three groups. Each group is shown the video and then is tested on the device. Scores range from 0 to 100. The data are in a snippet of SAS code (EX_9.2.SAS):

```
DATA DEVICE;
INPUT SUBJ $ GROUP SCORE;
DATALINES;
AE 1 99
DF 2 99
ED 1 82
FR 3 79
EE 1 89
EG 2 87
IS 3 69
OE 2 77
KY 1 100
WD 3 82
AD 2 89
TR 1 99
SS 2 83
WE 3 81
;
TITLE 'Exercise 9.2';
```

a. Which type of ANOVA is appropriate for this analysis?
b. Complete the code to perform the correct analysis.
c. Perform a multiple comparison test.
d. Produce boxplots.
e. What are your conclusions?

CHAPTER

10

CORRELATION AND REGRESSION

LEARNING OBJECTIVES

- To be able to use SAS procedures to calculate Pearson and Spearman correlations
- To be able to use SAS procedures to produce a matrix of scatterplots
- To be able to use SAS procedures to perform simple linear regression
- To be able to use SAS procedures to perform multiple linear regression
- To be able to use SAS procedures to calculate predictions using a model
- To be able to use SAS procedures to perform residual analysis

Correlation measures the association between two quantitative variables, and the closely related regression analysis uses the relationship between independent and dependent variables for predicting the dependent (response or outcome) variable using one or more independent (predictor or explanatory) variables. In simple linear regression, there is a single dependent variable and a single independent variable while in multiple linear regression there are two or more independent variables. In this chapter we discuss the use of SAS to perform correlation and regression analyses.

CORRELATION ANALYSIS USING PROC CORR

Before proceeding to the use of SAS to perform correlation analysis, we first provide a brief discussion of the basics of correlation analysis.

Correlation Analysis Basics

The correlation coefficient is a measure of the linear relationship between two quantitative variables measured on the same subject (or entity). For example, you might want to study the relationship between height and weight for a sample of teenage boys. For two variables of interest, say X and Y, the correlation, ρ, measures the extent to which a scatterplot of data from the bivariate distribution of X and Y tends to fall along a line. The correlation ρ is a unitless quantity (i.e., it does not depend on the units of measurement) that ranges from -1 to $+1$ where $\rho = -1$ and $\rho = +1$ correspond to perfect negative and positive linear relationships, respectively, and $\rho = 0$ indicates no linear relationship.

In practice it is often of interest to test the hypotheses:

$H_0: \rho = 0$: There is no linear relationship between the two variables.

$H_a: \rho \neq 0$: There is a linear relationship between the two variables.

The correlation coefficient ρ is typically estimated from data using the Pearson correlation coefficient, usually denoted r. PROC CORR in SAS provides a test of the above hypotheses designed to determine whether the estimated correlation coefficient, r, is significantly different from zero. This test assumes that the data represent a random sample from some bivariate normal population. If normality is not a good assumption, nonparametric correlation estimates are available, the most popular of which is Spearman's rho, which PROC CORR also provides. To examine the nature of the relationship between two variables, it is always good practice to look at scatterplots of the variables.

Using SAS PROC CORR for Correlation Analysis

The SAS procedure most often used to calculate correlations is PROC CORR. The syntax for this procedure is:

```
PROC CORR <options>; <statements>;
```

The most commonly used options are:

DATA= *datsetname*;
  Specifies dataset

SPEARMAN
  Requests Spearman rank correlations

NOSIMPLE
  Suppresses display of descriptive statistics

NOPROB
  Suppresses display of *p*-values

The most commonly used information statements are:

VAR *variable(s)*;
  Pairwise correlations are calculated for the variables listed

BY *variable(s)*;
  Produces separate set of pairwise correlations for variables in the VAR list for
  each level of the categorical variable in the BY list (data must be sorted prior
  to using the BY statement in PROC CORR)

WITH *variable(s)*;
  Correlations are obtained between the variables in the VAR list with variables
  in the WITH list

HANDS-ON
EXAMPLE

This example illustrates how to calculate Pearson correlations on several variables in a data set.

1. In the Editor window, open the program ACORR1.SAS.

```
ODS HTML;
PROC CORR DATA="C:\SASDATA\SOMEDATA";
     VAR AGE TIME1 TIME2;
TITLE "Example correlations using PROC CORR";
RUN;
ODS HTML CLOSE;
```

(Continued)

2. Run the program and observe the results, shown in Table 10.1. The output also includes descriptive statistics not shown here. Table 10.1 contains pairwise Pearson correlations between each of the three variables listed in the VAR statement. For example, the correlation between AGE and TIME1 is $r = 0.50088$, and the p-value associated with the test of $H_0: \rho = 0$ is $p = 0.0002$.

TABLE 10.1. **Output from PROC CORR**

Pearson Correlation Coefficients, N = 50 Prob > |r| under H0: Rho=0			
	AGE	**TIME1**	**TIME2**
AGE Age on Jan 1, 2000	1.00000	0.50088 0.0002	0.38082 0.0064
TIME1 Baseline	0.50088 0.0002	1.00000	0.76396 <.0001
TIME2 6 Months	0.38082 0.0064	0.76396 <.0001	1.00000

3. If normality is questionable, you may want to request that the rank correlations (Spearman) be calculated (either by themselves or in combination with the Pearson correlations). Use the following PROC CORR statement to request both Pearson and Spearmen correlations:

```
PROC CORR DATA="C:\SASDATA\SOMEDATA" PEARSON SPEARMAN;
```

Re-run the program and observe that a second table is output containing the Spearman correlations and associated p-values.

4. To simplify the output by suppressing the p-values and descriptive univariate statistics, change the PROC CORR statement to

```
PROC CORR DATA="C:\SASDATA\SOMEDATA"
SPEARMAN NOPROB NOSIMPLE;
```

Re-run the program and observe the output.

Producing a Matrix of Scatterplots

As indicated earlier, it is important to examine a scatterplot of the relationship between two variables to determine the nature of the relationship (e.g., is it linear?). Use of the ODS GRAPHICS mode provides a method for displaying a matrix of the scatterplots associated with correlation estimates. This is illustrated in the following Hands-on Example.

HANDS-ON EXAMPLE

This example illustrates how to create a matrix of scatterplots.

1. In the Editor window, open the program ACORR2.SAS.

```
ODS HTML;
ODS GRAPHICS ON;
PROC CORR DATA="C:\SASDATA\SOMEDATA";
     VAR AGE TIME1-TIME2;
TITLE "Example correlation calculations using PROC CORR";
RUN;
ODS GRAPHICS OFF;
ODS HTML CLOSE;
```

We've used the SAS code from the previous Hands-on Example, with the ODS GRAPHICS statements added. Notice that the first ODS GRAPHICS statement turns "on" the graphics option and the ODS GRAPHICS OFF statement turns the graphics "off."

2. Run the program and observe the matrix of scatterplots illustrated in Figure 10.1. Note that two scatterplots are produced for each pair of variables, so you need examine only the upper or lower half of the table.

FIGURE 10.1. *Matrix of scatterplots*

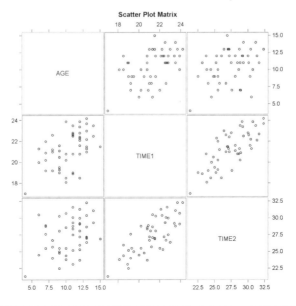

Calculating Correlations Using the WITH Statement

In the previous Hands-on Example, all pairwise correlations were calculated from the list of variables. At times you may want to produce a list of correlations of one or more variables (possibly outcome variables) with several other variables. Use the WITH statement to produce the abbreviated list of correlations, as illustrated in the following Hands-on Example.

HANDS-ON EXAMPLE

This example illustrates how to calculate correlations using a WITH statement.

1. In the Editor window, open the file ACORR3.SAS.

```
ODS HTML;
PROC CORR DATA="C:\SASDATA\SOMEDATA" NOSIMPLE;
    VAR TIME1-TIME4; WITH AGE;
TITLE "Example correlation calculations using a WITH
    statement";
RUN;
ODS HTML CLOSE;
```

Notice that the VAR statement contains TIME1-TIME4, and a WITH statement is included that requests correlations between AGE and the four variables in the VAR statement.

2. Run this example and observe the output shown in Table 10.2. Notice that the output includes only correlations between AGE and the other variables.

TABLE 10.2. Correlations using a WITH statement

Pearson Correlation Coefficients, $N = 50$ Prob > |r| under H0: Rho=0				
	TIME1	TIME2	TIME3	TIME4
AGE Age on Jan 1, 2000	0.50088 0.0002	0.38082 0.0064	0.44952 0.0011	0.48846 0.0003

SIMPLE LINEAR REGRESSION

Simple linear regression is used to predict the value of a dependent variable from the value of an independent variable. For example, in a study of factory workers you could use simple linear regression to predict a pulmonary measure, forced vital capacity (FVC), from asbestos exposure. That is, you could determine whether increased exposure to asbestos is predictive of diminished FVC. The following SAS PROC REG code produces the simple linear regression equation for this analysis:

```
PROC REG;
MODEL FVC=ASB;
RUN;
```

Notice that the MODEL statement is used to tell SAS which variables to use in the analysis. As in the ANOVA procedure discussed in Chapter 9, the MODEL statement has the following form:

```
MODEL dependentvar = independentvar;
```

where the dependent variable (*dependentvar*) is the measure you are trying to predict and the independent variable (*independentvar*) is your predictor.

The Simple Linear Regression Model

The regression line that SAS calculates from the data is an estimate of a theoretical line describing the relationship between the independent variable (X) and the dependent variable (Y). The theoretical line is

$$Y = \alpha + \beta x + \varepsilon$$

where α is the y-intercept, β is the slope, and ε is an error term that is normally distributed with zero mean and constant variance. It should be noted that $\beta = 0$ indicates that there is no linear relationship between X and Y. A simple linear regression analysis is used to develop an equation (a linear regression line) for predicting the dependent variable given a value (x) of the independent variable. The regression line calculated by SAS is given by

$$\hat{Y} = a + bx$$

where a and b are the least-squares estimates of α and β.

The null hypothesis that there is no predictive linear relationship between the two variables is that the slope of the regression equation is zero. Specifically, the hypotheses are:

$H_0: \beta = 0$

$H_a: \beta \neq 0$

A low *p*-value for this test (say, less than 0.05) indicates significant evidence to conclude that the slope of the line is not 0—that is, that knowledge of X would be useful in predicting Y.

> The *t*-test for slope is mathematically equivalent to the *t*-test of $H_0: \rho = 0$ in a correlation analysis.

Using SAS PROC REG for Simple Linear Regression

The general syntax for `PROC REG` is

```
PROC REG <options>; <statements>;
```

The most commonly used options are:

`DATA=datsetname`
    Specifies dataset.

`SIMPLE`
    Displays descriptive statistics.

The most commonly used statements are:

`MODEL dependentvar = independentvar </ options >;`
    Specifies the variable to be predicted (`dependentvar`) and the variable that is the predictor (`independentvar`)

`BY groupvariable;`
    Produces separate regression analyses for each value of the `BY` variable

Several `MODEL` options are available, but we will defer their discussion to the section on using SAS for multiple linear regression later in this chapter.

HANDS-ON
EXAMPLE

In this example, a random sample of fourteen elementary school students is selected from a school, and each student is measured on a creativity score (*X*) using a new testing instrument and on a task score (*Y*) using a standard instrument. The task score is the mean time taken to perform several hand–eye coordination tasks. Because administering the creativity test is much cheaper, the researcher wants to know if the CREATE score is a good substitute for the more expensive TASK score. The data are shown in Table 10.3.

TABLE 10.3.　Data for simple linear regression

SUBJECT	CREATE	TASK
AE	28	4.5
FR	35	3.9
HT	37	3.9
IO	50	6.1
DP	69	6.8
YR	75	8.6
QD	40	2.9
SW	65	5.5
DF	29	5.7
ER	25	3.0
RR	51	7.1
TG	45	7.3
EF	31	3.3
TJ	40	5.2

1. In the Editor window, open the file AREG1.SAS.

```
DATA ART;
INPUT SUBJECT $ CREATE TASK;
DATALINES;
AE    28    4.5
FR    35    3.9
HT    37    3.9
IO    50    6.1
DP    69    4.3
YR    84    8.8
QD    40    2.1
SW    65    5.5
```

(Continued)

```
DF      29      5.7
ER      42      3.0
RR      51      7.1
TG      45      7.3
EF      31      3.3
TJ      40      5.2
```

```
;
ODS HTML;
PROC REG;
MODEL TASK=CREATE;
TITLE "Example simple linear regression using PROC REG";
RUN;
ODS HTML CLOSE;
QUIT;
```

2. Examine the code for PROC REG. The MODEL statement indicates that you want to predict the TASK score (the old test) from the CREATE score (the new test). Run the program and observe the abbreviated output, shown in Table 10.4.

   Information of interest in the first table includes:

   ■ **R-Square:** This is a measure of the strength of the association between the dependent and independent variables. (It is the square of the Pearson correlation coefficient.) The closer this value is to 1, the stronger the association. In this case $R^2 = 0.31$ indicates that 31 percent of the variability in TASK is explained by the regression with CREATE.

TABLE 10.4. Output from PROG REG for a simple linear regression

Root MSE	1.60348	R-Square	0.3075
Dependent Mean	5.05000	Adj R-Sq	0.2498
Coeff Var	31.75213		

Parameter Estimates					
Variable	DF	Parameter Estimate	Standard Error	t Value	Pr > |t|
Intercept	1	2.16452	1.32141	1.64	0.1273
CREATE	1	0.06253	0.02709	2.31	0.0396

Several other measures are mentioned in this table that are not discussed here. The second table includes information related to the regression model.

- **Slope:** The statistical test on the "CREATE" row is for a test of $H_0: \beta = 0$, and $p = 0.04$ provides evidence to reject the null hypothesis and conclude that the slope is not zero. (The statistical test on the Intercept is generally of little importance.)
- **Estimates:** The column labeled "Parameter Estimate" gives the least squares estimates a and b of the regression equation. In this case, the equation is:

```
TASK = 2.16452 + 0.06235 * CREATE;
```

Thus, from this equation you can predict a value of the TASK score from the CREATE score. However, before making any predictions using this equation, you should analyze the relationship further.

Creating a Simple Linear Regression Plot

It is always a good idea to plot your data to examine the linearity of the relationship. In SAS, you can create a simple scatterplot by adding the following statements to the code:

```
SYMBOL1 V=STAR I=RL;
PROC GPLOT; PLOT TASK*CREATE;
```

In this code,

SYMBOL1

specifies information about how to plot the data. The 1 tells SAS that this information is for the first pair of values in the PLOT statement (TASK*CREATE).

V=STAR

indicates that stars are used for the points on the graph. (See Appendix A for more symbol options.)

I=RL

specifies interpolation for the points where R stands for regression and L stands for linear fit. Thus, it draws the line specified by the linear regression equation through the points.

PLOT

specifies which variables to plot. These are indicated as

DEPENDENTVAR*INDEPENDENTVAR

which places the dependent variables on the Y or vertical axis and the independent variable on the X or horizontal axis.

HANDS-ON EXAMPLE

This example illustrates how to create a simple scatterplot with a superimposed regression line.

1. In the Editor window, open the file AREG2.SAS. Notice that it is the SAS code in AREG1.SAS for predicting TASK from CREATE with the following lines added *before* the ODS HTML CLOSE statement:

```
SYMBOL1 V=STAR I=RL;
PROC GPLOT; PLOT TASK*CREATE;
RUN;
QUIT;
```

2. Run the program and observe the graph that is created, as shown in Figure 10.2. Note that the graph appears both in the ODS Output (Results Viewer) and in the Graph window.

    In the plot, the independent variable (CREATE) is on the *x*-axis and the dependent variable (TASK) is on the *y*-axis. By observing the scatterplot, you can see a positive correlation between the two variables (in this case *r* = 0.74), and it appears that knowing CREATE should help in predicting TASK. It is also clear that knowing CREATE does not in any way perfectly predict TASK. Additional information about creating graphics is presented in Chapter 14.

FIGURE 10.2. *Example simple linear regression using PROC REG*

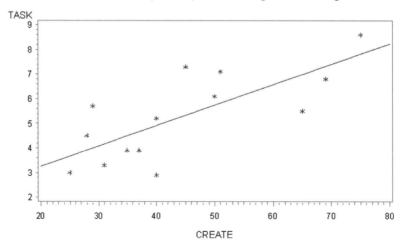

MULTIPLE LINEAR REGRESSION USING PROC REG

Multiple linear regression (MLR) is an extension of simple linear regression. In MLR there is single dependent variable (Y) and more than one independent (X_i) variable. As with simple linear regression, the multiple regression equation calculated by SAS is a sample-based version of a theoretical equation describing the relationship between the k independent variables and the dependent variable Y. The theoretical equation is of the form

$$Y = \alpha + \beta_1 x_1 + \beta_2 x_2 + L + \beta_k x_k + \varepsilon$$

where α is the intercept term and β_i is the regression coefficient corresponding to the ith independent variable. Also, as with simple linear regression, ε is an error term that is assumed to be normally distributed with zero mean and constant variance. From this model it is clear that if $\beta_i = 0$ the ith independent variable is not useful in predicting the dependent variable. The multiple regression equation calculated by SAS for predicting the dependent variable from the k independent variables is

$$\hat{Y} = a + b_1 x_1 + b_2 x_2 + \ldots + b_k x_k$$

whereas with simple linear regression, the coefficients a, b_1, b_2,..., and b_k are least squares estimates of the corresponding coefficients in the theoretical model.

As part of the analysis, the statistical significance of each of the coefficients is tested using a Student's t-test to determine if it contributes significant information to the predictor. These are tests of the hypotheses:

$$H_0 : \beta_i = 0$$

$$H_0 : \beta_i = 0$$

For these tests, if the p-value is low (say, less than 0.05), the conclusion is that the ith independent variable does not contribute significant information to the equation. Care must be taken because each variable in the equation may be related to other variables, so decisions about the inclusion or exclusion of a particular variable test must take these interrelationships into consideration.

As in the simple linear regression model, the R^2 (R-squared) statistic is used to measure the strength of the relationship between the set of independent variables and the dependent variable. The overall significance of the regression is tested using an analysis of variance approach. This is an overall test that all β_i's are equal to zero. The test statistic and the p-value are reported by SAS. If the p-value is low (say, less than 0.05), the conclusion is that some β_i's are not equal to zero, and thus the equation will have some predictive value for Y.

When there are several possible independent variables, you may want to determine what subset of them provides the best model. A number of model selection techniques, some manual and some automated, can help you arrive at a parsimonious set of predictors (i.e., those that provide good prediction with few predictors).

Using SAS PROC REG for Multiple Linear Regression

As mentioned in the section on simple linear regression, the general syntax for PROC REG is

```
PROC REG <options>; <statements>;
```
and the most commonly used options are

```
DATA= datsetname;
```
Specifies dataset

```
SIMPLE
```
Displays descriptive statistics

```
ID variable
```
The variable specified here is displayed beside each observation in certain output tables to identify observations

The most commonly used statements are:

```
MODEL dependentvar = independentvars</options>
```
Specifies the variable to be predicted (*dependentvar*) and the variables that are the predictors (*independentvars*)

```
MODEL STATEMENT OPTIONS
```
(Place after slash following the independent variable list.)

```
P
```
Requests a table containing predicted values from the model.

```
R
```
Requests that the residual be analyzed.

```
CLM
```
Prints the 95 percent upper and lower confidence limits for the expected value of the dependent variable (mean) for each observation.

```
CLI
```
Requests the 95 percent upper and lower confidence limits for an individual value of the dependent variable.

```
INCLUDE=k
```
Include the first k variables in the variable list in the model (for automated selection procedures).

```
SELECTION=
```
Options include BACKWARD, FORWARD, and STEPWISE.

```
SLSTAY=
```
Maximum p-value for a variable to stay in a model during automated model selection.

```
SLENTRY=
```
Minimum p-value for a variable to enter a model for forward or stepwise selection.

The selection options specify how variables will be considered for inclusion in the model. The `BACKWARD` method considers all predictor variables and eliminates the ones that do not meet the minimal `SLSTAY` criterion until only those meeting the criterion remain. The `FORWARD` method brings in the most significant variable that meets the `SLENTRY` criterion and continues entering variables until none meets the criterion. `STEPWISE` is a mixture of the two; it begins like the `FORWARD` method but reevaluates variables at each step and may eliminate a variable if it does not meet the `SLSTAY` criterion. Additional model selection criteria are also available in SAS.

HANDS-ON EXAMPLE

In this example, an employer wants to be able to predict how well applicants will do on the job once they are hired. He devises four tests that he thinks will measure the skills required for the job. Ten prospects are selected at random from a group of applicants and given the four tests. Then, they are given an on-the-job proficiency score (`JOBSCORE`) by a supervisor who observes their work.

1. In the Editor window, open the file `AREG3.SAS`.

```
DATA JOB;INPUT SUBJECT $ TEST1 TEST2 TEST3 TEST4 JOBSCORE;
CARDS;
```

1	75	100	90	88	78
2	51	85	88	89	71
3	99	96	94	93	85
4	92	106	84	84	67
5	90	89	83	77	69
6	67	77	83	73	65
7	109	67	71	65	50
8	94	112	105	91	107
9	105	110	99	95	96
10	74	102	88	69	63

```
;
ODS HTML;
PROC REG;
MODEL JOBSCORE=TEST1 TEST2 TEST3 TEST4;
TITLE "Job Score Analysis using PROC REG";
RUN;
ODS HTML CLOSE;
QUIT;
```

(Continued)

Notice that the dependent variable in the MODEL statement is JOBSCORE and that the TEST variables, listed on the right side of the equal sign, are the independent variables.

2. Run the program and observe the analysis of variance table, Table 10.5. This table includes an overall test of significance of the model. If this test is not significant, it suggests that the independent variables as a group are not predictive of the dependent variable. In this case, $p = 0.0003$, so you would reject the null hypothesis that all $\beta_i = 0$ and continue examining the model.

3. Examine the parameter estimates table, Table 10.6.

The parameter estimates table shows results for tests of the significance (Pr >|t|) of the intercept and each coefficient. In this case, the p-values for TEST2 and TEST4 are not significant ($p > 0.05$). Using this information, you might consider dropping the variables TEST2 and TEST4 from the model and re-running the program to see how the reduced model fits the data.

TABLE 10.5. Analysis of variance output for PROC REG

Analysis of Variance					
Source	DF	Sum of Squares	Mean Square	F Value	Pr > F
Model	4	2495.96648	623.99162	49.58	0.0003
Error	5	62.93352	12.58670		
Corrected Total	9	2558.90000			

Root MSE	3.54777	R-Square	0.9754
Dependent Mean	75.10000	Adj R-Sq	0.9557
Coeff Var	4.72407		

TABLE 10.6. Parameter estimates

Parameter Estimates					
Variable	DF	Parameter Estimate	Standard Error	t Value	Pr > |t|
Intercept	1	-95.55939	12.82483	-7.45	0.0007
TEST1	1	0.17631	0.06616	2.66	0.0446
TEST2	1	-0.22344	0.14354	-1.56	0.1803
TEST3	1	1.74602	0.27770	6.29	0.0015
TEST4	1	0.26865	0.18424	1.46	0.2046

Automated Model Selection

It is often the case in multiple regression analysis that one of your goals is to arrive at a model that gives you an optimal regression equation with the fewest parameters. In the previous Hands-on Example, the predictors TEST2 and TEST4 are not significant. As mentioned following the listing of MODEL options, a variety of automated model selection procedures are available in SAS. You can choose to select variables using manual or automated methods, or a combination of both. The various model selection techniques will not always result in the same final model, and the decision concerning which variables to include in the final model should not be based entirely on the results of any automated procedure. The researcher's knowledge of the data should always be used to guide the model selection process even when automated procedures are used.

The following Hands-on Example illustrates the BACKWARD elimination technique for model selection. In this technique, the full model is examined, and in successive steps the least predictive variable is eliminated from the model until all remaining variables show at least a $p < 0.10$ significance level.

HANDS-ON
EXAMPLE

This example illustrates how to use automated model selection techniques.

1. Using the code from AREG3.SAS, modify the model statement to use the backward elimination model selection technique. Notice that this option is in the MODEL statement and is preceded by a forward slash (/).

```
MODEL JOBSCORE=TEST1 TEST2 TEST3 TEST4
    /SELECTION=BACKWARD;
```

2. Run the modified program. This procedure examines the coefficients and drops independent variables that are not predictive. Examine the parameter estimates table, Table 10.7. Notice that the variables TEST1 and TEST3 remain in the model, while TEST2 and TEST4 were removed. In this table, TEST1 is highly significant ($p < 0.0001$) and TEST3 is marginally significant ($p = 0.0779$). Also, notice that $R^2 = 0.9528$, which indicates a good predictive model.

3. Because TEST1 is only marginally significant (and not significant at the 0.05 level) and if each test is expensive, then you might want to use a more stringent rule to retain variables (e.g., use a smaller value for SLSTAY). Change the MODEL statement to read:

(Continued)

TABLE 10.7. Parameter estimates for revised model

			Summary of Backward Elimination				
Step	Variable Removed	Number Vars In	Partial R-Square	Model R-Square	C(p)	F Value	Pr > F
1	TEST4	3	0.0105	0.9649	5.1261	2.13	0.2046
2	TEST2	2	0.0122	0.9528	5.6018	2.08	0.1989

```
MODEL JOBSCORE=TEST1 TEST2 TEST3 TEST4/
    SELECTION=BACKWARD
    SLSTAY=0.05;
```

SLSTAY=0.05 tells SAS to remove variables whose significance level is 0.05 or larger (the default is 0.10). Run the revised program and observe the parameter estimates table, Table 10.8, which now includes only the predictor variable TEST3. Also note that $R^2 = 0.924$. Thus, this model is still highly significant and appears to be strongly predictive of JOBSCORE.

TABLE 10.8. Parameter estimates for final model

Variable	Parameter Estimate	Standard Error	Type II SS	F Value	Pr > F
Intercept	-76.81121	15.47905	598.38485	24.62	0.0011
TEST3	1.71651	0.17402	2364.49377	97.30	<.0001

GOING DEEPER: CALCULATING PREDICTIONS

Once you decide on a "final" model, you may want to predict values from new subjects using this model. In the JOBSCORE example, you could use the model shown in Table 10.8 to predict how well a new job prospect will do on the job. The prediction equation is based on the parameter estimates shown in that table and given by

```
JOBSCORE = -76.81121 +1.71651*TEST3;
```

Using this equation, you can easily calculate manually a JOBSCORE for new applicants. However, you can program SAS to do the calculations for you. This becomes particularly helpful if your final model contains several predictor variables or if you want to make a lot of predictions. The following procedures can be used to predict new values:

■ Create a new data set containing new values for the independent variable.

■ Merge (append) the new data set with the old one.

- Calculate the regression equation and request predictions.

- Use the ID option to display the new values in the output.

The following Hands-on Example shows how to program SAS to predict JOBSCORE for ten applicants who received the following scores on TEST3: 79, 87, 98, 100, 49, 88, 91, 79, 84, 87.

HANDS-ON
EXAMPLE

This example illustrates how to calculate predictions for data following the development of a regression model.

1. In the Editor window, open the file named AREG4.SAS. Here is a partial listing of that program:

```
DATA NEWAPPS;
        INPUT SUBJECT $ TEST3;
        DATALINES;
101 79
102 87
103 98
104 100
105 49
106 88
107 91
108 79
109 84
110 87
    ;
DATA REPORT; SET JOB NEWAPPS;
PREDICT_ID=CATS(SUBJECT,": ",TEST3);
RUN;
PROC REG DATA=REPORT;
     ID PREDICT_ID;
     MODEL JOBSCORE=TEST3 /P CLI;
RUN;
SYMBOL1 V=STAR I=RL;
PROC GPLOT DATA=JOB; PLOT JOBSCORE*TEST3;
RUN;
```

(Continued)

```
ODS HTML CLOSE;
QUIT;
```

In the second DATA step, the data set named NEWAPPS is appended to the old JOB data set to create a data set named REPORT. Also, a new variable is created named PREDICT_ID using a CATS function that concatenates the two variables SUBJECT and TEST3 (see Appendix D). This variable is used as the ID variable in the output so that the predicted scores can be matched to a particular subject. The /P CLI options tell SAS to output a table containing the predicted values and confidence limits on the actual JOBSCORE values. (Actually, simply using CLI will also produce both predictions and confidence limits.)

2. Run this example, and observe the (abbreviated) output in Table 10.9. The first ten rows of the output table report information about the ten subjects

TABLE 10.9. Predictions using final model

			Output Statistics			
Obs	PREDICT_ID	Dependent Variable	Predicted Value	Std Error Mean Predict	95% CL Predict	Residual
1	1:90	78.0000	77.6748	1.5806	65.7371 89.6124	0.3252
2	2:88	71.0000	74.2417	1.5613	62.3176 86.1659	-3.2417
3	3:94	85.0000	84.5408	1.8292	72.4158 96.6658	0.4592
4	4:84	67.0000	67.3757	1.7445	55.3172 79.4342	-0.3757
5	5:83	69.0000	65.6592	1.8292	53.5342 77.7842	3.3408
6	6:83	65.0000	65.6592	1.8292	53.5342 77.7842	-0.6592
7	7:71	50.0000	45.0611	3.4211	31.2242 58.8980	4.9389
8	8:105	107.0000	103.4224	3.2671	89.7848 117.0601	3.5776
9	9:99	96.0000	93.1234	2.4018	80.4783 105.7685	2.8766
10	10:88	63.0000	74.2417	1.5613	62.3176 86.1659	-11.2417
11	101:79	.	58.7931	2.2722	46.2760 71.3103	.
12	102:87	.	72.5252	1.5806	60.5876 84.4629	.
13	103:98	.	91.4069	2.2722	78.8897 103.9240	.
14	104:100	.	94.8399	2.5367	82.0555 107.6243	.
15	105:49	.	7.2978	7.0482	-12.5361 27.1318	.
16	106:88	.	74.2417	1.5613	62.3176 86.1659	.
17	107:91	.	79.3913	1.6184	67.4267 91.3559	.
18	108:79	.	58.7931	2.2722	46.2760 71.3103	.
19	109:84	.	67.3757	1.7445	55.3172 79.4342	.
20	110:87	.	72.5252	1.5806	60.5876 84.4629	.

in the training data set from which the regression model is obtained. Starting with observation 11, the information relates to the new data that did not include a dependent variable (JOBSCORE). The new data were not used to calculate the regression equation, but their predicted values were calculated. Thus, for observation 11 (i.e., subject 101) you can see that this subject had a score on TEST3 of 79, which is used to calculate a predicted JOBSCORE of 58.79.

The "95% CL Predict" column indicates confidence limits for the actual value of JOBSCORE for the TEST3 values. For example, JOBSCORE for subject 101 could plausibly be as low as 46.2760 or as high as 71.3103.

3. Because the final model has only a single independent variable (i.e., it is a simple linear regression), we have used the above code to also plot a scatterplot of the data along with the fitted regression line in Figure 10.3. There it can be seen that there is a strong relationship between JOBSCORE and TEST3 and that this relationship appears to be linear.

FIGURE 10.3. *Scatterplot and regression line for final model*

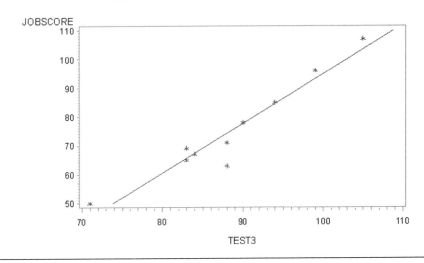

GOING DEEPER: RESIDUAL ANALYSIS

In the case of the simple linear regression model, a scatterplot such as those shown in Figure 10.1 and Figure 10.3 is a useful graphic for visually inspecting the nature of the association. The following Hands-on Examples provide related residual analysis techniques for assessing the appropriateness of a linear regression fit to a set of data that are appropriate for simple linear regression and multiple linear regression.

To produce output graphs for residual analysis, use the following syntax:

```
ODS HTML;   * (or RTF, PDF, etc);
ODS GRAPHICS ON;
PROC REG;
MODEL dependentvars = independentvars/R;
RUN;
ODS GRAPHICS OFF;
ODS HTML CLOSE;
RUN;
```

For more options, see the SAS documentation. In the following Hands-on Example, a residual analysis is applied to the final model obtained earlier using TEST3 to predict JOBSCORE.

HANDS-ON
EXAMPLE

This example illustrates how to examine model residuals as a part of model verification.

1. In the Editor window, open the file named AREG5.SAS. This program is based on the JOBSCORE example, with the following statements used for the analysis of TEST1 to predict JOBSCORE.

```
ODS HTML;
ODS GRAPHICS ON;
TITLE "Residual Analysis";
PROC REG DATA=JOB;
MODEL JOBSCORE=TEST3/R;
RUN;
ODS GRAPHICS OFF;
ODS HTML CLOSE;
QUIT;
```

The /R option requests graphs and diagnostics that assist with a residual analysis for this model.

2. Run the program and observe the output statistics table, Table 10.10. The "Residual" column gives the difference between the observed dependent variable and the predicted value using the regression equation. You can inspect this column to find out whether there are certain subjects whose scores were not as well predicted as others'. For example, subject 10's residual score is −11.24, the difference between the observed score from the JOBSCORE (63.0) and the predicted score (74.24). If a residual is much larger for one subject than for the others, examine the data for miscoding or to otherwise understand why the score for that subject is so different from its predicted value.

The "Student Residual" column contains *z*-scores for residuals that provide a measure of the magnitude of the difference. Generally, a residual greater than 2 or less than −2 can be seen as statistically significant and may need further investigation. Because the studentized residual for subject 10 is −2.404, this indicates that the prediction for this subject's JOBSCORE was substantially smaller than expected. The columns labeled "−2−1 0 1 2" are a crude graph of the studentized residuals. The "****" in that column for subject 10 are a visual indication that the prediction is substantially smaller than expected.

The Cook's D statistic gives an indication of the "influence" of a particular data point. A value close to 0 indicates no influence; and the higher the value, the greater the influence. Note that subject 7 had a larger influence on the estimates of the regression coefficients than did most other subjects.

TABLE 10.10. Output statistics for PROC REG

Output Statistics									
Obs	PREDICT_ID	Dependent Variable	Predicted Value	Std Error Mean Predict	Residual	Std Error Residual	Student Residual	−2−1 0 1 2	Cook's D
1	1:90	78.0000	77.6748	1.5806	0.3252	4.669	0.0697	I I I	0.000
2	2:88	71.0000	74.2417	1.5613	−3.2417	4.676	−0.693	I *I I	0.027
3	3:94	85.0000	84.5408	1.8292	0.4592	4.578	0.100	I I I	0.001
4	4:84	67.0000	67.3757	1.7445	−0.3757	4.611	−0.0815	I I I	0.000
5	5:83	69.0000	65.6592	1.8292	3.3408	4.578	0.730	I I* I	0.043
6	6:83	65.0000	65.6592	1.8292	−0.6592	4.578	−0.144	I I I	0.002
7	7:71	50.0000	45.0611	3.4211	4.9389	3.549	1.392	I I** I	0.900
8	8:105	107.0000	103.4224	3.2671	3.5776	3.691	0.969	I I* I	0.368
9	9:99	96.0000	93.1234	2.4018	2.8766	4.305	0.668	I I* I	0.069
10	10:88	63.0000	74.2417	1.5613	−11.2417	4.676	−2.404	I ****I I	0.322

(Continued)

Based on this residual analysis, you should examine why subject 7 had such a high Cook's D score and why the prediction for subject 10 was so much less than expected. Sometimes such an examination of the data turns up miscoded values or may indicate something different about some subjects that affect whether they should be included in the analysis.

3. Observe the graphs displayed in the Results Viewer. The first series of graphs is shown in Figure 10.4. This is an extensive set of graphs that can be used to assess the fit of the model. We will describe a few of these here:

- **Residual Plots:** The top two left plots are plots of the unstandardized and standardized residuals plotted against the predicted JOBSCORE variable (x-axis). For a good fit, both graphs should show points that are spread randomly around the zero line. There is one point (associated with subject 10) whose residual appears smaller than expected.

FIGURE 10.4. *ODS GRAPHICS output for PROC REG*

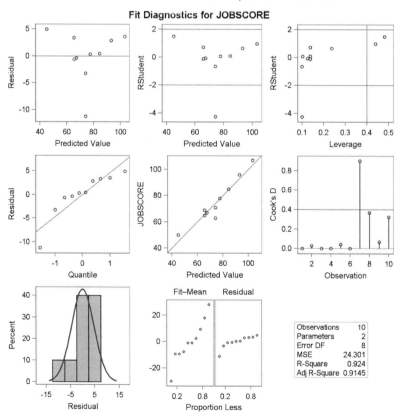

- **Quantile Plot:** For an unbiased fit, the quantile plot (second row, leftmost) should show a random scatter of points around the diagonal line.

- **Cook's D:** This plot (second row, rightmost) shows that observation 7 has a much larger Cook's D than the rest, and thus has a large influence on the model.

Two other plots are provided in the ODS GRAPHICS output. One is a larger version of the residual plot and the other is a plot of the regression line with mean and individual prediction limits. See Figure 10.5. The smaller, dark bands are 95 percent Confidence Limits for the mean of JOBSCORE given values of TEST3, and the larger dashed bands are 95 percent Prediction Limits for actual JOBSCORE values for given values of TEST3.

FIGURE 10.5. *Prediction limits*

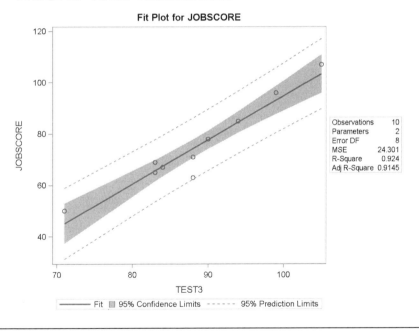

SUMMARY

This chapter showed you how to measure the association betwen two quantative variables (correlation analysis). It also discussed how to calculate a prediction equation using simple or multiple linear regression.

EXERCISES

10.1. Run a regression analysis involving U.S. crime data.

This exercise uses crime statistics for Washington, D.C., from the *United States Uniform Crime Report* to examine the rise in assaults for the years 1978 to 1993. In the early 1990s there was national concern about a greater-than-expected rise in crime. The media predicted that crime was spiraling up out of control and that cities would soon become war zones of violent crimes. They had the statistics to back them up.

a. Open the program EX_10.1.SAS, which performs a simple linear regression model. Run the program and observe the results, which are summarized in Figure 10.6.

b. If your job was to predict future crimes in order to budget for police personnel, how would these results influence your decision?

c. Based on the results in Table 10.11, fill in the blanks in the prediction equation below.

ASSAULTS = _____ + _____ * YEAR

FIGURE 10.6. *Washington, D.C., assaults, 1978–93*

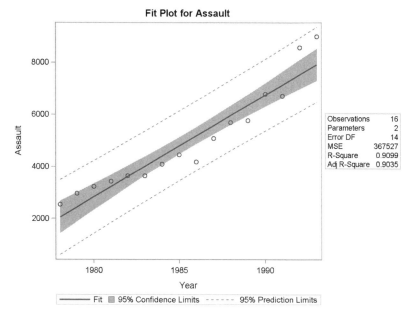

TABLE 10.11. **Regression estimates for Washington, D.C., crime data 1978–93**

Parameter Estimates						
Variable	Label	DF	Parameter Estimate	Standard Error	t Value	Pr > |t|
Intercept	Intercept	1	-771153	65279	-11.81	<.0001
Year	Year	1	390.90441	32.87797	11.89	<.0001

d. Using your prediction equation, predict the number of assaults for the years 1990, 1995, 2000, and 2007.

e. How good do you think predictions will be, given the fact that the result shows an impressive fit ($R^2 = 0.91$)?

f. Fill in the table below

Year	Actual number of assaults	Estimated number of assaults
1990	7365	_____
1995	7228	_____
2000	4582	_____
2007	3686	_____

g. Open the file EX_10.1B.SAS. This contains the same regression model, but with data through 2007. Run the model and observe the results.

    I. What is the R^2?

    II. Examine the scatterplot of year by number of assaults. How does it differ from the earlier version (Figure 10.6)?

    III. Using the data from 1973 to 1993 to predict number of assaults for 2000 and 2007 is called extrapolation. Based on these results, do you think extrapolation is a wise practice?

10.2. Perform variable selection in a multiple linear regression.

    The linear regression model in EX_10.2.SAS attempts to determine CITYMPG using the four variables AUTOMATIC, ENGINESIZE, CYLINDERS, and HYBRID. In this exercise you will find a "best" model.

a. In the Editor window, open the file EX_10.2.SAS.

b. Run the program and note which variables are selected for the BACKWARD selection procedure.

    c. Change the selection option to FORWARD. Run the program and note which variables are in the final model.

    d. Change the selection option to STEPWISE. Run the program and note which variables are in the final model.

    e. Are the results the same? What criteria would you use to select the "best" model?

10.3. Using the WITH statement

    a. In the Editor window, open the file ACORR3.SAS.

```
ODS HTML;
PROC CORR DATA="C:\SASDATA\SOMEDATA" NOSIMPLE;
     VAR TIME1-TIME4; WITH AGE;
TITLE "Example correlation calculations using a WITH
statement";
RUN;
ODS HTML CLOSE;
```

Notice that the VAR statement contains TIME1-TIME4, and a WITH statement is included that requests correlations between AGE and the four variables in the VAR statement.

    b. Run this exercise and observe the output shown in Table 10.2. Notice that the output includes only correlations between AGE and the other variables.

CHAPTER

NONPARAMETRIC ANALYSIS

LEARNING OBJECTIVES

- To be able to use SAS procedures to compare two independent samples (Wilcoxon-Mann-Whitney)

- To be able to use SAS procedures to compare k independent samples (Kruskal-Wallis)

- To be able to use SAS procedures to compare two dependent (paired) samples

- To be able to use SAS procedures to compare k dependent samples (Friedman's test)

- To be able to use SAS procedures to perform multiple comparisons following a significant Kruskal-Wallis test (macro)

An assumption for many statistical tests such as the *t*-tests and ANOVA is that the data are normally distributed. When this normality assumption is suspect or cannot be met, there are alternative techniques for analyzing the data.

Statistical techniques based on an assumption that data are distributed according to some parameterized distribution (such as the normal distribution) are referred to as parametric analyses. Statistical techniques that do not rely on this assumption are called nonparametric procedures. This chapter illustrates several nonparametric techniques. One nonparametric procedure, Spearman's rank correlation, was previously discussed in Chapter 10.

COMPARING TWO INDEPENDENT SAMPLES USING NPAR1WAY

A nonparametric test can be used to compare two or more independent groups when you cannot make the assumption that the observed data follow a normal distribution. Using a nonparametric test is also a useful technique if you do not have exact data values for the observations but you do have order statistics—that is, you don't know the actual response values, but you know which is largest, next largest, and so forth, to the smallest. In this case the smallest value is recoded as 1 and the next to smallest is recoded as 2 and so forth. Many nonparametric procedures are based on these ranks.

The tests discussed in this chapter for comparing two independent groups are the Wilcoxon (sometimes called Wilcoxon-Mann-Whitney) test and the Kruskal-Wallis test. The hypotheses tested are:

H_0: The two groups have the same distribution (they come from the same population).

H_a: The two groups do not have the same distributions (they come from different populations).

The SAS procedure for testing these hypotheses is PROC NPAR1WAY. The results of several tests are included in the SAS output. This discussion will also include information about the Wilcoxon Rank Sums (sometimes called the Wilcoxon-Mann-Whitney test). The syntax for NPAR1WAY is:

PROC NPAR1WAY <*options*>; *statements*;

Options illustrated in the following Hands-on Examples are:

DATA=*datsetname*;
　　Specifies dataset

WILCOXON
　　Limits output to Wilcoxon-type tests

MEDIAN
　　Requests median test

VW
　　Requests Van der Waerden test

Commonly used information statements include:

CLASS *variable(s)*;
    Specify grouping variable, character or numeric

VAR *variable(s)*;
    List numeric response or dependent variable

EXACT
    Request exact *p*-values

HANDS-ON
EXAMPLE

This example illustrates how to compare two independent groups using nonparametric methods.

In it, observations from two brands of fertilizer are compared to determine if one provides better overall growth (measured by height) than the other. (This is the same data used in ATTEST2.SAS, which was discussed in the Hands-on Example in the section "Running the Two-sample *t*-test in SAS" in Chapter 8.

1. In the Editor window, open the file ANPAR1.SAS.

```
DATA FERTILIZER;
INPUT BRAND $ HEIGHT;
DATALINES;
    A    20.00
    A    23.00
    A    32.00
    A    24.00
    A    25.00
    A    28.00
    A    27.50
    B    25.00
    B    46.00
    B    56.00
    B    45.00
    B    46.00
    B    51.00
```

(Continued)

```
     B    34.00
     B    47.50

;
ODS HTML;
PROC NPAR1WAY WILCOXON;
     CLASS BRAND;
     VAR HEIGHT;
     EXACT;
     Title Compare two groups using NPAR1WAY;
RUN;
ODS HTML CLOSE;
```

The WILCOXON option is included in the PROC NPAR1WAY statement to limit the output to Wilcoxon-type analyses.

2. Run the program and observe the output in Table 11.1.

TABLE 11.1. **Output from NPAR1WAY for a two-group analysis**

Wilcoxon Scores (Rank Sums) for Variable HEIGHT Classified by Variable BRAND					
BRAND	N	Sum of Scores	Expected Under H0	Std Dev Under H0	Mean Score
A	7	31.50	56.0	8.625543	4.50000
B	8	88.50	64.0	8.625543	11.06250
Average scores were used for ties.					

Wilcoxon Two-Sample Test	
Statistic (S)	31.5000
Normal Approximation	
Z	-2.7824
One-Sided Pr < Z	0.0027
Two-Sided Pr > |Z|	0.0054
t Approximation	
One-Sided Pr < Z	0.0073
Two-Sided Pr > |Z|	0.0147
Exact Test	
One-Sided Pr <= S	0.0012
Two-Sided Pr >= |S - Mean|	0.0025
Z includes a continuity correction of 0.5.	

Kruskal-Wallis Test	
Chi-Square	8.0679
DF	1
Pr > Chi-Square	0.0045

The "Wilcoxon Scores" table provides summary statistics for the data. The "Wilcoxon Two-Sample Test" table reports a variety of approximate *p*-values for the Wilcoxon test (both one- and two-sided). The Kruskal-Wallis test is an extension of the Wilcoxon-Mann-Whitney test that is applicable to two or more independent samples. The Kruskal-Wallis *p*-value reported in this table is a result of a chi-square approximation.

We recommend using the Exact Test *p*-values obtained as a result of the information statement EXACT. The two-sided *p*-value (appropriate for testing the hypotheses as stated above) is 0.0025, suggesting a difference between the two distributions (i.e., that the effects of the fertilizers are different). (See Desu and Raghavarao, 2004.) Use of the ODS GRAPHICS ON/ODS GRAPHICS OFF statements produces side-by-side box-plots (not shown here) that illustrate the difference between the two distributions.

A number of other tests are reported in the SAS output (when the WILCOXON option is not used) which are not described here. They include a median test and a Van der Waerden two-sample test. Which test is appropriate? Different disciplines often favor one test over another, or you may find that the type of analysis you are performing is commonly reported using one or another of these tests.

COMPARING *K* INDEPENDENT SAMPLES (KRUSKAL-WALLIS)

If more than two independent groups are being compared using nonparametric methods, SAS uses the Kruskal-Wallis test to compare groups. The hypotheses being tested are:

H_0: There is no difference among the distributions of the groups.

H_a: There are differences among the distributions of the groups.

This test is an extension of the Wilcoxon-Mann-Whitney test described earlier. It uses the WILCOXON procedure to calculate mean ranks for the data and uses that information to calculate the test statistic for the Kruskal-Wallis test.

HANDS-ON
EXAMPLE

This example illustrates how to compare three or more independent groups using nonparametric procedures. The data are weight gains of twenty-eight animals that are randomly assigned to four feed treatments with seven animals to a treatment type. Suppose you want to test whether there are differences among the effects of the different treatments. If you have reason to believe that the populations from which these samples are taken are not normally distributed, then the Kruskal-Wallis test would be appropriate. The data for this example are:

(Continued)

Group 1	Group 2	Group 3	Group 4
50.8	68.7	82.6	76.9
57.0	67.7	74.1	72.2
44.6	66.3	80.5	73.7
51.7	69.8	80.3	74.2
48.2	66.9	81.5	70.6
51.3	65.2	78.6	75.3
49.0	62.0	76.1	69.8

1. In the Editor window, open the program ANPAR2.SAS. (Notice that the DATA step uses the compact data entry technique. See the "@@" in the INPUT line. See Chapter 2.)

```
DATA NPAR;
INPUT GROUP WEIGHT @@;
DATALINES;
1 50.8 1 57.0 1 44.6 1 51.7 1 48.2 1 51.3 1 49.0
2 68.7 2 67.7 2 66.3 2 69.8 2 66.9 2 65.2 2 62.0
3 82.6 3 74.1 3 80.5 3 80.3 3 81.5 3 78.6 3 76.1
4 76.9 4 72.2 4 73.7 4 74.2 4 70.6 4 75.3 4 69.8

;
ODS HTML;
PROC NPAR1WAY WILCOXON;
      CLASS GROUP;
      VAR WEIGHT;
      Title 'Four group analysis using NPAR1WAY';
RUN;
ODS HTML CLOSE;
```

The SAS code for this program is very similar to that for the Wilcoxon-Mann-Whitney test in the previous Hands-on Example and, interestingly, you request the Kruskal-Wallis test using the WILCOXON option because Kruskal-Wallis is a k-group version of the Wilcoxon-Mann-Whitney test. The only real difference is that this data set includes four categories for the grouping variable. Also note that again, the WILCOXON option in the NPAR1WAY statement limits the amount of output.

2. Run the program and observe the output in Table 11.2.

   The first table provides summary information for the mean scores based on the ranks. The Kruskal-Wallis test reports $p < 0.0001$, indicating that there is a significant difference in the distribution of the groups. (Notice that because in this case there are four groups, NPAR1WAY does not produce output for the Wilcoxon Rank Sums test such as that in Table 11.1.) Also, you can request exact p-values, but the computing time involved will

TABLE 11.2. **Output from NPAR1WAY for a four-sample group comparison**

Wilcoxon Scores (Rank Sums) for Variable WEIGHT Classified by Variable GROUP					
GROUP	N	Sum of Scores	Expected Under H0	Std Dev Under H0	Mean Score
1	7	28.00	101.50	18.845498	4.000000
2	7	77.50	101.50	18.845498	11.071429
3	7	171.00	101.50	18.845498	24.428571
4	7	129.50	101.50	18.845498	18.500000
Average scores were used for ties.					

Kruskal-Wallis Test	
Chi-Square	24.4807
DF	3
Pr > Chi-Square	<.0001

be extensive even in the current case of four groups of seven. As with the two-group case, the use of the GRAPHICS option in ODS will produce side-by-side boxplots to assist you in understanding the differences.

Unlike in the PROC ANOVA procedure, there are no multiple comparison tests provided with NPAR1WAY. However, in the Going Deeper section later in this chapter, a method is provided to perform this follow-up procedure.

If you prefer not to use the method for multiple comparisons shown in the Going Deeper section, and the test for k-samples is significant, an acceptable procedure is to perform multiple pairwise comparisons across the groups and adjust the significance level from 0.05 using the Bonferroni technique of dividing the significant level by the total number of comparisons. For example, in the case with four groups, there are six pairwise comparisons, so you would perform six Wilcoxon-Mann-Whitney comparisons. For each test, you would use the significance level adjusted to (0.05/6 =.0083) as your criterion for rejecting the null hypothesis.

COMPARING TWO DEPENDENT (PAIRED) SAMPLES

Two nonparametric tests for paired data are available in the PROC UNIVARIATE procedure: the sign test and the signed rank test. These tests are nonparametric counterparts to the paired t-test. The sign test is simple. It counts the number of positive and negative differences and calculates a p-value based on this information. The (Wilcoxon) signed rank test bases its decision on the magnitude of the ranked differences. The hypotheses for these tests are:

H_0: The probability of a positive difference is the same as that of a negative difference.

H_a: The probability of a positive difference is different from that of a negative difference.

The following Hands-on Example illustrates how to perform these tests in SAS.

HANDS-ON EXAMPLE

This example illustrates how to compare paired observations using nonparametric techniques.

1. In the Editor window, open the program `AUNIPAIRED.SAS`.

```
DATA WEIGHT;
INPUT WBEFORE WAFTER;
* Calculate WLOSS in the DATA step *;
WLOSS=WBEFORE-WAFTER;
DATALINES;
200 185
175 154
188 176
198 193
197 198
310 275
245 224
202 188
;
ODS HTML;
PROC UNIVARIATE;
    VAR WLOSS;
    TITLE "Paired comparison using PROC UNIVARIATE";
RUN;
ODS HTML CLOSE;
```

Notice that the difference `WLOSS` is calculated in the `DATA` step. Because the test is based on the difference between `WBEFORE` and `WAFTER`, the variable `WLOSS` is the variable referenced in `PROC UNIVARIATE`.

2. Run the program and observe the (abbreviated) output in Table 11.3. The `PROC UNIVARIATE` procedure produces more output, but this is the table we are interested in for the paired comparison.

TABLE 11.3. **PROC UNIVARIATE to test paired difference**

Tests for Location: Mu0=0				
Test	**Statistic**		**p Value**	
Student's t	t	2.788474	**Pr > |t|**	0.0270
Sign	M	3	**Pr >= |M|**	0.0703
Signed Rank	S	17	**Pr >= |S|**	0.0156

In the "Tests for Location" table, three test results are given. The *p*-value for the Student's *t*-test is the same that is given in the PROC MEANS example in Chapter 8 (*p*= 0.056). The two nonparametric tests reported are the sign and signed rank tests. The sign test reports a *p*-value of 0.0703 and the signed rank test reports a *p*-value of 0.0156. All of the *p*-values are two-sided.

COMPARING *K* DEPENDENT SAMPLES (FRIEDMAN'S TEST)

When your data include more than two repeated measures and the normality assumption is questioned, you can perform a Friedman procedure to test the hypotheses:

H_0: The distributions are the same across the repeated measures.

H_a: There are some differences in distributions across the repeated measures.

Although no procedure in SAS performs a Friedman's test directly, you can calculate the statistic needed to perform the test using PROC FREQ.

Recall the repeated measures example in Chapter 9, in which four drugs were given to five patients in random order. In this crossover design, the observed value is a reaction to the drug, where a larger value is beneficial. The data are as follows:

Subj	Drug1	Drug2	Drug3	Drug4
1	31	29	17	35
2	15	17	11	23
3	25	21	19	31
4	35	35	21	45
5	27	27	15	31

The following Hands-on Example shows how these data are coded for input so that the Friedman's test may be performed, and how to perform the Friedman's test using PROC FREQ.

HANDS-ON EXAMPLE

This example illustrates how to compare three or more repeated measures using nonparametric techniques.

1. In the Editor window, open the file `AFRIEDMAN.SAS`.

```
DATA TIME;
INPUT SUBJ DRUG OBS;
DATALINES;
1   1    31
1   2    29
1   3    17
1   4    35
2   1    15
...ETC...
5   2    27
5   3    15
5   4    31
;
ODS HTML;
Title "Friedman Analysis";
PROC FREQ;
   TABLES SUBJ*DRUG*OBS / CMH2 SCORES=RANK NOPRINT;
RUN;
ODS HTML CLOSE;
```

Notice that in this analysis, the data set is structured differently from most data sets in this book, although it is set up the same here as for the repeated measures ANOVA analysis in Chapter 9. In a repeated measures analysis, each line contains the observed reading for a single experimental condition, in this case for each subject and each drug administered. Therefore, because each subject received the drug four times, there are four lines for each subject.

The PROC FREQ statement requests a three-way table. Statement options include CMH2, which requests Cochran-Mantel-Haenszel Statistics, and the SCORES=RANK option indicates that the analysis is to be performed on ranks. The NOPRINT option is used to suppress the output of the actual summary table because it is quite large and provides nothing needed for this analysis.

2. Run the analysis and observe the output shown in Table 11.4.

TABLE 11.4. **Friedman's test output using PROC FREQ**

Cochran-Mantel-Haenszel Statistics (Based on Rank Scores)				
Statistic	Alternative Hypothesis	DF	Value	Prob
1	Nonzero Correlation	1	1.2250	0.2684
2	Row Mean Scores Differ	3	14.1250	0.0027

The test statistic for a Friedman's test is found in the "Row Mean Scores Differ" row, where the Friedman Chi-Square = 14.125 with 3 degrees of freedom and $p = 0.0027$. Because the p-value is less than 0.05, you would conclude that there is a difference in the distributions across DRUGs.

As with the Kruskal-Wallis test, there is no built-in follow-up multiple comparison test available for this procedure. If you reject the null hypothesis, you can perform comparisons for each drug pair using the Wilcoxon test on the differences as discussed in the previous section on paired comparisons. As in the Kruskal-Wallis multiple comparisons discussed earlier, you should adjust your significance level using the Bonferroni technique. For example, in this case with four groups (measured in repeated readings) you would perform six pairwise comparisons, and for an overall 0.05 level test you would use the $0.05/6 = 0.0083$ level of significance for each individual pairwise comparison.

GOING DEEPER: NONPARAMETRIC MULTIPLE COMPARISONS

Because SAS is a flexible language, SAS programmers often create their own procedures for performing analyses that are not already in the SAS language. For the Kruskal-Wallis (KW) nonparametric analysis of variance described above, SAS provides no specific post hoc pairwise comparisons when the overall KW test is significant, indicating some difference among groups.

The following Hands-on Example illustrates how a procedure written in SAS code (called a macro) can be used to perform an analysis not included in the SAS program. This example utilizes a SAS macro implementation of a multiple comparison test (Nemenyi [Tukey-type] or Dunn's test) to be used along with SAS NPAR1WAY.

Although this example uses a SAS macro, the contents and procedure for constructing macros are beyond the scope of this book. (See Chapter 16.) However, because many macros are available in published papers and books, it is useful to understand how to use macros, and this is illustrated in the following example. (See Elliott and Hynan, 2007.)

HANDS-ON
EXAMPLE

This example shows how you can use a macro to calculate multiple comparisons following a Kruskal-Wallis test.

 This example is based on the previous independent four-group comparison earlier in the chapter, with the addition of code to run a macro procedure to perform multiple comparisons.

1. In the Editor window, open the file ANPAR3.SAS.

```
%INCLUDE C:\SASDATA\KW_MC.SAS;
DATA NPAR;
INPUT GROUP WEIGHT @@;
DATALINES;
1 50.8 1 57.0 1 44.6 1 51.7 1 48.2 1 51.3 1 49.0
2 68.7 2 67.7 2 66.3 2 69.8 2 66.9 2 65.2 2 62.0
3 82.6 3 74.1 3 80.5 3 80.3 3 81.5 3 78.6 3 76.1
4 76.9 4 72.2 4 73.7 4 74.2 4 70.6 4 75.3 4 69.8
;
* BEGIN INFORMATION FOR USING THE SAS MACRO KW>MC;
%LET NUMGROUPS=4;
%LET DATANAME=NPAR;
%LET OBSVAR=WEIGHT;
%LET GROUP=GROUP;
%LET ALPHA=0.05;
Title "Kruskal-Wallis Multiple Comparisons";
*******************************************************
*invoke the KW_MC macro
*******************************************************;
ODS HTML;
ODS GRAPHICS ON;
  %KW_MC(source=&DATANAME, groups=&NUMGROUPS,
  obsname=&OBSVAR, gpname=&GROUP, sig=&alpha);
ODS GRAPHICS OFF;
ODS HTML CLOSE;
```

 Notice the %INCLUDE statement at the top of the program. This statement tells SAS to get additional SAS code that is stored in a file in the indicated location. Thus, the file C:\SASDATA\KW_MC.SAS must be at the designated location, or you must change the file name to match the appropriate location.

The data set used in this program is the same as the one used in the previous Kruskal-Wallis example on weight gains of animals assigned randomly to four treatments.

The series of %LET statements are used to tell the SAS macro the values of certain parameters needed by the macro. In this case, the number of groups (NUMGROUPS) is 4. The names of the data set containing the data for analysis is NPAR. The variable containing the dependent variable is WEIGHT, and the grouping variable is named GROUP. The significance level used to perform the test is indicated by ALPHA=0.05.

The statement that begins with %KW_MC(source5 is the statement that "calls" the SAS macro. You do not need to change anything about this statement to use the macro for any other data set. If you use this procedure for another analysis, the only items you must change are the four values in the %LET statements.

2. Run the program and observe the results. The Kruskal-Wallis results are the same as those in the previous example. The multiple comparison test is shown in Table 11.5.

Table 11.5 describes a series of pairwise tests, performed at the overall 0.05 significance level. For example, the test indicates that for the comparison of groups 3 and 1, you reject the null hypothesis that the two groups are from the same distribution. The same conclusion is reached for the comparison of

TABLE 11.5. **Multiple comparison test for a Kruskal-Wallis analysis**

Group sample sizes not equal, or some ranks tied. Performed Dunn's test, alpha=0.05					
Comparison group = GROUP					
Compare	Diff	SE	q	Q(0.05)	Conclude
3 vs 1	20.43	4.4	4.64	2.638	Reject
3 vs 2	13.36	4.4	3.04	2.638	Reject
3 vs 4	5.93	4.4	1.35	2.638	Do not reject
4 vs 1	14.5	4.4	3.3	2.638	Reject
4 vs 2	7.43	4.4	1.69	2.638	Do not reject
2 vs 1	7.07	4.4	1.61	2.638	Do not reject

(Continued)

groups 3 and 2. Thus, your conclusion based on this test would be that weight gain for group 3 is different from that for groups 1 and 2, but not different from that for group 4. Weight gain for group 4 is significantly different from that for group 1 but not from that for group 2. Finally, weight gain for group 2 is not different from that for group 1. Because of the inclusion of the GRAPHICS ON and GRAPHICS OFF commands in the code, the output includes side-by-side boxplots as shown in Figure 11.1. These suggest that treatment 3 is preferred to treatments 1 and 2.

FIGURE 11.1. *Side-by-side boxplots for the weight-gain data*

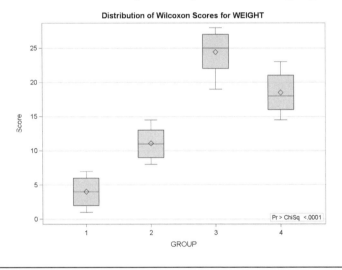

SUMMARY

This chapter introduced several nonparametric alternatives to standard parametric analyses. These procedures are useful when the normality assumption is questionable and particularly important when sample sizes are small.

EXERCISES

11.1. Run a median test.

a. Using the SAS program in ANPAR2.SAS, change the selection from the Wilcoxon (Kruskal-Wallis) test to the median test, as shown here:

```
PROC NPAR1WAY MEDIAN;
```

b. Run the program and observe the results. Do the results differ?

11.2. Run a nonparametric analysis.

A retail franchise is interested in stopping shrinkage (the loss of merchandise through theft) in its eleven stores in Denver, Colorado. The management believes that the presence of a uniformed police officer near the entrance will deter theft. Six of the eleven stores are randomly selected to have an officer present for a month. On the following month, the officers are assigned to the other five stores for a month. Shrinkage is determined at the end of each month, yielding the data shown in Table 11.6. (Note: The two months selected have historically had about the same sales volume per month.)

TABLE 11.6.   **Store shrinkage, in thousands**

Store Number	Without Officer	With Officer
001	1.3	0.9
002	0.9	0.46
003	2.6	2.5
004	8.2	4.1
005	2.2	2.1
006	0.89	0.9
007	1.6	1.5
008	2.4	2.2
009	3.2	1.1
010	0.5	0.4
011	1.1	0.5

a. Write a SAS program to analyze these data using an appropriate nonparametric procedure. Start with this code:

```
DATA STORES;
INPUT STORE $ WITHOUT WITH;
LOSSDIFF=WITH-WITHOUT;
DATALINES;
001 1.3 .9
002  .9 .46
...etc
;
PROC _____
VAR _____
RUN;
```

b. Observe the output and make a decision. Is there evidence that shrinkage is lower when an officer is present?

CHAPTER

12

LOGISTIC REGRESSION

LEARNING OBJECTIVES

- To be able to perform a logistic analysis using PROC LOGISTIC
- To be able to create a SAS program that will perform a simple logistic analysis
- To be able to create a SAS program that will perform multiple logistic analyses
- To be able to use SAS to assess a model's fit and predictive ability

Binary logistic regression models are based on a dependent variable that can take on only one of two values, such as presence or absence of a disease, deceased or not deceased, married or unmarried, and so on. In this setting, the independent (sometimes called explanatory or predictor) variables are used for predicting the probability of occurrence of an outcome (such as mortality).

The logistic regression model is sometimes called a logit model. Logistic analysis methods are available for cases in which the dependent variable takes on more than two values, but this topic is beyond the scope of this book. Logistic analysis is used to create an equation that can be used to predict the probability of occurrence of the outcome of interest, to assess the relative importance of independent variables, and to calculate odds ratios that measure the importance of an independent variable relative to the response. The independent variables can be either continuous or categorical.

LOGISTIC ANALYSIS BASICS

Before describing the SAS implementation of logistic regression, we briefly discuss some of the basic ideas underlying logistic analysis. We show the actual logistic regression equations here because we believe they provide insights about how logistic regression works.

The Logistic Regression Model

The basic form of the logistic equation is

$$p = \frac{e^{\beta_0 + \beta_1 X_1 + \beta_2 X_2 + \cdots + \beta_k X_k}}{1 + e^{\beta_0 + \beta_1 X_1 + \beta_2 X_2 + \cdots + \beta_k X_k}}$$

where $X_1, \ldots, X_k$ are the k independent variables, p is the probability of occurrence of the outcome of interest (which lies between 0 and 1), β_i is the coefficient on the independent variable X_i, and β_0 is a constant term. As in linear regression, the parameters of this theoretical model are estimated from the data, resulting in the prediction equation

$$\hat{p} = \frac{e^{b_0 + b_1 X_1 + b_2 X_2 + \cdots + b_k X_k}}{1 + e^{b_0 + b_1 X_1 + b_2 X_2 + \cdots + b_k X_k}}$$

where the b_i's are maximum likelihood estimates of the β's (calculated by SAS) and $\hat{p}$ is the estimated probability of occurrence of the outcome of interest. Of course, any variable with a zero coefficient in the theoretical model is not useful in predicting the probability of occurrence. SAS reports tests of the null hypothesis that all of the β_i's, $i = 1, \ldots, k$ are zero.

If this null hypothesis is not rejected, then there is no statistical evidence that the independent variables as a group are useful in the prediction. If the overall test is rejected, then we conclude that at least some of the variables are useful in the prediction. SAS reports individual tests of importance of each of the independent variables. That is, for each $i = 1, \ldots, k$, SAS reports the results of the tests.

$H_0:\beta_i = 0$: The ith independent variable is not predictive of the probability of occurrence.

$H_a:\beta_i \neq 0$: The ith independent variable is predictive of the probability of occurrence.

Understanding Odds and Odds Ratios

Another use of the logistic model is the calculation of odds ratios (OR) for each independent variable. The odds of an event measures the expected number of times an event will occur relative to the number of times it will not occur. Thus, if the odds of an event is 5, this indicates that we expect five times as many occurrences as non-occurrences. An odds of 0.2 ($=1/5$) would indicate that we expect five times as many non-occurrences as occurrences.

Suppose you have a dichotomous dependent variable such as mortality that is predicted using an independent variable which measures whether or not a person had a penetrating wound in an automobile accident. If you calculate that the odds of dying given a penetrating wound is 0.088 and the odds of dying given a nonpenetrating wound is 0.024, then the odds ratio of dying given a penetrating wound is OR = 0.088/0.0247 = 3.56. Thus, the odds of dying given a penetrating wound relative to a non-penetrating wound is about four times greater than if one does not have a penetrating wound. Odds ratios for quantitative independent variables (such as AGE, SBP, WEIGHT, etc.) are interpreted differently, and this interpretation is discussed in an upcoming example in the section "Using Simple Logistic Analysis."

PERFORMING A LOGISTIC ANALYSIS USING PROC LOGISTIC

PROC LOGISTIC is the SAS procedure that allows you to analyze data using a binary logistic model. An abbreviated syntax for this statement is:

```
PROC LOGISTIC < options ;
CLASS variables;
MODEL dependentvar < (variable_options) > =
      < independentvars> < / options >;
```

The PROC LOGISTIC and MODEL statements are required, and only one MODEL statement can be specified. The CLASS statement (if used) must precede the MODEL statement. Note that the dependent variable must be binary. For simplicity, all of the examples in this chapter use a response variable that takes on the values 0 or 1.

By default, SAS assumes that the outcome predicted (with p) in the logistic regression equation corresponds to the case in which the dependent variable is 0. If, for example, you have a variable such as DISEASE with DISEASE=0 indicating the disease is absent and DISEASE=1 indicating the disease is present, then SAS will predict the probability of "disease absent" by default. If you want to predict the probability of "disease present," use the DESCENDING option (given in the following list of options) or recode your DISEASE variable.

Following are the PROC LOGISTIC options:

DATA=
Defines the data set used for the analysis.

DESCENDING
Reverses the sorting order for the levels of the response variable. By default, the procedure will predict the outcome corresponding to the lower value of the dichotomous dependent variable. So, if the dependent variable takes on the values 0 and 1, then by default SAS predicts the probability that the dependent variable is 0.

MODEL *statement options* (place after the slash [/] following the independent variable list)

The MODEL statement names the dependent variable and the independent variables. Some of the options available for the MODEL statement are:

EXPB
Displays the exponentiated values ($e\beta^i$) of the parameter estimates $\hat{\beta}^i$ in the "Analysis of Maximum Likelihood Estimates" table for the logit model. These exponentiated values are the estimated odds ratios for the parameters corresponding to the continuous explanatory variables.

SELECTION=
Specifies variable selection method (examples are STEPWISE, BACKWARD, and FORWARD).

SLENTRY=
Specifies significance level for entering variables.

SLSTAY=
Specifies significance level for removing variables.

LACKFIT
Requests Hosmer-Lemershow goodness-of-fit test.

RISKLIMITS
Requests confidence limits for odds ratios.

CTABLE
Requests a classification table that reports how data are predicted under the model.

PPROB
Specifies limits for the values reported in the CTABLE.

INCLUDE=*n*

Includes first *n* independent variables in the model.

OUTROC=*name*

Outputs ROC values to a dataset (necessary for displaying an ROC curve when using ODS GRAPHICS).

The SELECTION options specify how variables will be considered for inclusion in the model. The BACKWARD method considers all predictor variables and eliminates the ones that do not meet the minimal SLSTAY criterion until only those meeting the criterion remain. The FORWARD method brings in the most significant variable that meets the SLENTRY criterion and continues entering variables until none of the remaining unused variables meets the criterion. STEPWISE is a mixture of the two. It begins like the FORWARD method and uses the SLENTRY criterion to enter variables but reevaluates variables at each step and may eliminate a variable if it no longer meets the SLSTAY criterion. A typical model statement would be something like this:

```
MODEL Y = X1 X2 ... Xk
              / EXPB
                SELECTION=STEPWISE
                SLENTRY=0.05
                SLSTAY=0.1
                RISKLIMITS;
```

where X1, X2, and so on to Xk are the *k* candidate independent variables and Y is the binary dependent variable. In this example, the STEPWISE procedure is used for variable selection. The *p*-value for variable entry is 0.05. Once variables are considered for the model, they must have a *p*-value of 0.1 or less to remain in the model. RISKLIMITS requests that an OR table be included in the output for the final model.

> If your binary outcome variable is not coded 0 and 1, you can still perform a logistic regression using PROC LOGISTIC. In this case you can specify the event to model in the MODEL statement. For example, if your outcome variable named STATUS takes on the values A and B and you want to use the independent variable to predict outcome A, you will use the model statement
>
> ```
> MODEL STATUS (EVENT = 'A') = independent variables;
> ```

USING SIMPLE LOGISTIC ANALYSIS

A simple logistic model is one that has only one predictor (independent) variable. This predictor variable can be either a binary or a quantitative measure. The following Hands-on Example illustrates the simple logistic model.

HANDS-ON
EXAMPLE

This example uses a simulated trauma dataset named ACCIDENTS to find a model to predict death (DEAD=1) using the variable PENETRATE (where a value of 1 represents a penetrating wound) observed at the trauma incident.

1. In the Editor window, open the file ALOG1.SAS.

```
ODS HTML;
PROC LOGISTIC DATA="C:\SASDATA\ACCIDENTS" DESCENDING;
   MODEL DEAD=PENETRATE / RISKLIMITS;
   TITLE 'Trauma Data Model Death by Penetration Wound ';
   RUN;
ODS HTML CLOSE;
```

    In this example, the independent variable PENETRATE, which is a 0,1 variable, is used to predict death (DEAD=1) so the DESCENDING option is used.

2. Run this program. Abbreviated output is shown in Table 12.1.

TABLE 12.1. **Output from logistic regression**

Response Profile		
Ordered Value	dead	Total Frequency
1	1	103
2	0	3580

Analysis of Maximum Likelihood Estimates					
Parameter	DF	Estimate	Standard Error	Wald Chi-Square	Pr > ChiSq
Intercept	1	-3.6988	0.1111	1108.0853	<.0001
penetrate	1	1.2697	0.2584	24.1519	<.0001

Odds Ratio Estimates		
Effect	Point Estimate	95% Wald Confidence Limits
penetrate	3.560	2.145 5.906

(Continued)

The Response Profile table indicates that there are 103 subjects with DEAD=1 (which is indicated as the modeled outcome) and 3,580 subjects who did not die (DEAD=0). The Maximum Likelihood Estimates table indicates that the variable PENETRATE is significantly associated with the outcome variable ($p < 0.0001$) and the Odds Ratio (OR) Estimates table reports that the odds ratio for PENETRATE is 3.56. This indicates that the odds of a person's dying who had a penetrating wound is 3.56 greater than that for a person who did not suffer this type of wound.

3. Change the binary variable PENETRATE to the quantitative variable ISS (Injury Severity Score) using the following statement:

```
MODEL DEAD=ISS/ RISKLIMITS;
```

Re-run the program and observe the output as shown in Table 12.2. In Table 12.2, the variable ISS is shown to be predictive of mortality ($p < 0.0001$) with an OR = 1.111. However, this OR is interpreted differently from the one for PENETRATE because ISS is a quantitative measure and PENETRATE is a binary measure. Interpret OR = 1.111 in this way: In this model, the odds of dying are 1.111 times greater for *each unit increase* in ISS.

TABLE 12.2. **Output for a continuous measure from logistic regression**

Analysis of Maximum Likelihood Estimates					
Parameter	DF	Estimate	Standard Error	Wald Chi-Square	Pr > ChiSq
Intercept	1	-5.4444	0.2105	668.7126	<.0001
ISS	1	0.1056	0.00721	214.5334	<.0001

Odds Ratio Estimates		
Effect	Point Estimate	95% Wald Confidence Limits
ISS	1.111	1.096 1.127

Graphing Simple Logistic Results

It is informative to examine a graph of the simple logistic regression analysis to understand how predictions are made using the logistic equation.

HANDS-ON
EXAMPLE

This example illustrates a simple logistic regression using a quantitative measure as the independent variable.

1. In the Editor window, open the file ALOG2.SAS.

```
ODS HTML;
PROC LOGISTIC DATA="C:\SASDATA\ACCIDENTS" DESCENDING;
    MODEL DEAD=ISS / RISKLIMITS;
    OUTPUT OUT=LOGOUT PREDICTED=PROB;
    TITLE "Simple binary logistic regession with plot.";
RUN;
*------------------------------------LOGISTIC PLOT;
GOPTIONS RESET=ALL;
PROC SORT DATA=LOGOUT;BY ISS;
TITLE 'LOGISTIC PLOT';
PROC GPLOT DATA=LOGOUT;
    PLOT PROB*ISS;
RUN;
ODS HTML CLOSE;
QUIT;
```

Notice the following statements

```
OUTPUT OUT=LOGOUT PREDICTED=PROB;
```

   Note that the DESCENDING option is used because death (i.e., DEAD=1) is the outcome of interest in the predictive model. Otherwise, the OR would by default be based on predicting DEAD=0. The OUTPUT statement creates a SAS data set named LOGOUT that contains the predicted values calculated by the logistic regression equation. The probabilities from the logistic equation (PROB) using the estimates of the coefficients are from the Estimate column in the Maximum Likelihood Estimates table in Table 12.2 to create the following prediction equation:

$$\hat{p} = \frac{e^{-5.444 + .1056 * ISS}}{1 + e^{-5.444 + .1056 * ISS}}$$

2. Run the program and observe the output. In particular, examine the "S-shaped" plot shown in Figure 12.1. The graph provides a way to estimate the probability of death for each Injury Severity Score. For example,

(Continued)

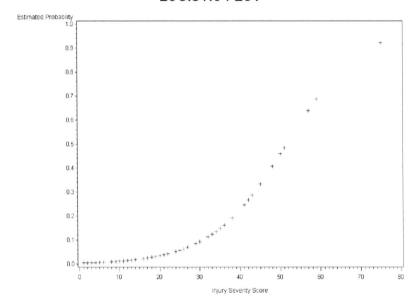

FIGURE 12.1. *A logistic plot from a simple logistic model*

LOGISTIC PLOT

locate ISS = 50 on the horizontal axis. Draw a vertical line to the plotted curve and from there draw a horizontal line to the vertical axis. This shows that for an ISS = 50, the probability of death is about 0.45 (or 45 percent).

$$\hat{p} = \frac{e^{-5.444 \,+\, .1056*ISS}}{1 + e^{-5.444 \,+\, .1056*ISS}} = 0.459$$

Notice that by substituting ISS=50 in the prediction equation, we obtain 0.459 which is consistent with the graphical estimate. It is typical that when $\hat{p} < 0.5$ you would predict non-occurrence of the event of interest (i.e., survival) and if $\hat{p} > 0.5$ you would predict occurrence (i.e., death). In this case we are pleased to predict that the subject would survive.

MULTIPLE BINARY LOGISTIC ANALYSIS

A multiple binary logistic regression model has more than one independent variable. As such, it is analogous to a multiple regression model in the case in which the dependent variable is binary. It is common to have several potential predictor variables. One of the tasks of the investigator is to select the best set of predictors to create a parsimonious and effective prediction equation.

Selecting Variables for Multiple Logistic Analysis

The procedure used to select the best independent variables is similar to the one used in multiple linear regression. You can choose to select variables using manual or automated methods, or a combination of both. It is often desirable for the investigator to use his or her knowledge to perform a preliminary selection of the most logically (plausibly) important variables. Automated procedures can then be used to select other potential variables.

The importance of each variable as a predictor in the final model depends on the other variables in the model. Confounding and interaction effects may need to be addressed in certain models, but these topics are beyond the scope of this book.

HANDS-ON
EXAMPLE

This example considers several potential predictors for mortality from the simulated ACCIDENTS dataset. Subjects range in age from very young to 18 years old. Recall that in this data set, the variable DEAD is coded as a 0/1 variable where 1 indicates that the subject died and 0 indicates that the subject survived. Also, ISS is an injury severity score where a larger score indicates a more severe injury, SBP is systolic blood pressure, and GCS is the Glasgow Coma Scale where a low value indicates a more severe injury.

1. In the Editor window, open the file ALOG3.SAS.

```
ODS HTML;
PROC LOGISTIC DATA="C:\SASDATA\ACCIDENTS" DESCENDING;
CLASS GENDER ;
MODEL DEAD =  PENETRATE ISS AGE GENDER SBP GCS
      / EXPB
       SELECTION=STEPWISE
       INCLUDE=1
       SLENTRY=0.05
       SLSTAY=0.05
       RISKLIMITS;
     TITLE 'LOGISTIC ON TRAUMA DATA WHERE AGE LE 18';
RUN;
ODS HTML CLOSE;
QUIT;
```

(Continued)

- Note that the DESCENDING option is used in order for the model to predict DEAD=1. Otherwise, the prediction and OR would be based on predicting DEAD=0 (survival).

- Seven possible independent variables are included in the MODEL statement: PENETRATE, ISS, AGE, RACE, GENDER, SBP, and GCS.

- Because GENDER is a text variable, it is indicated in a CLASS statement before the MODEL statement. SAS uses this information to create a design variable so GENDER can be used in the model. (Another option would be to recode GENDER into a 0/1 variable and use the recoded variable in the model.)

- Stepwise selection is requested with entry into the model set at 0.05 (SLENTRY) and removal from the model also set at 0.05 (SLSTAY).

- The INCLUDE=1 option indicates that the first variable in the independent variable list (PENETRATE) should always be in the model.

- RISKLIMITS requests odds ratios to be output.

2. Run this program. Notice that Table 12.3 shows how the CLASS variable GENDER has been transformed to allow it to be used in the model.

TABLE 12.3. CLASS variables

Class Level Information		
Class	Value	Design Variables
GENDER	Female	1
	Male	-1

3. In the output shown in Table 12.4, we see that the variables GCS, ISS, and AGE are entered into the model and then no other variables meet the entry criterion. The final model and odds ratio values are shown. Notice that the odds ratio for PENETRATE is different than it was in the simple logistic model because it is adjusted for the other variables in the model. The odds ratios for AGE and GCS indicate that, in general, older children and children with higher GCS scores are more likely to survive an injury.

TABLE 12.4. **Final model**

Analysis of Maximum Likelihood Estimates						
Parameter	DF	Estimate	Standard Error	Wald Chi-Square	Pr > ChiSq	Exp(Est)
Intercept	1	-0.4850	0.4661	1.0827	0.2981	0.616
penetrate	1	2.4072	0.4053	35.2776	<.0001	11.103
ISS	1	0.0673	0.00974	47.7172	<.0001	1.070
AGE	1	-0.1092	0.0245	19.9400	<.0001	0.897
GCS	1	-0.4193	0.0453	85.7115	<.0001	0.657

Odds Ratio Estimates		
Effect	Point Estimate	95% Wald Confidence Limits
penetrate	11.103	5.017 24.570
ISS	1.070	1.049 1.090
AGE	0.897	0.855 0.941
GCS	0.657	0.602 0.719

Other model selection options include BACKWARD and FORWARD selection. These options do not always result in the same "final" model, and the decision concerning variables to be included in the final model should not be entirely based on the results of any automated procedure. The researcher's knowledge of the data should always be used to guide the model selection process even when automated procedures are used.

GOING DEEPER: ASSESSING A MODEL'S FIT AND PREDICTIVE ABILITY

Once you decide on a final model, you should analyze that model for its predictive ability. One method of analyzing the predictive capabilities of the logistic equation uses the Hosmer and Lemeshow test. This test is based on dividing subjects into deciles on the basis of predicted probabilities. (See Hosmer and Lemeshow, 2000.) SAS reports chi-square statistics based on observed and expected frequencies for subjects within these ten categories.

The Hosmer and Lemeshow test is requested using the LACKFIT option in the MODEL statement. Another measure used to assess the fit is a Receiver Operator Curve (ROC), which provides a measure of how well the model predicts outcomes.

HANDS-ON
EXAMPLE

This example illustrates the Hosmer and Lemeshow test and an ROC curve.

1. In the Editor window, open the file `ALOG4.SAS`.

```
ODS HTML;
ODS GRAPHICS ON;
PROC LOGISTIC DATA="C:\SASDATA\ACCIDENTS" DESCENDING;
CLASS GENDER RACE;
MODEL DEAD = PENETRATE ISS AGE GCS
        / EXPB
          LACKFIT
          RISKLIMITS
          CTABLE
         OUTROC=ROC1;
TITLE 'Assess models predictive ability';
RUN;
ODS GRAPHICS OFF;
ODS HTML CLOSE;
QUIT;
```

- The `LACKFIT` option requests a Hosmer and Lemeshow analysis.

- `CTABLE` requests predictions for various probability cutoff points.

- The `OUTROC=ROC1` statement along with the `ODS GRAPHICS ON` and `ODS GRAPHICS OFF` statements produces an ROC curve.

2. Run the program. Observe the Hosmer and Lemeshow tables shown in Table 12.5. SAS computes a chi-square from observed and expected frequencies in the table.

   Large chi-square values (and correspondingly small p-values) indicate a lack of fit for the model. In this case we see that the Hosmer and Lemeshow chi-square test for the final model yields a p-value of 0.2532, thus suggesting a model with satisfactory predictive value. Note that the Hosmer and Lemeshow chi-square test is not a test of importance of specific model parameters. It is a separate post hoc test performed to evaluate a specific model.

TABLE 12.5. **Hosmer and Lemeshow results**

Partition for the Hosmer and Lemeshow Test					
		dead = 1		dead = 0	
Group	Total	Observed	Expected	Observed	Expected
1	366	0	0.08	366	365.92
2	370	0	0.11	370	369.89
3	369	0	0.13	369	368.87
4	369	0	0.17	369	368.83
5	369	1	0.22	368	368.78
6	369	0	0.29	369	368.71
7	368	0	0.40	368	367.60
8	368	0	0.71	368	367.29
9	368	10	4.94	358	363.06
10	367	92	95.96	275	271.04

Hosmer and Lemeshow Goodness-of-Fit Test		
Chi-Square	DF	Pr > ChiSq
10.1716	8	0.2532

3. Examine the Classification table (partially) shown in Table 12.6. As mentioned earlier, it is common practice to use 0.5 as the cutoff for predicting occurrence. That is, to predict non-occurrence of the event of interest whenever $\hat{p} < 0.5$ and to predict occurrence if $\hat{p} > 0.5$. The Classification table indicates how many correct and incorrect predictions would be made for a wide range of probability cutoff points used for the model. In this case, 98 percent of the cases are correctly classified using the 0.50 cutoff point.

Also note that at the 0.50 cutoff point, there is 38.8 percent sensitivity and 99.7 percent specificity. (Sensitivity is the probability of a positive result among subjects with the outcome of interest, and specificity is the probability of a negative result among subjects who do not exhibit the outcome.) If you desire to gain sensitivity, you can move the cutoff point to a lower probability level (at the sacrifice of specificity). Similarly, you can increase specificity by raising the cutoff probability. (For more information about selecting a cutoff point, see Cohen et al. [2002], p. 516, or Hosmer and Lemeshow [2000], pp. 160ff.)

(Continued)

TABLE 12.6. Classification table for logistic regression

	Correct		Incorrect		Percentages				
Prob Level	Event	Non-Event	Event	Non-Event	Correct	Sensi-tivity	Speci-ficity	False POS	False NEG
0.000	103	0	3580	0	2.8	100.0	0.0	97.2	.
0.020	97	3226	354	6	90.2	94.2	90.1	78.5	0.2
...etc...									
0.460	43	3567	13	60	98.0	41.7	99.6	23.2	1.7
0.480	41	3569	11	62	98.0	39.8	99.7	21.2	1.7
0.500	40	3569	11	63	98.0	38.8	99.7	21.6	1.7
0.520	38	3570	10	65	98.0	36.9	99.7	20.8	1.8
...etc...									
0.940	5	3580	0	98	97.3	4.9	100.0	0.0	2.7
0.960	1	3580	0	102	97.2	1.0	100.0	0.0	2.8
0.980	1	3580	0	102	97.2	1.0	100.0	0.0	2.8
1.000	0	3580	0	103	97.2	0.0	100.0	.	2.8

4. Examine the ROC curve, shown in Figure 12.2. This curve, which is a plot of 1-Specificity versus Sensitivity, measures the predictive ability of the model. Notice that the "Area Under the Curve" (AUC) is 0.9718. When the AUC is close to 1.0, a good fit is indicated. The closer the curve extends to the upper left corner, the closer the AUC is to 1. AUC approaches 0.50 as the curve gets closer to the diagonal line and would indicate a poor fit. The AUC statistic is often reported as an indicator of the predictive strength of the model. When you are considering competing "final" models, the Hosmer and Lemeshow test and AUC (larger is better) are criteria often used.

Another way to assess the model is to use the information in the Model Fit Statistics table (not shown). For example, note that in the example, the value of -2 times the log likelihood for the model is given by $-2\text{Log } L = 417.470$ (for intercept and covariates). In general, when comparing models, the lower the $-2\text{Log } L$ value, the better the fit. To determine whether the inclusion of an additional variable in a model gives a *significantly* better fit, you can use the difference in the $-2\text{Log } L$ values for the two models to compute a chi-square test statistic.

FIGURE 12.2. ROC curve

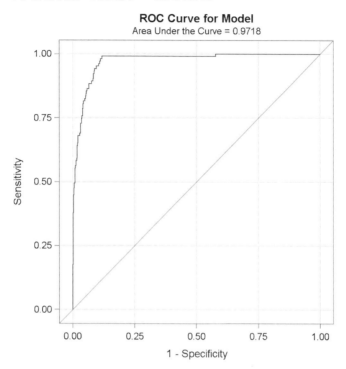

For example, for this model −2Log L is 417.470 (on the SAS output). By removing the AGE variable from the equation and rerunning the analysis, we get −2Log L = 438.094. The difference has a chi-squared distribution with one degree of freedom, and if this value is larger than the α-level critical value for a chi-square with one degree of freedom, then this is evidence at the α-level of significance that the variable AGE should be included in the model. For this example, the difference is 20.61, and thus at the $\alpha = 0.05$ level (critical value is 3.84) we conclude that AGE should be included in the model. Other criteria that can be used to assess competing models are the AIC (Akaike Information Criterion) or SC (Schwarz Criterion) values in the Model Fit Statistics table (smaller values indicate a better model in both cases).

SUMMARY

This chapter provided examples of the use of SAS for running simple and multi-variate logistic regression analysis. Also illustrated were techniques for selecting a model and for assessing its predictive ability.

EXERCISES

12.1. Run a multiple logistic regression.

Data were collected on 200 males. All had no evidence of coronary disease. After 10 years the subjects were examined for evidence of coronary disease. The researcher wants to know if the demographic information collected at the beginning of the study is helping in predicting if the subjects will develop coronary disease.

a. Using the following code as a beginning, use all three methods of model fitting to see what model looks the most promising.

```
PROC LOGISTIC DATA='C:\SASDATA\CORONARY' DESCENDING;
MODEL CORONARY= SBP DBP AGE BMI INSURANCE
    /_____;
RUN
```

b. What variables are in your final model?

c. Use SAS code to produce an ROC curve for the final model. What is the "Area under the curve" (AUC) for this model? How do you interpret this?

d. Use SAS code to produce a Hosmer and Lemeshow test on the final model. How do you interpret the results?

e. What are the Odds Ratios for the variables in the final model? How are they interpreted?

f. How well do you think this model predicts coronary disease in ten years?

g. If a 60-year-old man has a body mass index (BMI) of 25, what is your best guess of his probability of having coronary disease in 10 years? Hint: Use the following formula

$$\hat{p} = \frac{e^{b_0 + b_1 X_1 + b_2 X_2}}{1 + e^{b_0 + b_1 X_1 + b_2 X_2}}$$

13

ANALYSIS OF VARIANCE, PART II

LEARNING OBJECTIVES

- To be able to use SAS procedures to perform analysis of covariance
- To be able to use SAS procedures to perform two-factor ANOVA using PROC GLM
- To be able to perform two-factor ANOVA using PROC MIXED
- To be able to use SAS procedures to perform repeated measures with a grouping factor

SAS provides procedures that can analyze data from a wide range of experimental designs. This chapter illustrates three designs not previously discussed in Chapter 9 and provides you with a brief introduction to PROC MIXED.

ANALYSIS OF COVARIANCE

An analysis of covariance (ANCOVA) is a combination of analysis of variance and regression. The covariate is a quantitative variable that is related to the dependent variable. However, the covariate is not controlled by the investigator but is some value intrinsic to the subject (or entity). In ANCOVA the group means are adjusted by the covariate, and these adjusted means are compared with each other. Including this covariate variable in the model may explain some of the variability, resulting in a more powerful statistical test.

Consider an experiment designed to compare three medications for lowering systolic blood pressure (SBP). A potentially useful covariate would be age because it is known that there is a relationship between SBP and age. If SBP is the dependent variable in a model, it might be helpful to adjust SBP by the covariate age. Thus, in an ANCOVA, the adjusted means are compared rather than the raw means by group.

In the following Hands-on Example, we consider a data set in which a fifth-grade math teacher randomly assigns the eighteen students in her class to three different teaching methods for individualized instruction of a certain concept. The outcome of interest is the score on an exam over the concept after the instruction period. A pretest of basic math skills is given to the students prior to beginning the instruction. The data are shown in Table 13.1. The variable POSTTEST is compared across the three teaching methods. The covariate PRETEST is assumed to be linearly related to POSTTEST. Note that if there were no PRETEST used to adjust POSTTEST scores, the analysis would be a standard one-way analysis of variance comparing POSTTEST scores across the three teaching methods. However, with the addition of the PRETEST information, the analysis is potentially more powerful. The ANCOVA tests the null hypothesis that the POSTTEST means for the three methods adjusted by PRETEST are not different.

The procedure requires a multi-step approach.

1. Perform a test to determine if the POSTTEST-by-PRETEST linear relationships by METHOD are parallel—that is, when you compare the regression lines for each of the three METHODs, the lines should theoretically be parallel. If the lines are sufficiently nonparallel, ANCOVA is not the appropriate analysis to perform. The statistical test used for parallelism is an *F*-test.

2. If the *F*-test in step 1 does not reject parallelism, then another *F*-test is used to compare the adjusted means across METHOD.

3. If there are differences in means, then appropriate multiple comparisons can be performed to determine which groups differ.

TABLE 13.1. **Data from math course analysis**

Method	Pretest	Posttest
1	16	38
1	17	39
1	15	41
1	23	47
1	12	33
1	13	37
2	22	41
2	10	30
2	19	45
2	6	28
2	2	25
2	17	39
3	3	30
3	20	49
3	14	43
3	10	38
3	5	32
3	11	37

HANDS-ON
EXAMPLE

This example performs an analysis of covariance to compare three methods of teaching a fifth-grade math concept.

1. In the Editor window, open the file AGLM2.SAS.

(Continued)

```
DATA ANCOVA;
INPUT METHOD PRETEST POSTTEST @@;
DATALINES;
1    16    38    1    17    39    1    15    41
1    23    47    1    12    33    1    13    37
2    22    41    2    10    30    2    19    45
2     6    28    2     2    25    2    17    39
3     3    30    3    20    49    3    14    43
3    10    38    3     5    32    3    11    37
;
* CHECK THE ASSUMPTION THAT SLOPES ARE PARALLEL;
ODS HTML;
PROC GLM;
    CLASS METHOD;
    MODEL POSTTEST=PRETEST METHOD PRETEST*METHOD;
    TITLE 'Analysis of Covariance Example';
RUN;
* SINCE SLOPES ARE PARALLEL, DROP THE INTERACTION TERM;
PROC GLM;
    CLASS METHOD;
    MODEL POSTTEST=PRETEST METHOD;
    LSMEANS METHOD/STDERR PDIFF ADJUST=SCHEFFE;
RUN;
QUIT;
ODS HTML CLOSE;
```

Note that `PROC GLM` is run twice. The first instance is to test that the slopes are parallel. This is tested with the `MODEL` statement:

```
MODEL POSTTEST=PRETEST METHOD PRETEST*METHOD;
```

The `PRETEST*METHOD` factor in the model is the interaction (or parallel slopes) factor. When the test for this factor is not significant, it suggests that the slopes among types of `METHOD` can be treated as parallel.

2. Run the program. As mentioned in Chapter 9, we recommend using the Type III sums-of-squares. Observe these sums-of-squares in the output shown in Table 13.2. The row for the test of the interaction term (`PRETEST*METHOD`) is nonsignificant ($p = 0.6835$). This provides evidence that the slopes can be treated as parallel and that the ANCOVA is an appropriate analysis.

TABLE 13.2. **Test of slopes for analysis of covariance**

Source	DF	Type III SS	Mean Square	F Value	Pr > F
PRETEST	1	476.4504266	476.4504266	114.76	<.0001
METHOD	2	0.8199072	0.4099536	0.10	0.9067
PRETEST*METHOD	2	3.2623239	1.6311619	0.39	0.6835

3. Because the slopes are not significantly nonparallel, the second PROC GLM analysis is appropriate. Note that the interaction term has been removed from the MODEL statement, forcing the model to assume parallel regression lines.

```
MODEL POSTTEST=PRETEST METHOD;
```

   Table 13.3 shows the Type III SS output table for the second PROC GLM. The factor of interest in this table is METHOD, and the corresponding F is a statistical test comparing the three methods adjusting for PRETEST. Because $p = 0.0005$, we reject the null hypothesis that the adjusted means are equal and conclude that at least one pair of adjusted means are different from each other.

TABLE 13.3. **Analysis of covariance test of main effects**

Source	DF	Type III SS	Mean Square	F Value	Pr > F
PRETEST	1	627.9168352	627.9168352	165.60	<.0001
METHOD	2	105.9808664	52.9904332	13.98	0.0005

4. Because we found a difference in adjusted means, pairwise comparisons can be used to identify which adjusted means are different. The statement that provides that comparison is

```
LSMEANS METHOD/STDERR PDIFF ADJUST=SCHEFFE;
```

In this case we have chosen to use the Scheffe multiple comparisons, and the results are shown in Table 13.4.

   The Scheffe results provide p-values for each pairwise comparison. In this case, the comparisons of METHODs 1 and 3 ($p = 0.0056$) and 2 and 3 ($p = 0.0007$) indicate significant differences. METHODs 1 and 2 are not significantly different ($p = 0.68$).

   Because a high POSTTEST score is the goal, there is evidence to support the contention that the adjusted mean of 40.82 for METHOD 3 is a significantly higher score than for METHODs 1 and 2 and thus that METHOD 3 is the preferred method.

(Continued)

TABLE 13.4. Scheffe multiple comparisons for ANCOVA

METHOD	POSTTEST LSMEAN	Standard Error	Pr > |t|	LSMEAN Number
1	36.0946098	0.8300185	<.0001	1
2	35.0724100	0.7955731	<.0001	2
3	40.8329802	0.8215055	<.0001	3

Least Squares Means for effect METHOD
Pr > \|t\| for H0: LSMean(i)=LSMean(j)

Dependent Variable: POSTTEST

i/j	1	2	3
1		0.6837	0.0056
2	0.6837		0.0007
3	0.0056	0.0007	

5. It is always a good idea to supplement statistical results with graphics. In the Editor window, open the file AGLM3.SAS. This program is the same as the previous except for the addition of the code

```
ODS GRAPHICS ON;
```

and

```
ODS GRAPHCS OFF;
```

Run this program and observe the graphical output. The first plot, Figure 13.1, shows the three regression lines by METHOD. Note that the lines are near parallel, which confirms the findings in the first PROC GLM procedure.

When the model is run without the interaction term, we assume that the lines are parallel. Thus, the plot associated with the second PROC GLM uses a common slope estimate, and the lines in Figure 13.2 represent the adjusted means by METHOD.

These plots support our overall finding that the adjusted mean for METHOD 3 is higher than the means for the other methods. In addition, SAS provides a graphical display of the Scheffe results, as shown in Figure 13.3. This plot shows confidence intervals for the adjusted means indicated by lines at the intersection of the three methods. This graph indicates that the comparison of 3 versus 2 and 3 versus 1 are both significant because their lines do not cross the diagonal line. The comparison of 1 versus 2 is not significant.

6. Replace the Scheffe test in the LSMEANS line with a Bonferroni or Tukey test and compare the output and results.

FIGURE 13.1. *Regression lines for ANCOVA data*

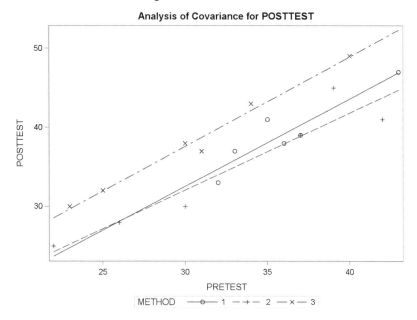

Analysis of Covariance for POSTTEST

FIGURE 13.2. *Parallel lines for ANCOVA data, for second model assuming parallel lines*

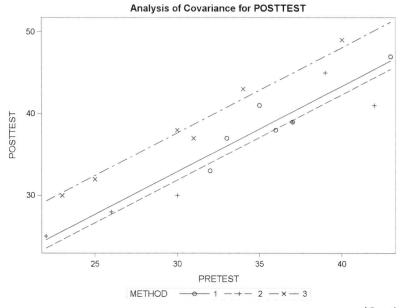

Analysis of Covariance for POSTTEST

(*Continued*)

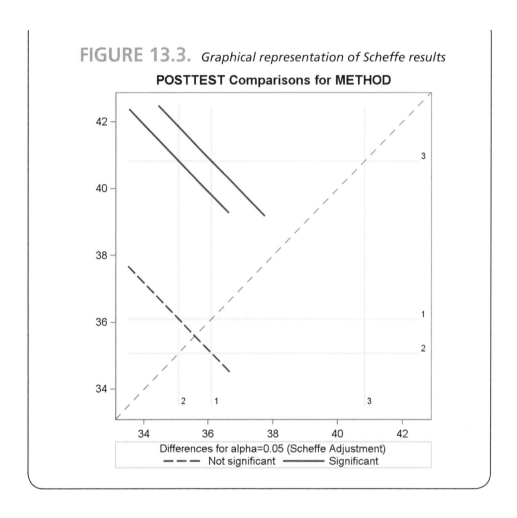

FIGURE 13.3. *Graphical representation of Scheffe results*

POSTTEST Comparisons for METHOD

Differences for alpha=0.05 (Scheffe Adjustment)
— — — Not significant ———— Significant

Two-Factor ANOVA Using PROC GLM

A two-way ANOVA is an analysis that allows you to simultaneously evaluate the effects of two experimental variables (factors). Each factor is a "grouping" variable such as type of treatment, gender, brand, and so on. The two-way ANOVA tests determine whether the factors are important (significant) either separately (called main effects) or in combination (via an interaction), which is the combined effect of the two factors.

As an example of interaction effects, suppose you are observing annual salary where the two factors are gender and job category. Figure 13.4 illustrates the difference between an interaction effect and no interaction effect. The left graph indicates that female salaried workers have a different pattern of income across hourly and salary categories from males. The right illustration indicates that the mean incomes for hourly and salaried personnel are parallel (non-interacting) across gender. When an interaction effect is present (left graph), you cannot easily compare means between male and female workers because they have different patterns. When there is no

FIGURE 13.4. *Example of an interaction effect*

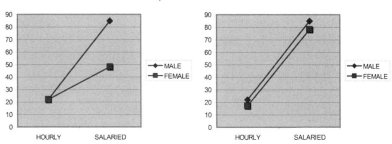

interaction effect (right graph), it makes sense to compare overall means between male and female workers.

The dimensions of a factorial design depend on how many levels of each factor are used. For example, a design where the first factor has two categories and the second has three categories is called a 2×3 (2 by 3) factorial design. Generally, the two-way ANOVA is called a $p \times q$ factorial design.

Understanding Fixed and Random Factors

Factors are classified as fixed or random. When the factor levels completely define all the classifications of interest, we have what is called a **fixed factor**. For example, GENDER (classified as male or female) is a fixed factor. When the levels used in the experiment are randomly selected from the population of possible levels, the factor is called a **random factor**. For example, a chemist interested in understanding the differences among laboratories that perform a certain assay may randomly select a sample of laboratories from among the large population of laboratories for his experiment. In this case, LAB would be a random effect. ANOVA models are classified with the following scheme:

- Both factors fixed: Model I ANOVA

- Both factors random: Model II ANOVA

- One random, one fixed: Model III ANOVA

In this section, we will assume that both factors (A and B) are fixed, and we illustrate an analysis for a Model I ANOVA. We will not provide an example of a Model II analysis, but a Model III ANOVA will be described in the next section.

When gathering data for this fixed-factor ANOVA design, within the $p \times q$ possible combinations of factors (cells), subjects should be randomly assigned to a treatment in such a way as to balance the number of subjects per cell. However, if the data are not balanced, an analysis can still be performed with PROC GLM (but not with PROC ANOVA).

There are some additional calculation issues involved with the unbalanced case that are not discussed here. Generally, in the unbalanced case, the Type III sums-of-squares from the PROC GLM output are recommended. Also, the dependent variable should be a quantitative variable whose distribution within each of the $p \times q$ (p by q) combinations is approximately normal with equal variances among combinations. (Some of these issues are relaxed when you are using PROC MIXED.)

There are two type of hypotheses used in a two-factor design: hypotheses about interaction effects and main effects. The interaction effect should be examined first:

H_0: There is no interaction effect.

H_a: There is an interaction effect.

Interaction implies that the pattern of means across groups is inconsistent (as was illustrated in the left graph in Figure 13.4). If there is an interaction effect, main effects cannot be examined directly because the interaction effect shows that differences across one main effect are not consistent across all levels of the other factor.

Thus, if there is no interaction effect, it makes sense to test hypotheses about main effects. The "main effects" hypotheses for factor A are:

$H_0 : \mu_{a1} = \mu_{a2} = \cdots = \mu_{ap}$: Means are equal across levels of A summed over B.

$H_a : \mu_{ai} \neq \mu_{aj}$ for some $i \neq j$: Means are not equal across levels of A summed over B.

Similarly, for factor B:

$H_0 : \mu_{b1} = \mu_{b2} = \cdots = \mu_{bp}$: Means are equal across levels of B summed over A.

$H_a : \mu_{bi} \neq \mu_{bj}$ for some $i \neq j$: Means are not equal across levels of B summed over A.

The results of these three tests (interaction, and two main effects tests) are given in an analysis of variance table as F-tests. A low p-value (usually less than 0.05) for a test indicates evidence to reject the null hypothesis in favor of the alternative.

HANDS-ON
EXAMPLE

This example (adapted from data set 404 in Hand, Daly, McConway, Lunn, and Ostrowski [1994]) concerns a study on weight loss for those attending meetings about dieting. A variable called CONDITION indicates whether the patient received a weight loss manual (CONDITION=1) or not (CONDITION=2). The STATUS variable indicates whether the patient had already been trying to lose weight before the series of meetings (STATUS=1) or not (STATUS=2).

Both factors are assumed to be fixed effects for this example, and there are an unequal numbers of subjects in each category. For this case, PROC GLM can be used.

1. In the Editor window, open the file AGLM4.SAS.

```
DATA SLIM;
INPUT CONDITION STATUS RESPONSE @@;
DATALINES;
1 1 -13.67 1 1 -12.85 1 1 -9.55 1 1 -17.03 1 1 13.61
1 2 .91 1 2 2.48 1 2 2.84 1 2 3.46 1 2 2.20 1 2 -.73
1 2 -3.05 1 2 -5.68 1 2 -3.44 1 2 -7.18 1 2 -3.40 1 2 -.74
2 1 -3.29 2 1 -4 2 1 -2.31 2 1 -3.4 2 1 -7.49 2 1 -13.62
2 1 -7.34 2 1 -7.39 2 1 -1.32 2 1 -12.01 2 1 -8.35
2 2 5.94 2 2 1.91 2 2 -4.0 2 2 -5.19 2 2 0 2 2 -2.8
;
ODS HTML;
TITLE "Two-Way ANOVA Example";
PROC GLM;
CLASS CONDITION STATUS;
    MODEL RESPONSE=CONDITION STATUS CONDITION*STATUS;
    MEANS CONDITION STATUS;
RUN;
ODS HTML CLOSE;
```

   Recall that in the MODEL statement, the dependent variable (RESPONSE) appears to the left of the equal sign and the independent variables (CONDITION and STATUS) appear to the right. The CONDITION*STATUS component of the MODEL statement is the interaction term. The two factors, CONDITION and STATUS, are listed in the CLASS statement because they are categorical variables.

2. Run this program and observe the output, partially illustrated in Table 13.5. This is output from the first PROC GLM statement in the code. Note that the overall model is significant ($p = .04$), indicating the presence of some differences in means. Notice also that because of the unequal number of observations per cell, the Type I and Type III sums-of-squares give different results. It is recommended that Type III SS be used.

3. For this analysis, first examine the interaction effect (the CONDITION*STATUS row) in the Type III ANOVA table. Because $p = 0.7872$, there is no evidence of interaction. As mentioned previously:

(Continued)

TABLE 13.5. **ANOVA results from a two-factor analysis using PROC GLM**

Level of STATUS	N	RESPONSE Mean	RESPONSE Std Dev
1	16	-6.87562500	7.17206058
2	18	-0.91500000	3.63062829

- If there is no interaction, examine the main effects tests in the ANOVA table by comparing marginal means.

- If there are interaction effects, the factor effects should not be interpreted in isolation from each other. It is usually more appropriate to compare effects of the first factor within levels of the second factor, and vice versa. That is, compare cell means rather than the marginal means using a post hoc analysis. Because there is no significant interaction in this example, it is appropriate to examine the main effects tests (STATUS and CONDITION):

- The test for the CONDITION main effect, $p = 0.6686$

- The test for STATUS, $p = 0.0056$.

Thus, you can reject the null hypothesis that there is no STATUS effect and conclude that there is evidence to support the hypothesis that STATUS (i.e., whether the subject was trying to lose weight) is a statistically significant factor in realized weight loss. Table 13.6 shows the marginal means for the two levels of STATUS. Because $p = 0.67$ for the CONDITION factor, we conclude that there is no significant CONDITION effect.

TABLE 13.6. **Marginal means for levels of STATUS**

				Analysis Variable : RESPONSE			
CONDITION	STATUS	N Obs	N	Mean	Std Dev	Minimum	Maximum
1	1	5	5	-7.90	12.31	-17.03	13.61
	2	12	12	-1.03	3.53	-7.18	3.46
2	1	11	11	-6.41	3.97	-13.62	-1.32
	2	6	6	-0.69	4.17	-5.19	5.94

Because there are only two categories of STATUS, we do not need to perform multiple comparisons, and the clear conclusion is that STATUS=1 (i.e., those who had previously been trying to lose weight) had significantly more weight loss on average than those in STATUS=2.

Viewing the Data Graphically

It is often helpful to use graphs to help visualize the results of a two-factor analysis. The following Hands-on Example illustrates how to use ODS Graphics to examine the means by factor.

HANDS-ON
EXAMPLE

This example (for SAS version 9.2.) uses ODS Graphics to display a plot that illustrates the results of the analysis.

1. In the Editor window, open the program GLM5.SAS. The analysis section of the code is shown here.

```
ODS HTML;
TITLE "Two-Way ANOVA Example";
ODS GRAPHICS ON;
PROC GLM;
CLASS CONDITION STATUS;
    MODEL RESPONSE= STATUS CONDITION CONDITION*STATUS;
RUN;
QUIT;
ODS GRAPHICS OFF;
ODS HTML CLOSE;
```

This program is runs the same as the PROC GLM in the previous example, with the addition of the ODS GRAPHICS ON and GRAPHICS OFF statements.

2. Run this program. The SAS ODS Graphics procedure produces the plot shown in Figure 13.5. This plot gives dot plots of the data for the four combinations of STATUS and CONDITION. The solid line connects the mean RESPONSE for subjects in STATUS=1 across CONDITION. The dashed line provides the same information for those in STATUS=2.

It can be seen that the lines are approximately parallel, supporting the finding of no significant interaction and indicating that RESPONSE scores are consistently higher for STATUS=2 across levels of CONDITION. Because RESPONSE is weight loss, this graphical representation supports the finding above that those who had previously been trying to lose weight (STATUS=1) had more success on the weight loss program.

(Continued)

FIGURE 13.5. *ODS Graphics interaction plot for the two-factor ANOVA example (SAS version 9.2)*

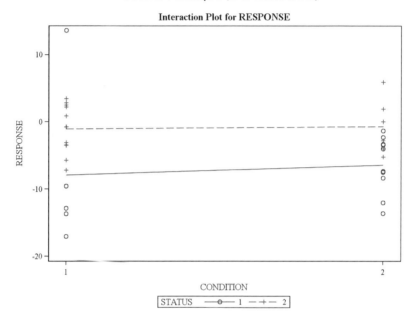

HANDS-ON EXAMPLE

This example (for all versions of SAS for Windows) uses PROC GPLOT to produce interaction plots for the two-factor analysis.

1. In the Editor window, open the program GLM5a.SAS. The analysis section of the code is shown here.

```
ODS HTML;
TITLE "TWO-WAY ANOVA EXAMPLE";
PROC MEANS MAXDEC=2; CLASS CONDITION STATUS;VAR RESPONSE;RUN;
* PRODUCE PLOTS;
PROC SORT;BY STATUS CONDITION;
```

```
PROC MEANS NOPRINT; BY STATUS CONDITION;
     OUTPUT OUT=FORPLOT MEAN=;
RUN;
AXIS1 OFFFSET=(5) ORDER=(1 TO 2);
PROC GPLOT;
PLOT RESPONSE*STATUS=CONDITION/HAXIS=AXIS1;
SYMBOL1 V=CIRCLE I=JOIN L=1 C=BLACK;
SYMBOL2 V=DOT I=JOIN L=2 C=BLACK;
RUN;
AXIS1 OFFSET=(5);
PROC GPLOT;
PLOT RESPONSE*CONDITION=STATUS/HAXIS=AXIS1;
SYMBOL1 V=CIRCLE I=JOIN L=1 C=BLACK;
SYMBOL2 V=DOT I=JOIN L=2 C=BLACK;
RUN;
QUIT;
ODS HTML CLOSE;
```

This program creates the necessary means for the plot using PROC MEANS. Note the code that produces the interaction plots. Means are output to a data set named FORPLOT. For more information on the AXIS and SYMBOL statements, see Chapter 14. PROC GPLOT creates the interaction plots, first for RESPONSE by STATUS and then for RESPONSE by CONDITION.

2. Run this program. The first PROC MEANS produces a table of descriptive statistics containing means by factor, as illustrated in Table 13.7.

   The program produces the interaction plots shown in Figure 13.6. The first plot gives information similar to that in Figure 13.5 (without the plotting of the actual points). The second plot graphs the means by STATUS with the two lines representing the two categories of CONDITION.

TABLE 13.7. Means by factor

				Analysis Variable : RESPONSE			
CONDITION	STATUS	N Obs	N	Mean	Std Dev	Minimum	Maximum
1	1	5	5	-7.90	12.31	-17.03	13.61
	2	12	12	-1.03	3.53	-7.18	3.46
2	1	11	11	-6.41	3.97	-13.62	-1.32
	2	6	6	-0.69	4.17	-5.19	5.94

(Continued)

FIGURE 13.6. *Interaction plots for two-way ANOVA*

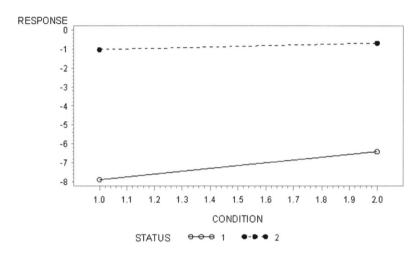

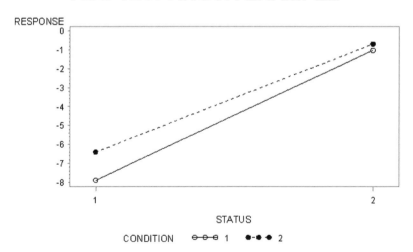

Again, the lines are close to parallel, indicating no interaction, and they are close together, which suggests little difference in marginal means by condition. This is consistent with the test results that found no significant difference in marginal means by CONDITION.

> Note that in a two-factor analysis, if an interaction effect exists you need to perform post hoc tests comparing means for status by each condition. Also, if there were more than two groups in a main effect, the decision concerning which marginal means are significantly different would require the use of post hoc comparisons.

GOING DEEPER: TWO-FACTOR ANOVA USING PROC MIXED

PROC MIXED performs mixed-model analysis of variance and repeated measures analysis of variance with covariance structure modeling. PROC MIXED has features not available in PROC GLM. Briefly, here are some of the major differences between PROC GLM and PROC MIXED in relation to two-factor ANOVA analysis:

PROC GLM:

- Is designed primarily for fixed effects models

- Calculates based on ordinary least squares and method of moments

- Defines all effects as fixed and adjusts for random effects after estimation

- Can perform mixed model analysis, but some results are not optimally calculated

PROC MIXED:

- Is designed for mixed effects models

- Uses generalized least squares for fixed effects and Restricted Maximum Likelihood Estimation (RMLE) to estimate variance components

- Allows selection of correlation models

Both PROC GLM and PROC MIXED can analyze fixed effects and mixed models. When all factors are fixed, the two approaches produce the same results. However, for mixed models (and some repeated measures models), the two different approaches can lead to differing answers. Because PROC MIXED uses a more general approach that is less restrictive (in terms of assumptions), its results are considered more reliable (Littell, Milliken, Stroup, and Wolfinger, 1996).

The following example is adapted from Chapter 41 of the SAS/STAT user's guide. The data include the response variable HEIGHT (in inches) of eighteen individuals. The individuals are classified according to FAMILY and GENDER. Because FAMILY consists of some selection of families, it is reasonable to consider FAMILY a random effect. Also, the interaction FAMILY*GENDER is a random effect. With this information in mind, we illustrate the use of PROC MIXED to analyze this Model III ANOVA in the following Hands-on Example. In this example the researcher wants to know if there is a difference in HEIGHT by GENDER and FAMILY.

HANDS-ON EXAMPLE

This example illustrates the use of PROC MIXED and assumes that FAMILY and FAMILY*GENDER are random factors.

1. In the Editor window, open the program AMIXED1.SAS.

```
DATA HEIGHTS;
INPUT FAMILY GENDER$ HEIGHT @@;
DATALINES;
   1 F 67    1 F 66    1 F 64    1 M 71    1 M 72    2 F 63
   2 F 63    2 F 67    2 M 69    2 M 68    2 M 70    3 F 63
   3 M 64    4 F 67    4 F 66    4 M 67    4 M 67    4 M 69
   ;
RUN;
ODS HTML;
PROC MEANS MAXDEC=2 MEAN DATA=HEIGHTS;
   CLASS FAMILY GENDER;
   VAR HEIGHT;
PROC MIXED;
      CLASS FAMILY GENDER;
      MODEL HEIGHT = GENDER;
      RANDOM FAMILY FAMILY*GENDER;
RUN;
ODS HTML CLOSE;
```

In this program, a table of means is created first, then the analysis is performed, as shown in Table 13.8. Make note of the following items in the PROC MIXED statement:

- FAMILY and GENDER appear in the CLASS statement because they are both grouping-type factors.
- The MODEL statement includes only the fixed factor GENDER, and the random factors FAMILY and FAMILY*GENDER are in a RANDOM statement.
- If both FAMILY and GENDER were fixed, the model statement would have been

```
MODEL HEIGHT = GENDER FAMILY GENDER*FAMILY;
```

2. Run the program. Observe the (abbreviated) output shown in Table 13.8

TABLE 13.8. **Output from PROC MIXED using random effects**

Analysis Variable : HEIGHT			
FAMILY	GENDER	N Obs	Mean
1	F	3	65.67
	M	2	71.50
2	F	3	64.33
	M	3	69.00
3	F	1	63.00
	M	1	64.00
4	F	2	66.50
	M	3	67.67

Type 3 Tests of Fixed Effects				
Effect	Num DF	Den DF	F Value	Pr > F
GENDER	1	3	7.95	0.0667

We are going to discuss only the final table, "Type 3 Tests of Fixed Effects." This table contains a significance test for the fixed effect, GENDER, which is marginally significant ($p=0.07$).

3. To illustrate why it is important to properly classify a random factor as random, change the MODEL statement to

```
MODEL HEIGHT = GENDER FAMILY GENDER*FAMILY;
```

as if FAMILY were a fixed factor. Eliminate the RANDOM statement. Run the program. The (abbreviated) output is shown in Table 13.9. Notice that in this case the test for a GENDER effect is significant ($p = 0.0018$). However, in the fixed effects model the FAMILY effect applies only to the families in the study (fixed effect). When FAMILY is classified as a random factor, the test results are applicable to families in general, not just to the ones in the study.

TABLE 13.9. **Model run as if all factors were fixed**

Type 3 Tests of Fixed Effects				
Effect	Num DF	Den DF	F Value	Pr > F
GENDER	1	10	17.63	0.0018
FAMILY	3	10	5.90	0.0139
FAMILY*GENDER	3	10	2.89	0.0889

GOING DEEPER: REPEATED MEASURES WITH A GROUPING FACTOR

A common design in medical research and other settings is to observe data for the same subject under different circumstances or over time (longitudinal). The one-way repeated measures design is illustrated in Chapter 9, "Analysis of Variance." When the design also includes a grouping variable, the analysis becomes a little more complicated. This "repeated measures design with a grouping factor" can be analyzed in SAS using PROC MIXED. Although it is also possible to perform this analysis using PROC GLM, the approach used in PROC MIXED is more mathematically general. Additionally, a distinct advantage of using PROC MIXED is that it allows missing values in the design whereas PROC GLM deletes an entire record from analysis if there is one missing observation.

Suppose you observe a response to a drug over four hours for seven subjects, three male and four female. In this case, the repeated measure, HOUR, is longitudinal. The effect across hours, because it is a measurement on the same individual four times, is called a within-subject factor. GENDER is a between-subject factor because it a measurement between independent groups. In this example, we'll assume that both GENDER and HOUR are fixed factors because they include all levels of interest. The observed data are shown in Table 13.10. Note that there is one missing value and an unequal number of subjects by GENDER.

TABLE 13.10.   **Original data set of repeated measures data**

SUB	GENDER	HOUR1	HOUR2	HOUR3	HOUR4
1	M	1	1.5	6	5.1
2	M	4	2.2	6.1	5.2
3	M	5.2	4.1	6.8	3.2
4	F	5.1	3.3	4.2	4.8
5	F	6.3	4.9	6.9	6.9
6	F	8.2	5.9	9.5	9.1
7	F	8.3	6.1	Missing	9.2

The data set for this analysis is initially set up like most data sets in this book, with one subject's data per record. However, for repeated measures, the SAS PROC MIXED procedure requires that the data be set up with one observation per record. The following Hands-on Example illustrates how to rearrange the data and perform the repeated measures analysis using PROC MIXED.

HANDS-ON EXAMPLE

This example uses PROC MIXED to analyze a repeated measures design that includes one grouping factor.

1. In the Editor window, open the file AREPEAT.SAS. The SAS code used to read in and rearrange the data set for the analysis is shown here.

```
DATA REPMIXED(KEEP= SUBJECT GENDER TIME OUTCOME);
INPUT SUBJECT GENDER $ HOUR1-HOUR4 ;
OUTCOME = HOUR1;   TIME = 1; OUTPUT;
OUTCOME = HOUR2;   TIME = 2; OUTPUT;
OUTCOME = HOUR3;   TIME = 3; OUTPUT;
OUTCOME = HOUR4;   TIME = 4; OUTPUT;
DATALINES;
1      M      1      1.5    6      5.1
2      M      4      2.2    6.1    5.2
3      M      5.2    4.1    5.8    3.2
4      F      5.1    3.3    5.2    4.8
5      F      6.3    4.9    7.9    6.9
6      F      8.2    5.9    9.5    9.1
7      F      8.3    6.1    .      9.2
;
```

The data set is initially set up with one subject per line. However, PROC MIXED requires that there be only one record per data line. That is, there should be one record per line with four records per subject. This necessary rearrangement is accomplished in the SAS code by

a. assigning each of the four HOUR values to the variable OUTCOME

b. creating a variable called TIME that contains the time marker (1 to 4)

c. for each of these assignments, outputting the variables to the new data set REPMIXED using the OUTPUT statement

(Continued)

The KEEP statement in parentheses after REPMIXED in the DATA statement tells SAS which variables to include in the final data set. The resulting data set is in the form shown in Table 13.11. Compare this data set to the original data setup shown in Table 13.10. Notice that for each row in the original data set, there are four rows in the REPMIXED data set.

2. The following code is used to perform three repeated measures analyses using PROC MIXED:

```
PROC MIXED DATA=REPMIXED;
      CLASS GENDER TIME SUBJECT;
      MODEL OUTCOME=GENDER TIME GENDER*TIME;
      REPEATED / TYPE=UN SUB=SUBJECT;
RUN;
PROC MIXED DATA=REPMIXED;
      CLASS GENDER TIME SUBJECT;
      MODEL OUTCOME=GENDER TIME GENDER*TIME;
      REPEATED / TYPE=CS SUB=SUBJECT;
RUN;
PROC MIXED DATA=REPMIXED;
```

TABLE 13.11.　REPMIXED data for use in PROC MIXED

SUBJECT	GENDER	TIME	OUTCOME
1	M	1	1
1	M	2	1.5
1	M	3	6
1	M	4	5.1
2	M	1	4
2	M	2	2.2
2	M	3	6.1
etc	Etc	etc	etc

```
CLASS GENDER TIME SUBJECT;
MODEL OUTCOME=GENDER TIME GENDER*TIME;
REPEATED / TYPE=AR(1) SUB=SUBJECT;
RUN;
```

These three `PROC MIXED` analyses are identical except for the `TYPE=` statement. Each `TYPE` statement includes a different specification for the within-subject covariance matrix. A few commonly used structures include:

- VC (Variance Components) is the default and simplest structure with all off-diagonal variances equal to 0.

- AR(1) (Autoregressive) assumes that nearby variances are correlated and decline exponentially with distance.

- CS (Compound Symmetry) assumes homogeneous variances that are constant regardless of how far apart the measurements are.

- UN (Unstructured) allows all variances to be different.

See the SAS/STAT manual (`PROC MIXED` chapter) for more options and details regarding covariance specifications.

The `CLASS` option indicates that the three factor variables are all classification (categorical) variables. (We include `SUBJECT` here even though we are not generally interested in a `SUBJECT` effect, in order to fully define the model.) The `MODEL` statement indicates that `OUTCOME` is the dependent variable and `GENDER`, `TIME`, and the interaction term `GENDER*TIME` are independent variables used to predict outcome.

The `REPEATED` statement indicates the `TYPE` of covariance structure to use in the analysis, and the `SUB=SUBJECT` indicates the name of the subject variable.

3. Run the program. A lot of output is created by SAS for this analysis, much of it dealing with the iterations required to fit the model. This output will not be discussed here. Initially, take note of the value of AIC (Akaike Information Criterion) in the Fit Statistics output table. This is a measure of the fit of the model, with smaller AIC values considered best. (There are other criteria you could also use, such as BIC and AICC, but we'll limit our discussion to AIC.) You can fit any number of covariance structures to the data with the `TYPE=` statement, and you then typically select the best fitting model. In this example, using the AIC criterion the AR(1) specification best fits the data. For these three models, the AIC results from the Fit Statistics tables associated with each covariance structure considered are

(Continued)

- AIC(unstructured) = 71.0

- AIC(compound symmetry) = 77.6

- AIC(autoregressive) = 70.2

TABLE 13.12. Results from PROC MIXED for AR(1) Structure

| | Type 3 Tests of Fixed Effects | | | |
Effect	Num DF	Den DF	F Value	Pr > F
GENDER	1	5	5.22	0.0710
TIME	3	14	29.67	<.0001
GENDER*TIME	3	14	1.48	0.2637

4. The primary tests for this model are found in the table titled "Type 3 Test of Fixed Effects." Because the AIC for the AR(1) model is lowest, we'll examine the results in that table, as shown in Table 13.12.

In this case, the results indicate that there is no interaction (GENDER*TIME, $p = 0.26$) effect. In the presence of no interaction, it is appropriate to examine the main effects tests for TIME and GENDER. For these results, there is a significant TIME ($p < 0.0001$) effect and a nonsignificant (but marginal) GENDER ($p = 0.071$) effect.

The other two models (unstructured and compound symmetry) report a significant GENDER effect (both $p < 0.05$). Thus, the structure selected can affect the outcome of the statistical tests.

Using the AR(1) results, we conclude that there is at most marginal evidence of a GENDER effect. There is (in all models) evidence to assume a significant TIME effect. To examine these results more closely, we'll look at plots of the means.

5. In the Editor window, open the program AREPEAT2.SAS. This is the same program used previously in this example with the addition of code that produces two graphs.

```
*------------------PRODUCE GRAPHS OF MEANS;
ODS HTML;
PROC SORT DATA=REPMIXED;BY GENDER TIME;
PROC MEANS noprint; BY GENDER TIME;
     OUTPUT OUT=FORPLOT MEAN=;
RUN;
PROC GPLOT;
```

```
PLOT OUTCOME*GENDER=TIME;
SYMBOL1 V=CIRCLE I=JOIN L=1 C=BLACK;
SYMBOL2 V=DOT I=JOIN L=2 C=BLUE;
SYMBOL3 V=STAR I=JOIN L=2 C=RED;
SYMBOL4 V=SQUARE I=JOIN L=2 C=GREEN;
RUN;

PROC SORT DATA=REPMIXED;BY TIME GENDER;
PROC MEANS noprint; BY TIME GENDER;
    OUTPUT OUT=FORPLOT MEAN=;
RUN;
PROC GPLOT;
PLOT OUTCOME*TIME=GENDER;
SYMBOL1 V=CIRCLE I=JOIN L=1 C=BLACK;
SYMBOL2 V=DOT I=JOIN L=2 C=BLUE;
RUN;
ODS HTML CLOSE;
```

This code calculates the means by GENDER and TIME (then TIME and GENDER) and plots the results. For more information about PROC GPLOT, see Chapter 14, Creating Graphs. Run the program and observe the plots, shown in Figure 13.7.

Although there (visually) appears to be a difference in means across GENDER, it is at most marginally significant (probably because of the small sample size). From the graph, observe that the mean at TIME3 is the highest and the mean at TIME2 is lowest.

6. To determine which TIMEs are significantly different, include the following option in the section of code related to the AR(1) covariance structure.

LSMEANS TIME/PDIFF;

This statement produces confidence limits on the differences in the (least square) means. Open and run the SAS program AREPEAT3.SAS. This program is similar to the original but includes only the AR(1) model (and the LSMEANS statement). Observe the results in Table 13.13. As we observed in Figure 13.7, the difference between TIME2 and TIME3 is the greatest difference ($p < 0.0001$) from the Pr >|t| column. Note also that there are significant differences between all other TIMEs except between TIME1 and TIME4 ($p = 0.17$).

(Continued)

FIGURE 13.7. *Plots for repeated measures analysis*

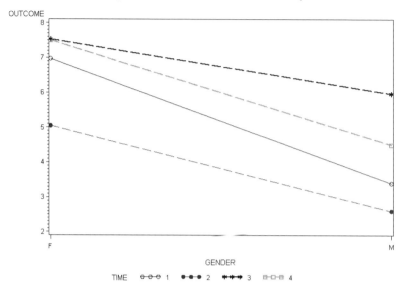

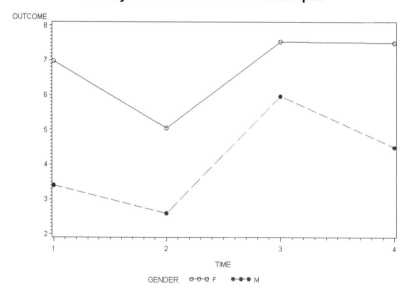

Performing a repeated measures analysis of variance with a grouping factor is an iterative procedure which requires that you determine which variance structure best fits the model. It is also advantageous to plot the means and, when there are more then two means in a significant factor, to compare means using the LSMEANS statement.

TABLE 13.13.   **Comparing pairwise times**

				Differences of Least Squares Means				
Effect	TIME	_TIME	Estimate	Standard Error	DF	t Value	Pr > |t|
TIME	1	2	1.3625	0.3507	14	3.89	0.0016
TIME	1	3	-1.7890	0.4879	14	-3.67	0.0025
TIME	1	4	-0.8125	0.5651	14	-1.44	0.1725
TIME	2	3	-3.1515	0.3638	14	-8.66	<.0001
TIME	2	4	-2.1750	0.4781	14	-4.55	0.0005
TIME	3	4	0.9765	0.3638	14	2.68	0.0178

SUMMARY

This chapter discussed the use of PROC GLM to perform analysis of covariance and two-factor ANOVA with fixed effects. We also introduced PROC MIXED and discussed its use on the two-factor mixed model and a repeated measures analysis with a grouping variable.

EXERCISES

13.1. Use multiple comparisons in PROC MIXED.

Another way to determine difference in means in a PROC MIXED model such as in AREPEAT3.SAS is to request multiple comparison tests using a statement such as

LSMEANS/ADJUST=TUKEY;

(you can optionally use BON, SCHEFFE or SIDAK as the comparison method). Replace the PDIFF command in AREPEAT3.SAS with one of these options and rerun the analysis.

13.2. **Use PROC MIXED with missing data.**

Notice that the analysis using PROC MIXED was able to handle a missing value in the data as well as unbalanced data (more females than males). To do this analysis in PROC GLM, use the program EX_13.2.SAS. Run this program and observe the interaction and main effects tests for GENDER and TIME in the Type III GLM results tables (P > F column.) Although the results are similar to those of PROC MIXED, note that one entire subject was eliminated from the analysis because it contained a missing value. The loss of subjects with missing values plus the fact that PROC GLM uses a less sophisticated calculation for random effects makes it desirable to use PROC MIXED.

CHAPTER

14

CREATING GRAPHS

LEARNING OBJECTIVES

- To be able to use SAS to create scatterplots and line graphs using GPLOT
- To be able to use SAS to create bar charts
- To be able to use SAS to create boxplots (box-and-whiskers plots)
- To be able to use ODS Graphics

SAS provides several procedures for creating graphs, which are an essential part of data analysis. In this chapter, graphs that are often used to complement the data analyses discussed in this book are illustrated by example. Some of these were discussed in previous chapters. This chapter provides more details and introduces graphs that have not been previously discussed.

In fact, SAS provides a number of other sophisticated techniques for creating a variety of graphs that are not discussed in this chapter. However, you should be able to take what you learn here and adapt it to other SAS graphs.

CREATING SCATTERPLOTS AND LINE GRAPHS USING GPLOT

PROC GPLOT is the basic routine used to obtain several types of graphs in SAS. This section illustrates how to create scatterplots and line graphs using PROC GPLOT, with an emphasis on creating graphs that are useful for data analysis. The abbreviated syntax for this procedure is:

```
PROC GPLOT <DATA=datasetname>; <PLOT plot-request(s)/
   option(s)>;
```

It is a good idea to include the following command to reset all SAS graphics options before you use PROC GPLOT or other SAS graph procedures:

```
GOPTIONS RESET=ALL;
```

Also, it is good practice to include a QUIT statement after a plot to tell the SAS program that the graph is complete. Otherwise you will notice a "Proc Gplot Running" warning in the Editor window, indicating that SAS is waiting for more information about the plot. Some of these options are illustrated in this chapter's Hands-on Examples.

Creating a Simple Scatterplot

The basic plot-request technique consists of indicating the variables used for the *x*-axis and *y*-axis in the statement

```
PLOT  y-axisvariable*x-axisvariable;
```

HANDS-ON
EXAMPLE

This example illustrates how to produce a simple scatterplot using PROC GPLOT.

1. In the Editor window, open the file AGRAPH1.SAS.

```
GOPTIONS RESET=ALL;
Title "Simple Scatterplot";
PROC GPLOT DATA="C:\SASDATA\CARS";
      PLOT HWYMPG*ENGINESIZE;
RUN;
QUIT;
```

This simple program requests a scatterplot of the variables HWYMPG (highway miles per gallon) by ENGINESIZE in the CARS data set.

2. Run the program and observe (in the Graph window) the results shown in Figure 14.1. This graph shows a decrease in MPG as engine size increases. Note that the variable names are displayed on the x- and y-axes and that the limits for each axis are selected by the program.

FIGURE 14.1. *Default scatterplot using PROC GPLOT*

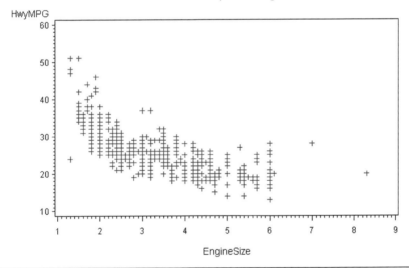

Managing Your SAS Graph

As mentioned previously, when you create a graph in SAS, the results are placed in the Graph window. Here are some handy tips for working in the Graph window.

Copy Graph: To copy the graph to the Clipboard so it can be pasted into Word, PowerPoint, or some other program, click on the graph and select Edit ⇒ Copy from the menu bar.

Export Graph: To export the graph to a standard graphics format file (such as JPG or TIF), click on the graph, select File ⇒ Export as Image, and select Files of Type according to the output type you need. Journals often want graphs in JPG or TIF formats for publication.

Edit Graph: SAS includes a simple editor you can use to include annotations to your graph. Click on the graph and select Edit ⇒ Edit Current Graph. For example, when editing a graph, select the "I-beam" icon, click within the graph where you want the annotation to appear, and enter text.

Print: Use the File ⇒ Print menu option to print a hard copy of the graph.

Enhancing a GPLOT Using the SYMBOL statement

Often, the purpose of displaying a scatterplot is to illustrate an association between two variables. You may also want to include a regression line through the scatter of points to emphasize the relationship, or you may want to use improvements to the plot that are also available. The following example shows how to use the SYMBOL statement to enhance your plot. This statement may appear before or within the PROC GPLOT statement. The abbreviated syntax for the SYMBOL statement is:

```
SYMBOL<1...255>
<COLOR=symbol-color>
<appearance-option(s)>
<INTERPOLATION=interpolation-option> ;
```

The symbol number indicates the plot to which the options will be applied. COLOR selects a color for the selected symbol options. INTERPOLATION indicates how to fit a curve through the scatter of points. Some commonly used appearance options (such as LINE or VALUE) for SYMBOL are:

COLOR= (or C=)

Indicates the color used for the dot in the plot. For example, C=BLUE causes the dots in the graph to be blue. Other common color options are RED, GREEN, and BLACK. See Appendix A for a more extensive list of available colors.

INTERPOLATION= (or I=)

Instructs SAS to include an interpolation curve in the plot. Several types of interpolation curves are available. A commonly used option is the **RL** or "regression, linear" fit. Other common options are:

RQ
    Quadratic regression

RC
    Cubic regression

STDk
    Standard error bars of length k* STDEV (add J = join at mean, B = Bars, T = tops on error bars). For example, STDkJ to join the bars.

STDM

Same as STDk but uses standard error of the mean

JOIN

Joins dots

BOXT

Display boxplots with tops on the whiskers

LINE= (or L=)

Indicates the pattern of the line drawn in the graph. For example, 1 is a solid line, 2 is small dots, 3 is larger dots, and so on. See Appendix A for other options.

VALUE= (or V=)

Indicates the symbol to be used for the dots on the plot. For example, V=STAR uses a star instead of the default character (+). Some commonly used symbols are square, star, circle, plus, and dot. See Appendix A for other options.

HANDS-ON
EXAMPLE

This example illustrates how to change the style of a plot's points and regression line.

1. In the Editor window, open the file AGRAPH2.SAS.

```
GOPTIONS RESET=ALL;
Title "Simple Scatterplot, Change symbol";
PROC GPLOT DATA="C:\SASDATA\CARS";
     PLOT HWYMPG*CITYMPG;
     SYMBOL1 V=STAR I=RL C=BLUE L=2;
RUN;
QUIT;
```

2. Run this program and observe the output, shown in Figure 14.2.

   Notice on your screen that the following items are specified for this plot:

   ■ The dot color is blue (C=BLUE).

   ■ The displayed symbol is a star (V=STAR).

(Continued)

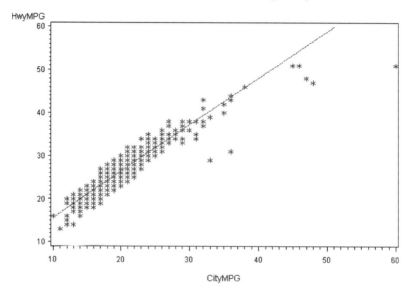

FIGURE 14.2. *PROC GPLOT with dots and line Specified*

■ A linear regression line is displayed (I=RL).

■ The displayed line is dotted (L=2).

3. Change the C, V, and L options and re-run the plot to observe how changing these options modifies the plot.

Customizing Axes in a Plot

If you are preparing a plot for use in a project presentation or publication, you may
want to change the characteristics of the plot axes. The following Hands-on Example
illustrates some of the basic techniques. The AXIS statement follows the syntax

```
AXIS<1...99><options>;
```

Common options used for the AXIS statement include the following and are illustrated in the Hands-on Example.

COLOR= (or C=)
Indicates the color used for the axis in the plot. For example, C=BLUE causes the axis to be blue. Other common color options are RED, GREEN, and BLACK. See Appendix A for a comprehensive list of available colors.

LABEL=(*text-arguments*)
Modifies an axis label. The text arguments define specific parts of the label's appearance. These include angle, color, font, justification, and rotation angle (A=), where A=90 means to display the label at a 90 degree angle (vertical).

OFFSET =(<n1><,n2>)<units >
Specifies the distance from the first and last major tick marks or bars to the ends of the axis line.

ORDER=(*value-list*)
Specifies the order of the values on the axis. For example, ORDER=(1 to 100 by 5) specifies that the axis will contain the numbers 1 to 100 with axis label increments of 5.

VALUE=(*options*)
Specifies the height of text (among other items)—for example, VALUE=(H=4).

WIDTH=*thickness-factor*
Specifies width of the axis (affects the width of the entire frame unless a NOFRAME option is used as defined below).

The AXIS statement is used in conjunction with an axis option in the PLOT statement. The syntax is

PLOT yaxis*xax is </options>;

Some common AXIS options used for the PLOT statement include the following and are illustrated in the Hands-on Example that follows.

HAXIS=AXIS*k*
Indicates which AXIS*k* definition to apply to the horizontal axis. For example, HAXIS=AXIS1indicates that the AXIS1 definition is to be applied.

VAXIS=AXIS*k*
Indicates which AXIS*k* definition to apply to the vertical axis. For example, VAXIS=AXIS2 indicates that the AXIS2 definition is to be applied.

NOFRAME
Suppresses the default frame around the graph.

HANDS-ON EXAMPLE

This example illustrates how to format axes using PROC GPLOT.

1. In the Editor window, open the program AGRAPH2A.SAS.

```
GOPTIONS RESET=ALL;
AXIS1 C=RED ORDER=(0 TO 80 BY 5)
      LABEL=('City Miles Per Gallon' FONT=SWISS)
        OFFSET=(5) WIDTH=2 VALUE=(H=2);
AXIS2 C=GREEN ORDER=(0 TO 80 BY 5)
      LABEL=(A=90 'Highway Miles Per Gallon' FONT=SWISS)
        OFFSET=(5) WIDTH=4 VALUE=(H=1);
TITLE "Enhanced Scatterplot";
ODS HTML;
PROC GPLOT DATA="C:\SASDATA\CARS";
      PLOT HWYMPG*CITYMPG/HAXIS=AXIS1 VAXIS=AXIS2 NOFRAME;
        SYMBOL1 V=DOT I=RL C=PURPLE L=2;
RUN;
ODS HTML CLOSE;
QUIT;
```

   This program obviously will create a plot with unappealing colors, but it illustrates the possibilities. Notice that there are two axis definitions (AXIS1 and AXIS2) and that these axis definitions are applied in the PLOT statement where VAXIS=AXIS2 and HAXIS=AXIS1.

2. Run the program and observe the output as shown in Figure 14.3.

   Because of the NOFRAME option, there is no frame around the entire plot (the frame is the default border that surrounds the plot as in Figure 14.2), but the colors of the axes are defined in the AXIS statements.

3. Clean up this plot by doing the following:

   a. Remove the definition for AXIS color in the AXIS1 and AXIS2 statements.

   b. Remove the NOFRAME option.

   c. Change the COLOR for the dots to GRAY.

   d. Change the LINE style (L=) to 5 (long dashes).

   e. Change the OFFSET to 2.

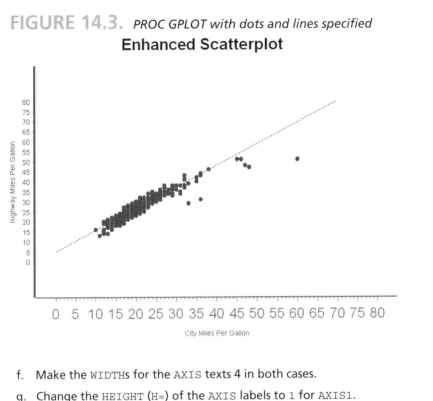

FIGURE 14.3. *PROC GPLOT with dots and lines specified*

f. Make the WIDTHs for the AXIS texts 4 in both cases.

g. Change the HEIGHT (H=) of the AXIS labels to 1 for AXIS1.

Re-run the program and observe the changes in the graph.

Displaying Error Bars in GPLOT

For some data presentations it is helpful to display data by groups with error bars on the graph to indicate the variability of data within a group. Displaying error bars (and other types of bars) is accomplished with the I= statement. For example:

INTERPOLATION= (or I=)

To employ this option to display error bars, use one of the following techniques:

■ I=STD1JT means include error bars that are 1 standard deviation (STD1) and that are joined (J) at the means with tops (T) on each bar. STD also supports values of 2 and 3.

■ I=BOXT means include boxplots with tops (T) on each whisker.

HANDS-ON
EXAMPLE

In this example you will create a graph that plots means and error bars.

FIGURE 14.4. *PROC GPLOT showing error bars*

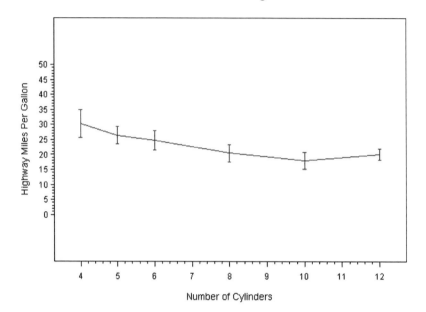

1. In the Editor window, open the program `AGRAPH3.SAS`.

```
GOPTIONS RESET=ALL;
AXIS1 ORDER=(4 TO 12 BY 1)
      LABEL=('Number of Cylinders' FONT=SWISS HEIGHT=4)
       OFFSET=(5);
AXIS2 ORDER=(0 TO 50 BY 5)
        LABEL=(A=90 'Highway Miles Per Gallon' FONT=SWISS
              HEIGHT=4)
        OFFSET=(5);
ODS HTML;
PROC GPLOT DATA="C:\SASDATA\CARS";
     PLOT HWYMPG*CYLINDERS/HAXIS=AXIS1 VAXIS=AXIS2;
```

```
          SYMBOL1 I=STD1JT H=1 LINE=1 VALUE=NONE;
  RUN;
  ODS HTML CLOSE;
  QUIT;
```

This plot is for highway miles per gallon (HWYMPG) by the number of CYLINDERs in the car's motor. Notice that the I=STD1JT interpolation option in the SYMBOL1 statement requests 1 standard deviation error bars. The VALUE=NONE option suppresses the graph of individual points. The AXIS1 statement requests that the *x*-axis contain only the values from 4 to 12 because that is the number of CYLINDERs in the data set.

2. Run the program and observe the output in Figure 14.4.

3. Change the interpolation option to request boxplots with tops on the ends of the whiskers:

   ```
   I=BOXT
   ```

   Run the revised program and observe the output.

There are several other methods for customizing a SAS GPLOT. Refer to Appendix A and the SAS documentation for additional options.

CREATING BAR CHARTS AND PIE CHARTS

You can produce bar and pie charts to display counts or percentages for frequency data. These charts are created with the SAS GCHART procedure. The abbreviated syntax is:

```
PROC GCHART<DATA=input-data-set>
HBAR|HBAR3D|VBAR|VBAR3D chart-variable(s) </
option(s)>;
PIE|PIE3D|DONUT chart-variable(s) </ option(s)>;
```

Chart-type specifications such as HBAR and VBAR refer to horizontal and vertical bar charts, pie charts, and three-dimensional (3D) versions of the charts. A first simple example of PROC GCHART is a horizontal bar chart (HBAR), shown in the following Hands-On Example.

HANDS-ON EXAMPLE

This example illustrates how to create a horizontal bar chart.

1. In the Editor window, open the file AGRAPH4.SAS.

```
GOPTIONS RESET=ALL;
Title "Horizontal Bar Chart";
ODS HTML;
PROC GCHART DATA="C:\SASDATA\SOMEDATA";
HBAR STATUS/DISCRETE;
RUN;
ODS HTML CLOSE;
QUIT;
```

This code requests a horizontal bar chart on the variable STATUS. The /DISCRETE option tells SAS that the numeric values for the STATUS variable should be treated as discrete values. Otherwise, SAS may assume that the numeric values are a range and create a barchart using midpoints instead of the actual values.

2. Run the program and observe the output in Figure 14.5. Note on your screen that blue is the default bar color.

3. Change HBAR to VBAR and re-run the program. Observe the output.

FIGURE 14.5. *Horizontal bar chart using PROC GCHART*

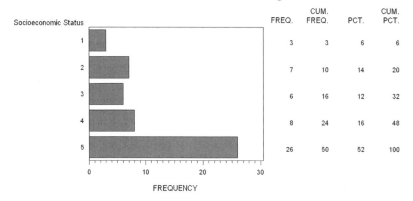

4. Change VBAR to PIE and re-run the program. Observe the output. Experiment with HBAR3D and PIE3D.

5. Include a PATTERN and COLOR statement to change the look of the graph. For example:

```
HBAR STATUS;
PATTERN1 VALUE=R1 COLOR=GREEN;
```

PATTERN and COLOR choices are described in Appendix A. Run the revised program and observe the output.

In the next Hands-on Example, we create a bar chart using two grouping variables. This is accomplished with a /GROUP option as illustrated here:

```
VBAR INJTYPE/GROUP=GENDER;
```

HANDS-ON EXAMPLE

This example illustrates how to modify axes in a bar chart.

1. In the Editor window, open the program AGRAPH5.SAS.

```
GOPTIONS RESET=ALL;
AXIS1 LABEL=NONE VALUE=(H=1.2);
AXIS2 LABEL=(A=90 "Count");
TITLE "Vertical Bar Chart";
ODS HTML;
PROC GCHART DATA="C:\SASDATA\SOMEDATA";
VBAR GENDER/GROUP=GP MAXIS=AXIS1 AXIS=AXIS2;
PATTERN1 VALUE=R1 COLOR=GREEN;
RUN;
ODS HTML CLOSE;
QUIT;
```

(Continued)

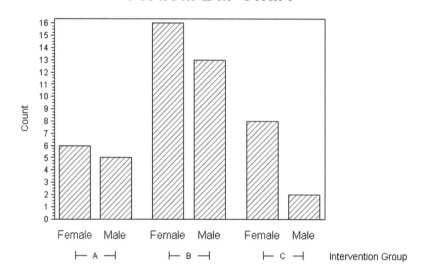

FIGURE 14.6. *PROC GCHART showing groups bars*

Note that AXIS= controls the frequency (vertical) axis for GCHART and MAXIS= controls the appearance of the midpoint (horizontal) axis.

2. Run the program and observe the output in Figure 14.6. This type of plot can be used to display cross-tabulation analyses.

3. The visual impact of this graph might be more dramatic if the Female and Male bars were in different colors. To accomplish this, use a SUBGROUP=GENDER command and define the second bar color using a PATTERN2 statement. In the Editor window, open the file AGRAPH6.SAS.

```
GOPTIONS RESET=ALL;
TITLE 'Bar Chart by Group with different bar colors';
ODS HTML;
PROC GCHART DATA="C:\SASDATA\SOMEDATA";
VBAR GENDER/GROUP=GP SUBGROUP=GENDER;
PATTERN1 VALUE=R1 COLOR=RED;
PATTERN2 VALUE=R1 COLOR=BLUE;
RUN;
ODS HTML CLOSE;
QUIT;
```

Notice the added SUBGROUP= statement. This tells SAS to color the bars for each subgroup using a different color. The PATTERN2 statement specifies the color for males because the patterns are assigned by alphabetical order.

4. Run the program and observe the output. Notice that the bars for each GENDER are now in different colors. The PATTERN remains the same because of the VALUE=R1 specification in both PATTERN statements.

5. Change the statement in PATTERN1 to VALUE=X4 and re-run the program to see how that change alters the output.

6. Change VBAR to VBAR3D. Notice that the colors for the bars remain, but the PATTERN option no longer has any effect.

If you want the bars to appear in an order other than alphabetical, you can create a format for the variable and apply that format to the variable for the PROC GCHART statement.

CREATING STACKED BAR CHARTS

Another often-used type of bar chart is a stacked bar chart. The change in the PROC GCHART code is that you do not use the GROUP option. This is illustrated in the following Hands-on Example.

HANDS-ON
EXAMPLE

This example illustrates how to create stacked bar charts using PROC GCHART.

1. In the Editor window, open the file AGRAPH7.SAS.
```
GOPTIONS RESET=ALL;
PATTERN1 V=R1 C=RED; * FOR BUS;
PATTERN2 V=R2 C=BLUE; * FOR CAR;
PATTERN3 V=R3 C=BLACK; * FOR WALK;
```

(Continued)

```
TITLE C=RED 'Stacked Bars, Method of Arrival';
ODS HTML;
PROC GCHART DATA="C:\SASDATA\SURVEY";
     VBAR GENDER / SUBGROUP=ARRIVE;
RUN;
ODS HTML CLOSE;
QUIT;
```

Notice that this plot is set up a little differently from previous GCHART examples, in that the PATTERN statement occurs before the PROC GCHART statement. The PATTERNs are set up for the three arrival types that will be graphed: Bus, Car, and Walk.

2. Run this program and observe the output in Figure 14.7.

FIGURE 14.7 *Stacked bar chart*

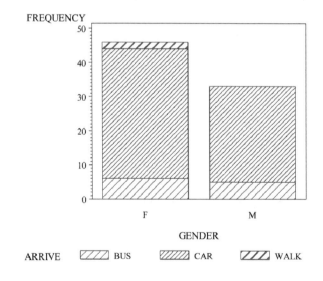

3. Change the SUBGROUP=ARRIVE statement to GROUP=ARRIVE. Re-run the program and observe the difference.

4. Suppose that for a publication that doesn't print in more than one color, you want the bars to be in different shades of gray. Change the PATTERN and V statements to read as follows:

```
PATTERN1 V=S C=GRAYAA; * FOR BUS(Dark Gray);
PATTERN2 V=S C=GRAYCC; * FOR CAR (Medium Gray);
PATTERN3 V=S C=GRAYEE; * FOR WALK (Light GRAY);
```

V=S indicates solid, and the various shades of gray are given as GRAYAA, GRAYCC, and so on to GRAYFF, which is white.

There are many options for customizing these plots, only a few of which have been discussed here. Several of the options (for example, AXIS and LEGEND) are similar to those used in PROC GPLOT.

CREATING MEAN BARS USING GCHART

An often-used analysis graphic is one that displays means as bars with error bars around the mean indicating a level of variability. PROC GCHART can produce this graph with a little help. The following Hands-on Example shows how this is accomplished.

HANDS-ON
EXAMPLE

In this example you will produce a bar chart with error bars representing means by group.

1. In the Editor window, open the file AGRAPH8.SAS.

```
%LET SS=50; *SAMPLE SIZE;
%LET CE=1; * PLOT ONE STANDARD ERROR;
DATA _NULL_;                                    (Continued)
```

```
   C=&CE;
   N=&SS;
   LEVEL=100 * (1 - 2 * (1 - PROBT(C,N-1)));
   CALL SYMPUT('LEVEL', PUT(LEVEL,BEST12.));
RUN;
GOPTIONS RESET=ALL;
PATTERN1 VALUE=SOLID C=LIGHTBLUE;
TITLE "MEANS WITH ERROR BARS";
PROC GCHART DATA='C:\SASDATA\SOMEDATA';
   VBAR GP/ WIDTH=15
            TYPE=MEAN
            SUMVAR=TIME1
            ERRORBAR=BOTH CLM=&LEVEL CERROR=RED;
RUN;
ODS HTML CLOSE;
QUIT;
```

Notice the %LET statements at the beginning of the program. These are macro (%LET) variables used to define two numbers needed for this program to calculate the appropriate error bars for the graph. SS is the sample size and CE is the size of the interval (1 means one standard error).

The DATA _NULL_ section is a specialized data set (_NULL_ allows you to perform calculations but does not create a data set) used here to define the value of the variable LEVEL, which is calculated using the PROBT function (Student's *t*-test probability function).

The CALL SYMPUT statement is a SAS language function that assigns a value produced in a DATA step to a macro variable. Thus, the macro variable &LEVEL created by the SYMPUT statement is later used in CLM=&LEVEL, which specified the value for the Confidence Limits on the Mean (CLM). (See Appendix B, "SAS Function Reference," for more about the SYMPUT function.)

Patterns and colors are discussed in Appendix A. The WIDTH statement sets the width of the bars. The TYPE statement indicates the statistics on which the height of the bars will be based. The ERRORBAR=BOTH statement indicates that the error bars will include a top and bottom. Run this program and observe the output, as shown in Figure 14.8.

2. Change the error bars to two standard errors by changing the value of CE. Also change the width of the bars to 20, and the color of the bars (C=). Re-run the program and observe the changes. Because CE is larger, you should see that the bars are longer.

FIGURE 14.8. *Means with error bars*

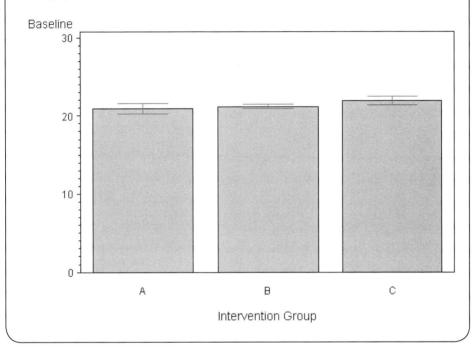

CREATING BOXPLOTS

Examples in previous chapters have illustrated a simple use of PROC BOXPLOT to create boxplots. This section provides information on methods for creating and enhancing the boxplots. The abbreviated syntax for this procedure is:

```
PROC BOXPLOT <DATA=datasetname>; <options>;
             PLOT analysis-variable*group-
             variable < (block-variables )>
             < =symbol-variable > < /
             options > ;
```

Creating a Simple Boxplot

The basic plot request consists of indicating the variables used for the analysis and grouping in the statement:

```
PLOT analysisvariable*groupingvariable;
```

HANDS-ON
EXAMPLE

This example illustrates a simple use of `PROC BOXPLOT`.

1. In the Editor window, open the file `AGRAPH9.SAS`.

```
GOPTIONS RESET=ALL;
ODS HTML;
Title "Simple Box Plot";
* You must sort the data on the grouping variable;
PROC SORT DATA="C:\SASDATA\CARS"
     OUT=CARDATA;BY CYLINDERS;
PROC BOXPLOT DATA=CARDATA;
     PLOT HWYMPG*CYLINDERS;
     WHERE CYLINDERS GT 1;
RUN;
ODS HTML CLOSE;
```

Notice that when creating side-by-side boxplots, you must sort the data on the grouping variable before running the `PROC BOXPLOT` procedure. Also note that the `WHERE` statement is necessary because one car (the Mazda RX-8) is listed as -1 cylinders as it uses a rotary engine. You could have also recoded the -1 as a missing value to obtain the same result.

2. Run this program and observe the output in Figure 14.9.

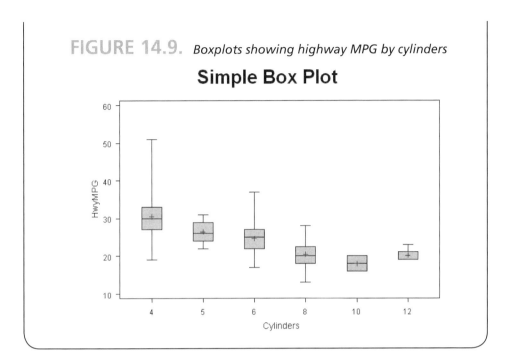

FIGURE 14.9. *Boxplots showing highway MPG by cylinders*

There are a number of options for the PLOT statement within PROC BOXPLOT, a few of which are illustrated in the following Hands-on Example.

HANDS-ON
EXAMPLE

This example illustrates how to change the appearance of the boxplot and modify the default colors used in the plot.

1. In the Editor window, open the program AGRAPH10.SAS.

```
GOPTIONS RESET=ALL;
ODS HTML;
Title "Simple Box Plot";
* You must sort the data on the grouping variable;
PROC SORT DATA="C:\SASDATA\CARS"
     OUT=CARDATA;BY CYLINDERS;
PROC BOXPLOT DATA=CARDATA;
     PLOT HWYMPG*CYLINDERS/
```

(Continued)

```
                    CBOXFILL=VLIGB
                  CBOXES=BLACK
                  BOXSTYLE=SCHEMATIC
                  NOTCHES;
              WHERE CYLINDERS GT 1;
      RUN;
      ODS HTML CLOSE;
      QUIT;
```

CBOXFILL and CBOXES specify the fill color and outline color of the boxes, respectively. BOXSTYLE requests the SCHEMATIC style plot, which specifies the type of outliers displayed in the plot.

2. Run the program and observe the output in Figure 14.10.

Notice that potential outliers are marked at the top of two of the boxplots. The SCHEMATIC option defines outliers as those values greater than the absolute value of 1.5*(InterquartilebRange) from the top or bottom of the box.

FIGURE 14.10. *Boxplots with enhancements*

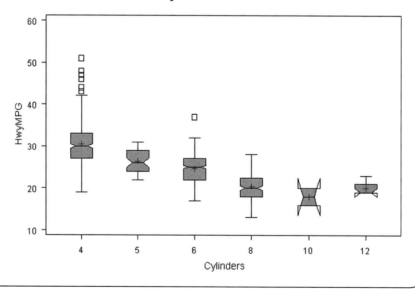

GOING DEEPER: ODS GRAPHICS

A few examples of the Output Delivery System (ODS) GRAPHICS were presented in previous chapters. This section provides additional information about how to use this option. To use ODS GRAPHICS, you must first turn on an output stream to an ODS output that supports graphics. These include HTML, PDF, RTF, LaTeX, PCL, and PS. ODS graphics are requested for a particular procedure by defining the ODS output stream and then "turning on" the graphics option with the statement

```
ODS HTML;
ODS GRAPHICS ON;
```

Once graphics have been turned on, run the SAS procedure, then turn off the graphics (and the ODS output stream) using these statements:

```
ODS GRAPHICS OFF;
ODS HTML CLOSE;
```

The following SAS procedures discussed in this book that support ODS graphics include:

■ PROC TTEST (Chapter 8)

■ PROC CORR (Chapter 10)

■ PROC ANOVA (Chapter 9)

■ PROC GLM (Chapters 9 and 13)

■ PROC LOGISTIC (Chapter 12)

■ PROC REG (Chapter 10)

ODS graphics are also supported by a number of other SAS procedures not mentioned in this book.

We recommend using ODS GRAPHICS ON/ODS GRAPHICS OFF to see what type of graphics output SAS provides with a procedure because new graphics types are routinely introduced in new versions of SAS.

ODS Graphics for PROC ANOVA and PROC GLM

ODS graphics output for the PROC ANOVA procedure includes a boxplot similar to the one previously described using PROC BOXPLOT. The difference is that with ODS the colors and style are usually of a higher quality than those created with the default PROC BOXPLOT options. (Using SAS graphics programming options, you can create a highly refined plot without using ODS.)

HANDS-ON
EXAMPLE

This example illustrates how to use ODS to create comparative box plots for an independent group ANOVA.

1. In the Editor window, open the program AGRAPH11.SAS.

```
GOPTIONS RESET=ALL;
Title "Output Box plot using ODS Graphics";
ODS HTML;
ODS GRAPHICS ON;
PROC ANOVA DATA="C:\SASDATA\CARS";
    CLASS CYLINDERS;
     MODEL HWYMPG=CYLINDERS;
     WHERE CYLINDERS GT 1;
RUN;
ODS GRAPHICS OFF;
ODS HTML CLOSE;
```

Notice that ODS output is opened for HTML followed by the ODS GRAPHICS ON command. The graphics and ODS output are turned off at the end of the program. Results appear in the Results Viewer.

2. Run the program and observe the output in Figure 14.11.

FIGURE 14.11. *Graphics output from ODS*

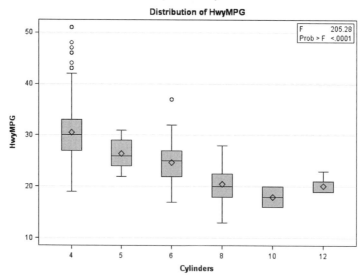

When you use PROC GLM instead of PROC ANOVA, all of the other syntax in the example and the ODS GRAPHICS output are the same. However, more complicated models can be defined in PROC GLM, which, depending on the model described, can create additional ODS GRAPHICS not described here.

ODS GRAPHICS for PROC CORR

For the PROC CORR procedure, there are two options for ODS GRAPHIC. They are

```
PLOTS=SCATTER
PLOTS=MATRIX
```

The PLOT=MATRIX statement is optional in SAS version 9.2 but required in previous versions to display the matrix of scatterplots. In Chapter 10 we showed an example using PROC CORR to create a scatterplot matrix using ODS. The following Hands-on Example illustrates ODS GRAPHICS with the PLOTS=SCATTER option.

HANDS-ON
EXAMPLE

This example illustrates ODS GRAPHICS options for PROC CORR.

1. In the Editor window, open the program AGRAPH12.SAS.

   ```
   GOPTIONS RESET=ALL;
   ODS HTML;
   ODS GRAPHICS ON;
   TITLE "ODS Scatterplot in PROC CORR";
   PROC CORR DATA="C:\SASDATA\CARS" PLOTS=SCATTER;
       VAR HWYMPG CITYMPG ENGINESIZE;
   RUN;
   ODS GRAPHICS OFF;
   ODS HTML CLOSE;
   ```

   Notice the PLOTS=SCATTER option in the PROC CORR statement.

2. Run the program and observe the output. One of the graphs in the output is shown in Figure 14.12. The output includes scatterplots for all pairs of variables in the VAR statement. Each scatterplot includes a 95 percent prediction ellipse, which marks a region that indicates with 95 percent confidence where a new observation might occur.

   (Continued)

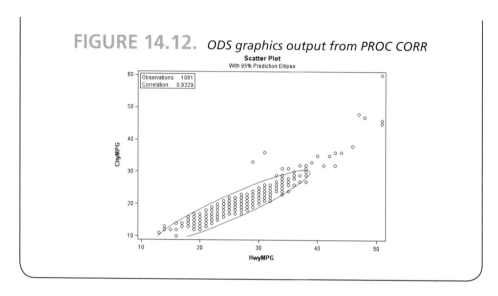

FIGURE 14.12. *ODS graphics output from PROC CORR*

SUMMARY

This chapter described a small portion of the graphical options available in SAS. However, the discussion of graphs in this chapter (and elsewhere in the book) covered many of the commonly used graphs in data analysis. Certain fields of study may have specialty graphs that are used for analysis, but many of them will use the same ingredients as were discussed here.

EXERCISES

14.1. Graph a comparison of means.

   Using the data in the file ANNOVA1.SAS and the example illustrated by AGRAPH8.SAS, create a graph that displays means as bars, and standard error markers.

14.2. Display comparative box plots.

   Using AGRAPH9.SAS as a guide, create a plot of comparative box plots by CYLINDERS (where CYLINDERS > 1) for CITYMPG in the CARS data set.

```
GOPTIONS RESET=ALL;
ODS HTML;
PROC SORT DATA="C:\SASDATA\CARS" OUT=MPGFILE;
     BY _____ ;
PROC _____ DATA=MPGFILE;
     PLOT _____*CYLINDERS;
     WHERE CYLINDERS GT _____ ;
RUN;
ODS HTML CLOSE;
QUIT;
```

CHAPTER

15

CONTROLLING OUTPUT USING ODS

LEARNING OBJECTIVES

- To be able to specify ODS output format and destination
- To be able to specify ODS style
- To be able to use ODS graphics from SAS procedures
- To be able to select specific tables for output
- To be able to enhance graphics using ODS and to create hyperlinks
- To be able to capture information from ODS tables

ODS, or Output Delivery System, is a method for controlling the output from SAS procedures. ODS began with version 8 and continues with added enhancements in versions 9.1 and 9.2. Throughout this book, our examples have illustrated how to use ODS graphics output. This topic was also discussed in Chapter 14, "Creating Graphs." The current chapter illustrates additional features of ODS that can help you send output for reports, graphs, and SAS data sets to a variety of output formats.

There are many more features of ODS than those discussed here. If you want to learn more about this topic, refer to the SAS documentation.

SPECIFYING THE ODS OUTPUT FORMAT AND DESTINATION

The SAS Output Delivery System is set up so that you "turn on" or initiate output into a designated output format. Once the output format has been initiated, SAS procedures send information to that output format. You can send output from one or more procedures to the output stream. Following the procedures for which you want the ODS output, you "turn off" or end the output. To initiate output using ODS, use the statement

```
ODS OUTPUT-FORMAT <OPTIONS>;
```

To end the ODS output, use the statement

```
ODS OUTPUT-FORMAT CLOSE;
```

Here are several output formats and options:

```
ODS LISTING
ODS HTML FILE=' HTML-FILE-PATHNAME.HTML ';
ODS PDF FILE=' PDF-FILE-PATHNAME.PDF ';
ODS RTF FILE=' RTF-FILE-PATHNAME.RTF ';
ODS PS FILE=' PS-FILE-PATHNAME.PS ';
ODS PLC FILE=' PCL-FILE-PATHNAME.PCL ';
```

Note that most of the output formats specify a filename with a FILE= option, and the HTML format uses either a FILE= or BODY= option. (The BODY= option is used when you are creating frames for Web pages—a topic not discussed in this book.) These output formats are described more fully as:

LISTING: The standard /default SAS Output window format.

HTML: HyperText Markup Language (HTML) is the standard format for displaying Web pages on the Internet and is also recognized by most word processors such as Microsoft Word. It is used for many of the examples in this book because it is the simplest to use and the output can be almost universally read.

PDF: Portable Document Format (PDF) is widely used to distribute documents by e-mail or via Internet downloads. Use of a PDF document requires that the (free) Adobe Reader or a similar program be installed on your computer. One of the benefits of the PDF format is that the contents of your document will appear the same when viewed under many types of computer operating systems, such as Windows, Mac OS X, and UNIX and its Linux derivations.

RTF: Rich Text Format (RTF) is a common language for word processors. When you capture information in this format it can be opened and edited by most word processors such as Microsoft Word or even Wordpad.

PS: Postscript (PS) is a printer language, and output captured in this format is usually designed to be printed on a Postscript printer.

PCL: Print Command Language (PCL) is a printer language, and output captured in this format is usually designed to be printed on a PCL printer.

Other specialty output formats are DOCUMENT, MARKUP, and WML (Wireless Markup Language).

The file names following the ODS output format are optional, but SAS may prompt you for a file name if it is omitted. Note that when you specify a file name in Windows, it must include the correct extension if Windows is to recognize the output file type. For example, to send data to a PDF file, you could use the syntax:

```
ODS PDF file='WINDOWS-PATH\Filename.PDF';
```

or, as a specific example:

```
ODS PDF FILE='C:\SASDATA\MYOUTPUT.PDF';
```

If you leave off the destination, as in

```
ODS PDF;
...some procedures
ODS CLOSE PDF;
```

SAS will send the output to the SAS Results Viewer window without prompting you for a file name. For output formats such as PDF and RTF, if you do not indicate a file name, you will be prompted to enter one (or you may choose to have the results go into the SAS Results Viewer). When you use the HTML output format, you are not prompted for a file name.

It is good programming practice to close standard output before using another ODS format. The following code closes the standard output listing before another ODS output format is initiated:

```
ODS LISTING CLOSE;
ODS HTML;
...some procedures
ODS CLOSE HTML;
ODS LISTING;
```

It is also a good idea to turn the LISTING (the standard SAS output) back on (`ODS LISTING`) after using another ODS output format, because if you do not, and later you create SAS output, it has no specified destination and may not appear in the Output window for the current SAS session.

SPECIFYING ODS OUTPUT STYLE

When you output information to a SAS ODS format, the tables, graphs, and text are defined with default colors and fonts. You can select from several built-in ODS styles. Each style is based on some theme or a format appropriate for a specific purpose. For example, the JOURNAL style formats your output in black and white that is appropriate for inclusion in a journal article. The option to specify a style is

```
STYLE=styletype;
```

This option appears in the ODS statement. For example:

```
ODS RTF STYLE=JOURNAL;
...some procedures
ODS RTF CLOSE;
```

To see a listing of the available SAS styles, use the code:

```
PROC TEMPLATE; LIST STYLES; RUN;
```

The default style is Styles.Default. The SAS format styles for version 9.2 as displayed in the output table generated by PROC TEMPLATE are shown in Table 15.1.

TABLE 15.1. ODS output styles

Obs	Path	Type			
1	Styles	Dir			
2	Styles.Analysis	Style	28	Styles.Money	Style
3	Styles.Astronomy	Style	29	Styles.NoFontDefault	Style
4	Styles.Banker	Style	30	Styles.Normal	Style
5	Styles.BarrettsBlue	Style	31	Styles.NormalPrinter	Style
6	Styles.Beige	Style	32	Styles.Ocean	Style
7	Styles.Brick	Style	33	Styles.Printer	Style
8	Styles.Brown	Style	34	Styles.Rsvp	Style

9	Styles.Curve	Style	35	Styles.Rtf	Style
10	Styles.D3d	Style	36	Styles.Sasweb	Style
11	Styles.Default	Style	37	Styles.Science	Style
12	Styles.EGDefault	Style	38	Styles.Seaside	Style
13	Styles.Education	Style	39	Styles.SeasidePrinter	Style
14	Styles.Electronics	Style	40	Styles.Sketch	Style
15	Styles.Festival	Style	41	Styles.Solutions	Style
16	Styles.FestivalPrinter	Style	42	Styles.Statdoc	Style
17	Styles.Gears	Style	43	Styles.Statistical	Style
18	Styles.Harvest	Style	44	Styles.Theme	Style
19	Styles.HighContrast	Style	45	Styles.Torn	Style
20	Styles.Journal	Style	46	Styles.Watercolor	Style
21	Styles.Journal2	Style	47	Styles.blockPrint	Style
22	Styles.Journal3	Style	48	Styles.fancyPrinter	Style
23	Styles.Listing	Style	49	Styles.grayscalePrinter	Style
24	Styles.Magnify	Style	50	Styles.monochromePrinter	Style
25	Styles.Meadow	Style	51	Styles.sansPrinter	Style
26	Styles.MeadowPrinter	Style	52	Styles.sasdocPrinter	Style
27	Styles.Minimal	Style	53	Styles.serifPrinter	Style

HANDS-ON
EXAMPLE

This example illustrates outputting information to a specific HTML file.

1. In the Editor window, open the file ODS2.SAS.

```
DATA TEST; SET "C:\SASDATA\SOMEDATA";
* DEFINE WHERE HTML LISTING WILL GO;
ODS HTML FILE='C:\SASDATA\ODS.HTML';
* CLOSE THE NORMAL OUTPUT LISTING;
ODS LISTING CLOSE;
PROC MEANS MAXDEC=2; VAR AGE TIME1-TIME4;
TITLE 'ODS HTML Example';
RUN;
* CLOSE THE HTML OUTPUT;
ODS HTML CLOSE;
* REOPEN THE NORMAL LISTING;
ODS LISTING;
RUN;
```

As defined above, the ODS HTML FILE= statement specifies the file name where the HTML output is stored on disk.

2. Run the program. Observe the HTML output in the Results Viewer.

3. Open Internet Explorer or another browser, select File ⇒ Open, and open the file C:\SASDATA\ODS.HTML. Notice that the SAS output has been saved locally in HTML format, viewable in a Web browser. (It could also be uploaded to a remote server and made available on the Internet. And it can also be opened in most word processors, including Micosoft Word, that "understand" the HTML language.)

4. Either in the SAS Results Viewer or in a Web browser, observe the output in Table 15.2. Notice (on screen) that the table has a light blue background.

5. Close the Results Viewer, return to the Editor window, and add a STYLE option to the ODS statement:

```
ODS HTML FILE='C:\SASDATA\ODS.HTML' STYLE=JOURNAL;
```

6. Re-run the program and observe the output. Notice that the new program produces output based on this black-and white "journal" style. See Table 15.3.

7. Change the ODS statement to

```
ODS PDF FILE='C:\SAS_ODS\ODS.PDF' STYLE=STATISTICAL;
```

TABLE 15.2. **HTML output using SAS ODS**

ODS HTML Example

The MEANS Procedure

Variable	Label	N	Mean	Std Dev	Minimum	Maximum
AGE	Age on Jan 1, 2000	50	10.46	2.43	4.00	15.00
TIME1	Baseline	50	21.27	1.72	17.00	24.20
TIME2	6 Months	50	27.44	2.66	21.30	32.30
TIME3	12 Months	50	30.49	3.03	22.70	35.90
TIME4	24 Months	50	30.84	3.53	21.20	36.10

TABLE 15.3. **ODS HTML output using JOURNAL style**

The MEANS Procedure

Variable	Label	N	Mean	Std Dev	Minimum	Maximum
AGE	Age on Jan 1, 2000	50	10.46	2.43	4.00	15.00
TIME1	Baseline	50	21.27	1.72	17.00	24.20
TIME2	6 Months	50	27.44	2.66	21.30	32.30
TIME3	12 Months	50	30.49	3.03	22.70	35.90
TIME4	24 Months	50	30.84	3.53	21.20	36.10

TABLE 15.4. **Output in PDF format with the statistical style**

The MEANS Procedure

Variable	Label	N	Mean	Std Dev	Minimum	Maximum
AGE	Age on Jan 1, 2000	50	10.46	2.43	4.00	15.00
TIME1	Baseline	50	21.27	1.72	17.00	24.20
TIME2	6 Months	50	27.44	2.66	21.30	32.30
TIME3	12 Months	50	30.49	3.03	22.70	35.90
TIME4	24 Months	50	30.84	3.53	21.20	36.10

Change the closing ODS statement to

```
ODS PDF CLOSE;
```

Also change the `TITLE` statement to reflect PDF output and re-run the program. Verify that the output file is in PDF format by opening the file using Adobe Reader or another PDF viewer program. The results are shown in Table 15.4. This output is created in the default format because no style has been specified. Similar results can be observed by outputting information in other ODS formats.

USING ODS TO SELECT SPECIFIC OUTPUT TABLES FOR PROCEDURES

SAS procedures often output a lot of information you don't want or need. In ODS output, each part of the output is contained in a table. Using ODS options, you can customize which tables you want SAS to output to the ODS destination. For example, suppose you are calculating a number of 2×2 cross-tabulations in a chi-square analysis. SAS automatically includes the Fisher's Exact test results. If you do not want that part of the output (maybe you want to save paper when you print results), you can use ODS to instruct SAS to exclude it from the analysis.

To include or exclude a table from the output, you first need to know the table's name. You can discover this information by using the ODS TRACE command in the following way:

```
ODS TRACE ON;
    procedure specifications;
ODS TRACE OFF;
```

This ODS option places information in the Log window that indicates the name of each output table. Once you've discovered the name of one or more tables you want to include (in this example) in the output, you can use the following code to make that request (using HTML as the example output destination):

```
ODS HTML;
ODS HTML SELECT tables-to-include;
PROC FREQ CODE;
ODS HTML CLOSE;
```

When you run this program, only the tables requested in the SELECT statement are included in the output. Similarly, you can use an ODS EXCLUDE statement to exclude tables from output.

HANDS-ON
EXAMPLE

This example illustrates how to use ODS to limit output from a SAS analysis.

1. In the Editor window, open the program ODS3.SAS. This program performs a chi-square analysis on a 2×2 contingency table.

```
DATA TABLE;
INPUT A B COUNT;
DATALINES;
```

```
0 0 12
0 1 15
1 0 18
1 1 3

;

ODS TRACE ON;
PROC FREQ;WEIGHT COUNT;
    TABLES A*B /CHISQ;
    TITLE 'CHI-SQUARE ANALYSIS FOR A 2X2 TABLE';
RUN;
ODS TRACE OFF;
```

2. Run the program and observe the results. Notice that the results consist of the following tables:

   a. The A by B cross-tabulation table

   b. Statistics for the A by B analysis

   c. Fisher's Exact test

   Examine the information in the Log window. The portion of the Log file shown in Figure 15.1 is the information created as a result of the ODS TRACE ON and ODS TRACE OFF statements.

   FIGURE 15.1. *ODS TRACE output*

```
Output Added:
-------------
Name:         CrossTabFreqs
Label:        Cross-Tabular Freq Table
Template:     Base.Freq.CrossTabFreqs
Path:         Freq.Table1.CrossTabFreqs
-------------

Output Added:
-------------
Name:         ChiSq
Label:        Chi-Square Tests
Template:     Base.Freq.ChiSq
Path:         Freq.Table1.ChiSq
-------------

Output Added:
-------------
Name:         FishersExact
Label:        Fisher's Exact Test
Template:     Base.Freq.ChisqExactFactoid
Path:         Freq.Table1.FishersExact
-------------
```
                                                        (Continued)

Notice the names of the tables:

- CrossTabFreqs
- ChiSq
- FishersExact

Knowing these names (they are not case-sensitive), you can, for example, limit your output to only the CrossTabFreqs and ChiSq tables.

3. In the Editor window, open the program ODS4.SAS.

```
DATA TABLE;
INPUT A B COUNT;
DATALINES;
0 0 12
0 1 15
1 0 18
1 1 3
;
ODS HTML;
ODS HTML SELECT CROSSTABFREQS CHISQ;
PROC FREQ;WEIGHT COUNT;
    TABLES A*B /CHISQ;
    TITLE 'CHI-SQUARE ANALYSIS FOR A 2X2 TABLE';
RUN;
ODS HTML CLOSE;
```

4. Run this program. Notice that it produces the same output as the previous code, but without the Fisher's table. You would get the same results by using the EXCLUDE option as in the following code:

```
ODS HTML EXCLUDE FISHERSEXACT;
```

GOING DEEPER: ENHANCING GRAPHICS USING ODS AND CREATING HYPERLINKS

You can use ODS to capture standard output from SAS GRAPHICS procedures or use the ODS GRAPHICS option to output graphs specifically designed for certain SAS procedures. Not all SAS procedures create graphs, but many of the analysis procedures do produce graphs designed for that analysis. Several examples of this option were presented in Chapter 14. This section presents several additional examples showing how ODS GRAPHICS can be used.

An additional feature is that ODS can be used to create an interactive "Drill Down Chart" using SAS ODS HTML. To define a link to a portion of a SAS graph, use a statement like the following:

```
IF GP="A" THEN HTMLLINK='HREF="GPA.HTM"';
```

The strange-looking HTMLLINK='HREF="GPA.HTM"' designation is an HTML command that specifies a reference name for an HTML link. (Note that the HREF is included in single quotation marks and the file name is in double quotation marks.) In SAS, this defines a link for category "A". This technique is illustrated in the following Hands-on Example.

HANDS-ON
EXAMPLE

This example illustrates how to use HTML links in a SAS graph using ODS.

1. In the Editor window, open the file ODS5.SAS.

```
ODS HTML;
PROC GCHART DATA="C:\SASDATA\SOMEDATA";
     HBAR GP/ DISCRETE;
RUN; QUIT;
ODS HTML CLOSE;
```

2. Run this program and observe that it creates a standard horizontal bar chart that consists of three categories of the variable GP. See Figure 15.2.

3. Suppose for each "group," represented by one of the bars on the plot, you want to make available a set of background statistics. You can use ODS to

FIGURE 15.2. *Drill-down plot, first run*

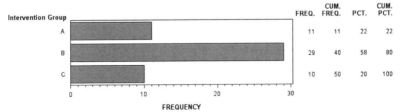

(Continued)

associate a link for each bar on the graph to a separate Web page. Thus, each bar becomes a Web page link, and when you click on a bar on the graph, you open an HTML page. In the Editor window, open the file ODS6.SAS.

```
* CREATE OUTPUT FOR EACH SECONDARY ANALYSIS;
ODS HTML FILE="C:\SASDATA\GPA.HTM";
PROC MEANS DATA= "C:\SASDATA\SOMEDATA" MAXDEC=2 N MEAN STD;
VAR AGE TIME1-TIME4;
WHERE GP="A";
TITLE 'Summary for GROUP A';
RUN;
ODS HTML FILE="C:\SASDATA\GPB.HTM";
PROC MEANS DATA= "C:\SASDATA\SOMEDATA" MAXDEC=2 N MEAN STD;
VAR AGE TIME1-TIME4;
WHERE GP="B";
TITLE 'Summary for GROUP B';
RUN;
ODS HTML FILE-"C:\SASDATA\GPC.HTM";
PROC MEANS DATA= "C:\SASDATA\SOMEDATA" MAXDEC=2 N MEAN STD;
VAR AGE TIME1-TIME4;
WHERE GP="C";
TITLE 'Summary for GROUP C';
RUN;
*....................................CREATE THE BARCHART;
DATA BARCHART;SET "C:\SASDATA\SOMEDATA";
LENGTH HTMLLINK $40;
IF GP="A" THEN HTMLLINK='HREF="GPA.HTM"';
IF GP="B" THEN HTMLLINK='HREF="GPB.HTM"';
IF GP="C" THEN HTMLLINK='HREF="GPC.HTM"';
ODS HTML FILE="C:\SASDATA\GCHART.HTM" GPATH="C:\SASDATA\";
ODS LISTING CLOSE;
PROC GCHART;
     HBAR GP/ HTML=HTMLLINK;
       TITLE 'Summary information for each GP.';
RUN; QUIT;
ODS HTML CLOSE;
ODS LISTING;
```

Notice the first three sections of the code, starting with

```
ODS HTML FILE="C:\SASDATA\GPA.HTM";
```

```
PROC MEANS DATA= "C:\SASDATA\SOMEDATA" MAXDEC=2 N MEAN STD;
VAR AGE TIME1-TIME4;
WHERE GP="A";
TITLE 'Summary for GROUP A';
RUN;
```

This code creates an HTML output file containing statistics from the GP "A" category. These HTML files will be used to display underlying information about each bar in the bar chart. Similar code relates to GP "B" and GP "C."

The second section of the code creates a data set called BARCHART. It includes a new variable named HTMLLINK that is defined for each of the categories. In the GCHART statement, the OPTION in the line

```
HBAR GP/ HTML=HTMLLINK;
```

relates the HTML link (HTMLLINK) to each category of GP.

4. Run the program and observe the output in the Results Viewer (or view GCHART.HTM in a Browser). The graph is virtually identical to the one illustrated in Figure 15.3.

5. Click on the bar for group A and the information shown in Table 15.5 appears. With the information shown in Table 15.5 in the Results Viewer, find the left arrow at the top of the window and click it once to return to the graph (or use the "back" arrow in a browser). Try the links for the other two bars. Using this technique, you can create graphs with drill-down capabilities that allow you to display background information for each category in a graph.

TABLE 15.5. Output from drilling down from a bar chart

Variable	Label	N	Mean	Std Dev
AGE	Age on Jan 1, 2000	11	10.36	2.87
TIME1	Baseline	11	20.90	2.08
TIME2	6 Months	11	27.00	2.93
TIME3	12 Months	11	30.35	3.20
TIME4	24 Months	11	30.44	3.96

(Continued)

6. Change the last `IF` statement in the code to

```
IF GP="C" THEN HTMLLINK='HREF="http://www.cnn.com"';
```

   or to some other Web page. Re-run the program and click on the third bar. The contents of the indicated Web page should be displayed.

GOING DEEPER: CAPTURING INFORMATION FROM ODS TABLES

Another way to use the information from `ODS TRACE` is to capture output from procedures and save that information in a SAS output file. Once you know the name of the output table, you can use ODS to output the table as a SAS data file using the command

```
ODS OUTPUT NAMEOFTABLE=OUTPUTDATASET;
```

After outputting the information to a new data set, you can merge that information into the current SAS data set using the following code:

```
DATA NEW; SET ORIGINAL;
IF _N_=1 THEN SET OUTPUTDATASET;
```

The `_N_` is a special variable that is the record number of a data set. Thus the statement

```
IF _N_=1 then SET OUTPUTDATASET;
```

tells SAS to merge the information from record 1 of `OUTPUTDATASET` into the `NEW` data set (along with the information from `ORIGINAL`). This is illustrated in the following Hands-on Example.

Although certain SAS procedures allow you to save information from an analysis, the advantage of this ODS method is that *any* value in *any* output table can be captured.

HANDS-ON EXAMPLE

This example illustrates how to capture a specific statistic from the output of a procedure and save that information in a SAS data set.

1. In the Editor window, open the file `ODS7.SAS`.
   ```
   DATA WT;
   INPUT WEIGHT @@;
   ```

```
DATALINES;
64 71 53 67 55 58
77 57 56 51 76 68

;
ODS TRACE ON;
PROC MEANS DATA=WT;
RUN;
ODS TRACE OFF;RUN;
QUIT;
```

2. Run this program. It uses the TRACE option to display the names of the output tables for PROC MEANS, as shown in Table 15.6. Notice that the name of the output table is "Summary."

3. Close the Results Viewer and clear the output and log files. Open the SAS program ODS8.SAS. Notice that the SAS code has been modified by the removal of the TRACE ON and TRACE OFF commands and the addition of the following statement just before the PROC MEANS statement, as shown here:

```
ODS OUTPUT SUMMARY=STATS;
PROC MEANS;
```

SUMMARY in the ODS OUTPUT statement is the name of the table, and STATS is the name of the output data set you are creating.

4. Run the edited SAS program. Look in the Log window and see the following statement, which tells you that SAS created the requested data set.

TABLE 15.6.   **Trace output from a PROC REG**

```
Output Added:
-----------------
Name:          Summary
Label:         Summary statistics
Template:      base.summary
Path:          Means.Summary
-----------------
```

(Continued)

```
NOTE: The data set WORK.STATS has 1 observation and 5 variables.
```

Examine the Results Viewer window to see the contents of the new data set created, as shown in Table 15.7.

TABLE 15.7. The SAS Data set created using ODS OUTPUT

Obs	WEIGHT_N	WEIGHT_Mean	WEIGHT_StdDev	WEIGHT_Min	WEIGHT_Max
1	12	62.75	8.9861003778	51	77

This information can now be used in other calculations, as illustrated in the next step.

5. In the Editor window, open the file ODS9.SAS.

```
DATA WT;
INPUT WEIGHT @@;
DATALINES;
64 71 53 67 55 58
77 57 56 51 76 68
;
DATA WTDIFF;SET WT;
IF _N_=1 THEN SET STATS;
DIFF=WEIGHT-WEIGHT_MEAN;
Z=DIFF/WEIGHT_STDDEV;    *    CREATES    STANDARDIZED    SCORE
    (Z-SCORE);
RUN;
ODS HTML;
PROC PRINT DATA= WTDIFF;VAR WEIGHT DIFF Z;
RUN;
ODS HTML CLOSE;
```

This program creates a new data set called WTDIFF that consists of the original data set WT and the first (and only) row of the new STATS data set (specified by the IF _N_=1 THEN SET STATS statement). A calculation is then made to create the Z variable.

6. Run this program and observe the output, which contains z-scores for each record, as shown in Table 15.8. Using this technique, you can capture any statistic from a SAS output table, merge it into another data set, and use that information to calculate new variables.

TABLE 15.8.   **Results of calculating Z-Score**

Obs	WEIGHT	DIFF	Z
1	64	1.25	0.13910
2	71	8.25	0.91808
3	53	-9.75	-1.08501
4	67	4.25	0.47295
5	55	-7.75	-0.86244
6	58	-4.75	-0.52859
7	77	14.25	1.58578
8	57	-5.75	-0.63988
9	56	-6.75	-0.75116
10	51	-11.75	-1.30757
11	76	13.25	1.47450
12	68	5.25	0.58424

EXTENDED ODS FEATURES

This chapter has introduced a number of features available in SAS ODS. However, there are many features not covered here. For example, every ODS table output by a SAS procedure uses a template to control the way it is created. Using `PROC TEMPLATE`, you can modify these templates to customize the content and look of each output table.

You can store the components of any ODS report in order to modify and replay them using `PROC DOCUMENT`. These tasks are beyond the scope of this book, and we refer you to the SAS documentation if you want to learn more about these topics.

SUMMARY

The SAS Output Delivery System (ODS) provides a number of ways to manipulate output from SAS procedures. Many examples in the book have used ODS to output results from procedures into HTML and other formats. This chapter introduced other ways to use ODS, including additional options for outputting procedure results, outputting SAS data sets, and using ODS to enhance graphic output.

EXERCISES

15.1. Use `ODS PDF`.

Using the `FIRST.SAS` program, include output to the `ODS PDF` format using the `STATISTICAL` style.

15.2. Use an interactive `ODS` **graph.**

a. Open `ODS6.SAS`. Change the type of chart from `HBAR` to `PIE` and run the program. Test to verify that the HTML links work.

b. Change the type of chart to `VBAR` and run the program. Test to verify that the HTML links work.

c. Change the type of chart to a `VBAR3D` and run the program. Test to verify that the HTML links work.

d. Similarly, try the graph types `BLOCK`, `HBAR3D`, `PIE3D`, and `STAR`.

15.3. Use `ODS TRACE`.

Open the file `EX_15.3.SAS`. Notice the `TRACE ON` and `TRACE OFF` commands. Run this program to discover the names of the output tables (in the Log window). They are:

a. Statistics

b. Conflimits

c. _____

d. _____

Use this information in an `ODS SELECT` statement to limit output of the procedure to the tables for statistics and *t*-tests only.

15.4. Use `ODS SELECT`.

Using the data from the following 2 × 2 table, write a program that will display the cross-tabulation program and a Fisher's Exact test (and not display the chi-square table).

		DISEASED	
		YES	NO
	YES	24	8
EXPOSED	NO	9	19

Here is how the program might begin:

```
DATA TABLE;
   INPUT EXPOSURE DISEASE COUNT;
   DATALINES;
0 0 24
```

Finish writing the code to read in the data and calculate the desired statistics.

15.5. Use `ODS` to extract table statistics.

Using the data from Exercise 15.4, write a program that will use `TRACE ON` and `TRACE OFF` to discover the name of the table that contains the Fisher's Exact test.

Use the command

```
ODS OUTPUT nameoftable=STATSOUT;
```

where `nameoftable` is the name of the Fisher's Exact test you discovered using the `TRACE` commands.

a. Use Viewtable to examine the output SAS data set named `STATSOUT` (or use a `PROC PRINT`).

b. Notice the name of the variable that contains the values `XP2_FISH`. It is

_____.

c. Notice the name of the variable that contains the *p*-value for the `XP2_FISH` value. It is _____.

d. In order to minimize the amount of output for the test, suppose you want to see only the *p*-value for the two-sided Fisher's Exact test. Use the following code to print out the *p*-value from the Fisher's Exact test.

```
PROC PRINT LABEL DATA=TABLE;
LABEL CVALUE1='P-VALUE' NAME1='TEST';
WHERE NAME1="XP2_FISH";
VAR NAME1 CVALUE1;
ID TABLE;
RUN;
```

This program uses several features that were discussed in previous chapters.

    a. Why is the LABEL option included in the PROC PRINT statement? (See Chapter 4, the section "Labeling Variables with Explanatory Names.")

    b. What does the WHERE statement do?

    c. What does the ID statement do?

CHAPTER

16

ADVANCED SAS PROGRAMMING TOPICS

LEARNING OBJECTIVES

- To be able to read and write data using Dynamic Data Exchange (DDE)
- To be able to use the RETAIN statement
- To be able to use Arrays and DO loops
- To be able to transpose data sets
- To be able to perform advanced merging, appending, and updating of data sets
- To be able to perform data recoding using SELECT
- To be able to use SAS macro variables and macros

The SAS programming language is extensive and flexible, and there are many features of the language that were not discussed in the previous chapters of this book. This chapter is included for those who want to go deeper into SAS programming. It introduces several other topics that are commonly used in preparing data for analysis. However, it is not exhaustive. For additional information, please refer to the SAS documentation.

READING AND WRITING DATA USING DDE

Dynamic Data Exchange (DDE) is a communication system built into Microsoft Windows that allows two software programs to access the same data file. In SAS, this means that you can dynamically read in data from another application, such as Microsoft Excel.

To use DDE in Excel and SAS, you must have Excel installed on your computer. There are several ways to use DDE in SAS. They include:

- Reading data from the clipboard

- Utilizing the DDE "triplet" to access data

- Controlling the Windows application from SAS

Reading Excel Data from the Windows Clipboard

The simplest way to dynamically read data into SAS from an Excel file is to use the clipboard method. This technique will also work for any program that allows you to copy a table of data onto the Windows clipboard.

HANDS-ON
EXAMPLE

In this example you will copy data onto the Windows clipboard and then read that data into SAS.

1. In Excel, open the file SAMPLEDATA.XLS.

2. Copy the data range (from cell A2 to cell H19) by highlighting it. You do this by clicking in cell A2, holding the left button on the mouse, and then dragging the highlighted material to cell H19 as shown in Figure 16.1.

3. Select Edit ⇒ Copy (or press CtrlC) to copy these cells to the Windows clipboard.

4. Switch to the SAS program and in the Editor window, open the program DDE1.SAS.

FIGURE 16.1. *Excel data to import into SAS via the clipboard*

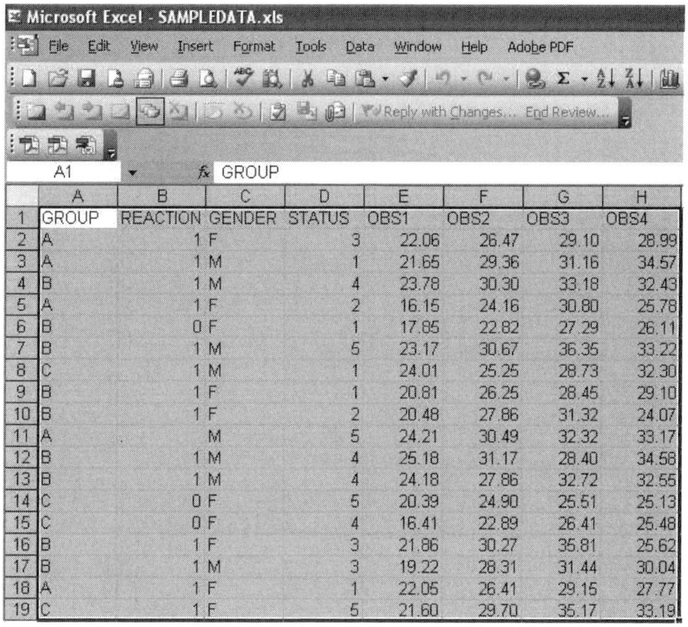

	A	B	C	D	E	F	G	H
1	GROUP	REACTION	GENDER	STATUS	OBS1	OBS2	OBS3	OBS4
2	A	1	F	3	22.06	26.47	29.10	28.99
3	A	1	M	1	21.65	29.36	31.16	34.57
4	B	1	M	4	23.78	30.30	33.18	32.43
5	A	1	F	2	16.15	24.16	30.80	25.78
6	B	0	F	1	17.85	22.82	27.29	26.11
7	B	1	M	5	23.17	30.67	36.35	33.22
8	C	1	M	1	24.01	25.25	28.73	32.30
9	B	1	F	1	20.81	26.25	28.45	29.10
10	B	1	F	2	20.48	27.86	31.32	24.07
11	A		M	5	24.21	30.49	32.32	33.17
12	B	1	M	4	25.18	31.17	28.40	34.58
13	B	1	M	4	24.18	27.86	32.72	32.55
14	C	0	F	5	20.39	24.90	25.51	25.13
15	C	0	F	4	16.41	22.89	26.41	25.48
16	B	1	F	3	21.86	30.27	35.81	25.62
17	B	1	M	3	19.22	28.31	31.44	30.04
18	A	1	F	1	22.05	26.41	29.15	27.77
19	C	1	F	5	21.60	29.70	35.17	33.19

```
FILENAME MYFILE DDE 'CLIPBOARD';
DATA FROMXL;
     INFILE MYFILE;
     INPUT GROUP $1. REACTION GENDER $1. STATUS OBS1 OBS2
     OBS3 OBS4;
ODS HTML STYLE=JOURNAL;
PROC PRINT; RUN;
ODS HTML CLOSE;
```

In this program the `FILENAME` command line defines a file reference in SAS called `MYFILE` as a DDE using the Windows clipboard. In other words, it tells SAS that you will be referencing data using the filename `MYFILE` and that these data are currently on the Windows clipboard.

- The `"DATA"` command specifies the name of the SAS data file (`FROMXL`).
- The `INFILE` command line tells SAS to read data from the previously defined file reference called `MYFILE` (defined in the `FILENAME` line above).
- The `INPUT` command defines the data by listing the variables to read: Note the `INFORMAT`s used for the text variables (`$1`).

(Continued)

5. Run the program. The abbreviated SAS output is shown in Table 16.1.

TABLE 16.1. **Data from windows clipboard import**

Obs	Group	Reaction	Gender	Status	Obs1	Obs2	Obs3	Obs4
1	A	1	F	3	22.06	26.47	29.10	28.99
2	A	1	M	1	21.65	29.36	31.16	34.57
3	B	1	M	4	23.78	30.30	33.18	32.43
4	A	1	F	2	16.15	24.16	30.80	25.78
5	B	0	F	1	17.85	22.82	27.29	26.11
6	B	1	M	5	23.17	30.67	36.35	33.22
7	C	1	M	1	24.01	25.25	28.73	32.30
8	B	1	F	1	20.81	26.25	28.45	29.10
9	B	1	F	2	20.48	27.86	31.32	24.07
10	A	.	M	5	24.21	30.49	32.32	33.17

Note the missing values for REACTION in observation number 10. This value was coded as a dot (.) in the Excel spreadsheet.

Reading Data into SAS Using the DDE Triplet Method

Another way to read data from an Excel file is the DDE triplet method. To use this method,

- Excel must be running on your computer.
- The file you want to access must be an Excel file.

■ You do not have to copy the data to the clipboard.

■ You need to know the range of data you want to import.

The DDE triplet designation is in the form (application π topic !item). For Excel it is of the form:

```
Excel|path\[filename.xls]sheetname!R1C1:R2C2
```

For example, the triplet for the spreadsheet SAMPLEDATA.XLS would be

```
Excel|C:\SASDATA\[sampledata.xls]sheet1!R2C1:R19C8
```

Of course, the path (C:\SASDATA) should be changed to match the location of the file you want to access. Note that the cell range begins on row 2—it does not include the variable names that are listed in row 1 of the spreadsheet. To read the data from the SAMPLEDATA.XLS file into SAS, use the FILENAME command:

```
FILENAME MYFILE DDE 'Excel|C:\SASDATA\[sampledata.
xls]sheet1!R2C1:R19C8';
```

To use this method in a SAS program, replace this FILENAME command with code in previous example (see DDE2.SAS). (Excel must be running for this example to work.)

Starting Excel within SAS (and Reading Data Using DDE)

You can save yourself the trouble of having to launch Excel before reading your data by opening the Excel program from within SAS. The commands to do this are:

```
OPTIONS NOXSYNC NOXWAIT;
X '"C:\SASDATA\sampledata.xls"';
```

The options NOXSYNC and NOXWAIT in the OPTIONS command tell SAS not to wait for input from the user. The X command tells SAS to run the indicated command in Windows, which invokes the Excel program and opens the SAMPLEDATA.XLS spreadsheet. Once Excel is running, you can use the FILENAME command as in the previous example. See DDE3.SAS.

Putting Data into Excel from SAS

Using DDE, you can also write information to Excel from SAS. In the following Hands-on Example, data are written to Excel, including the variable names. Note that the Excel spreadsheet must be opened or SAS must invoke the spreadsheet as in the previous example using the X command.

HANDS-ON
EXAMPLE

This example writes data from SAS to an Excel file.

1. Open a blank spreadsheet and save it as FROMSAS.XLS.

2. In the Editor window, open the program DDE4.SAS.

```
DATA TEMP;
INPUT ID SBP DBP SEX $ AGE WT;
DATALINES;
1 120 80 M 15 115
2 130 70 F 25 180
3 140 100 M 89 170
4 120 80 F 30 150
5 125 80 F 20 110

;
RUN;
* NOTE: TARGET SPREADSHEET MUST BE OPEN;
FILENAME TOEXCEL DDE
   'EXCEL|C:\SASDATA\[FROMSAS.XLS]SHEET1!R1C1:R7C6';
DATA _NULL_;
   FILE TOEXCEL;
      PUT 'ID SBP DBP SEX AGE WT';
   RUN;
FILENAME TOEXCEL DDE
   'EXCEL|C:\SASDATA\[FROMSAS.XLS]SHEET1!R2C1:R8C6';
DATA _NULL_;
   SET TEMP;
   FILE TOEXCEL;
      PUT ID SBP DBP SEX AGE WT;
RUN;
```

Notice that the FILENAME command is used twice. The first of the FILENAME commands writes the variable labels to row 1 of the spreadsheet. The second of these commands writes the data to the spreadsheet.

3. Run the program. The resulting spreadsheet (note that it is SPREAD1 in the Excel file FROMSAS.XLS) is shown in Figure 16.2.

FIGURE 16.2. *Data written to an Excel spreadsheet from SAS*

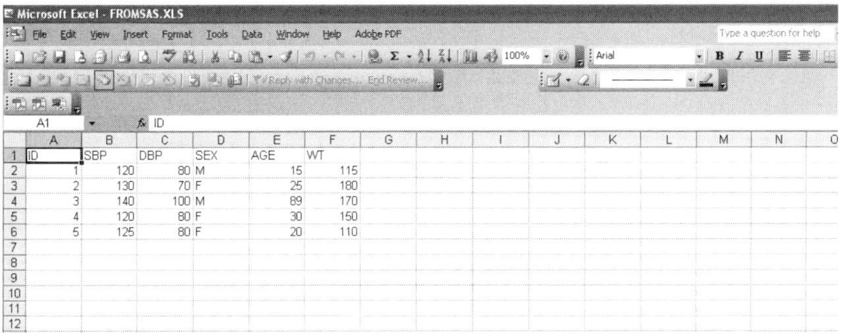

USING THE RETAIN STATEMENT

The RETAIN statement, used in a DATA step, allows you to retain values of a variable across iterations as values of the data are added to the data set. For example, suppose you have a series of observations that includes a date variable and you want to calculate the number of days since the first date. One way to do that is with the RETAIN statement. Assuming the data are sorted by date, consider the following code:

```
DATA DAYS;SET MYDATA;
IF _N_=1 THEN FIRST=VISIT_DATE;
RETAIN FIRST;
DAYS=VISIT_DATE-FIRST;
```

■ The IF _N_=1 statement creates a new variable called FIRST that contains the value of the first date in the dataset.

■ The RETAIN statement tells SAS to keep the value of FIRST the same on subsequent observations (otherwise it will be missing).

■ The DAYS= statement uses the FIRST variable to calculate a difference between the current record's VISIT_DATE value and FIRST—giving you the number of days since the first visit.

HANDS-ON
EXAMPLE

This example calculates the number of days since a first visit.

1. In the Editor window, open the program DRETAIN.SAS.

```
DATA MYDATA;
INPUT VISIT_DATE ANYDTDTE8.;
DATALINES;
01/04/05
01/29/05
03/07/05
04/25/05
07/06/05
08/30/05
;
DATA DAYS;SET MYDATA;
IF _N_=1 THEN FIRST=VISIT_DATE;
RETAIN FIRST;
DAYS=VISIT_DATE-FIRST;
ODS HTML STYLE=JOURNAL;
PROC PRINT;
Title 'These are the contents of the dataset DAYS';
FORMAT VISIT_DATE FIRST DATE8.;
RUN;
ODS HTML CLOSE;
```

2. Run this example and observe the output in Table 16.2.

3. Remove the RETAIN statement and re-run the program. Notice that the variable FIRST loses its value after the first iteration and the variable DAYS has a missing value for all records after the first record.

TABLE 16.2.   **Results of calculation using the RETAIN statement (these are the contents of the dataset DAYS)**

Obs	Visit_Date	First	Days
1	04JAN05	04JAN05	0
2	29JAN05	04JAN05	25
3	07MAR05	04JAN05	62
4	25APR05	04JAN05	111
5	06JUL05	04JAN05	183
6	30AUG05	04JAN05	238

ARRAYS AND DO LOOPS

A SAS ARRAY statement is a way to place a series of observations into a single variable called an array. Often these variables are referenced as part of a DO loop, which is a technique for iterating through a set of data. A simplified syntax for SAS arrays is:

```
ARRAY ARRAY-NAME(SUBSCRIPT) <$> ARRAY-VALUES
```
One-dimensional arrays are specified with an ARRAY statement, such as

```
ARRAY TIME(1:6) TIME1-TIME6;
    TIME(1)=TIME1, TIME(2)=TIME2, and so on
```

```
ARRAY TIME(6) TIME1-TIME6;
```
Same as above

```
ARRAY TIME(0:5) A B C D E F;
    TIME(0)=A, TIME(1)=B, and so on
```

```
ARRAY ANSWER(*) Q1-Q50;
    ANSWER(1)=Q1, and so on
```

```
ARRAY ANSWER(1:5) $ Q1-Q5;
    Where Q1-Q5 are text values
```

(There are a number of other more complex array statements that are not discussed here.)

A SAS DO loop is a way of incrementing through an array for the purpose of calculation, observation, or conditional assignment. Its syntax is:

```
DO I = X to Y < BY Z>;
    statements;
END;
```

where I is the index (select any variable name not in use) and X and Y are the lower and upper bounds of the loop—this could be an actual number or a variable name. (The optional Z increment allows you to change the increment from the default 1 unit to some other unit.) For example, suppose you take five blood pressure readings on each subject. If any of these readings is above 140, you want to classify the subject with the value HIGHBP=1, or else the subject will have the value HIGHBP=0. The following code could perform that task:

```
DATA NEW:SET OLD;
ARRAY SBP(5) READING1-READING5;
HIGHBP=0;
DO I=1 TO 5;
    IF SBP(I) GT 140 THEN HIGHBP=1;
END;
```

■ The ARRAY statement sets up an array named SBP that contains the values of the variables READING1 through READING5.

■ The DO statement begins a loop wherein the variable I iteratively takes on the values from 1 to 5. The DO loop ends with the END statement.

■ Within the DO loop, if any of the five readings is greater than (GT) 150, the variable HIGHBP is set to 1. Otherwise, the value of HIGHBP for that subject remains at 0.

Suppose you have a questionnaire in which the variables (answers) are named Q1 to Q50 and the answers recorded are YES, NO. Missing answers were originally coded in the data set as NA. You want to change these values to the value " " (a blank, which is typically a missing value for a character's variable). Using ARRAYs and a DO loop, you can quickly perform this task within a DATA step.

```
DATA NEW;SET OLD;
ARRAY ANSWER(1:50) $ Q1-Q50;
DO I=1 TO 50;
    IF ANSWER(I)="NA" then ANSWER(I)="";
END;
```

■ The ARRAY statement sets up an array named ANSWER that contains the text values of the variables Q1–Q50.

■ The DO statement begins a loop wherein the variable I iteratively takes on the values from 1 to 50. The DO loop ends with the END statement.

- Within the `DO` loop, the `IF` statement is performed 50 times, each time with a different value of `ANSWER(I)` representing the different values of `Q1`, `Q2`, and so on.

- Thus, for the first subject, each of the 50 questions is examined. If an answer is "NA", it is recoded with value `" "`.

```
IF ANSWER(1)="NA" THEN ANSWER(1)="";
```

which can be interpreted as

IF Q1 has an answer NA then recode Q1 as " ".

In a similar way, if your answers are numeric—1=Yes, 0=No and -9=Missing—then you could use the following code to set all -9 missing values to the standard SAS missing value code dot (.). In this case note that the variables `Q1-Q50` are numeric.

```
DATA NEW;SET OLD;
ARRAY ANSWER(1:50)Q1-Q50;
DO I=1 to 50;
     IF ANSWER(I)= -9 then ANSWER(I)=.;
END;
```

For a more complex example, suppose you have a number of observations on a subject over time and you want to know the last value for a certain variable—and that last value could have happened anytime within the number of patient visits. You can capture this "last" value using a combination of an `ARRAY` statement and a `DO` loop.

For example, suppose you have a number of measurements on a subject by visit named `VISIT1`, `VISIT2`, `VISIT3`, and so on. You can put these values into an array using the statement

```
ARRAY TIME (5) VISIT1-VISIT5;
```

which is equivalent to the more complete statement specifying the beginning and ending index

```
ARRAY TIME (1:5) VISIT1-VISIT5;
```

In both cases the array named `TIME` contains five values that are referenced as `TIME(1)`, `TIME(2)`, and so on. Or to make your indices go from 0 to 4, use

```
ARRAY TIME (0:4) VISIT1-VISIT5;
```

In this example, to find out the last actual value in the array (the last visit for which you have information), you could look at each value of `TIME` until you reached a value that contains no information, and then you would know that the previous value was the last valid number. To search though the array, you can use a DO loop. For example:

```
ARRAY TIME (1:5) VISIT1-VISIT5;
LAST=VISIT1;
DO I=1 TO 5;
    IF TIME(I) GT 0 THEN LAST=TIME(I);
END;
DROP I;
```

- The statement LAST=VISIT1 sets the initial value of LAST to the observation for the first VISIT (VISIT1).

- The DO loop iterates through the five possible values. As long as a good value is observed (TIME(I) GT 0), the variable LAST is set to the appropriate values of TIME. If TIME contains a 0 or a missing value, LAST is not set to that value.

- At the end of the loop, the last good value of TIME has been put into the variable LAST.

- The DO loop is ended by the statement END; at the end of the loop.

The temporary variable named I is dropped because we have no use for it once the loop is completed.

HANDS-ON
EXAMPLE

This example illustrates how to use ARRAYs and DO loops in a SAS program.

1. In the Editor window, open the program DDOLOOP.SAS.

```
DATA CLINIC;
INPUT @1 ID $3. @4 VISIT1 4. @7 VISIT2 4.
      @10 VISIT3 4. @13 VISIT4 4. @16 VISIT5 4.;
ARRAY TIME (5) VISIT1-VISIT5;
LAST=VISIT1;
DO I=1 TO 5;
    IF TIME(I) > 0 THEN LAST=TIME(I);
END;
DROP I;
DATALINES;
```

```
001 34 54 34 54 65
002 23 43 54 34
003 23 43 .  43
004 45 55 21 43 23
005 54
```

```
;
ODS HTML STYLE=JOURNAL;
Title "Example of ARRAYS and DO loops";
PROC PRINT;
RUN;
ODS HTML CLOSE;
```

2. Run this program and observe the output in Table 16.3. Notice that the variable LAST contains the value of the observation for the last "good" value from the list of visits.

TABLE 16.3. **Example of ARRAYs and DO loops**

Obs	ID	VISIT1	VISIT2	VISIT3	VISIT4	VISIT5	LAST
1	001	34	54	34	54	65	65
2	002	23	43	54	34	.	34
3	003	23	43	.	43	.	43
4	004	45	55	21	43	23	23
5	005	54	.	.	.	.	54

More Information about DO Loops

Another type of DO loop is the DO UNTIL. The syntax is:

```
DO UNTIL (condition);
    Statements;
END;
```

This statement is used to tell SAS to stay in a loop until a specific criterion is met. For example, a more efficient version of the previous program would be:

```
LAST=VISIT1;
FLAG=0;
```

```
DO I=1 TO 5 UNTIL (FLAG=1);
   IF TIME(I)>0 THEN DO
           LAST=TIME(I);
               FLAG=1;
   END;
END;
DROP I FLAG;
```

In this version of the program, the testing for the last visit stops once the test fails (a missing visit is encountered). Also, notice another use of the DO statement in this example:

```
IF (CONDITION) THEN DO;
    STATEMENTS;
END;
```

The DO WHILE is another type of DO loop. It is similar to the DO UNTIL:

```
DO WHILE (CONDITION);
    STATEMENTS;
END;
```

HANDS-ON
EXAMPLE

This program illustrates the used of the DO WHILE loop.

1. In the Editor window, open the program DWHILE.SAS.

```
DATA TMP;
N=0;
DO WHILE(N<5);
  OUTPUT;
  N+1;
END;
RUN;
PROC PRINT;
RUN;
```

This program includes a DO WHILE loop that outputs values into the TMP data set at each iteration of the DO WHILE loop.

2. Run the program and observe the output data set. Why do the values of N range from 0 to 4?

TRANSPOSING DATA SETS

PROC TRANSPOSE allows you to restructure the values in your data set by transposing (or reorienting) the data. This is typically performed when your data are not in the structure required for an analysis. For example, if your data are listed with subjects as columns you can transpose the data so the subjects represent rows. The simplified syntax for PROC TRANSPOSE is:

```
PROC TRANSPOSE DATA=input-data OUT=output-data;
<PREFIX=prefix>;
<BY <variables>;
VAR variables;
```

■ The input data set is the data set to be transposed.

■ The output data set is the resulting data set.

■ PREFIX specifies a prefix to the names of variables created in the transposition. The default names are COL1, COL2, and so on.

■ The BY variable, when specified, indicates the variable that is used to form BY groups. The VAR statement specifies which variables are to be transposed.

HANDS-ON
EXAMPLE

Suppose you have been given a data set in which each line represents a variable and each subject's data are in a single column. This example illustrates how to use PROC TRANSPOSE to restructure this data set. Notice that because some of the data are text, you must indicate that with a $ for each variable name in the INPUT statement.

1. In the Editor window, open the program DTRANSPOSE1.SAS.

```
DATA SUBJECTS;
INPUT SUB1 $ SUB2 $ SUB3 $ SUB4 $;
DATALINES;
12 21 13 14
13 21 12 14
15 31 23 23
15 33 21 32
 M  F  F  M
```

(Continued)

```
;
PROC TRANSPOSE DATA=SUBJECTS OUT=TRANSPOSED;
  VAR SUB1 SUB2 SUB3 SUB4;
RUN;
ODS HTML;
PROC PRINT DATA=TRANSPOSED;
RUN;
ODS HTML CLOSE;
```

2. Run the program. The OUT=TRANSPOSED statement creates a data set named OBS_TRANSPOSED from the procedure. The resulting data set is shown in Table 16.4.

3. You can control the names of the columns with a PREFIX statement. Change the PROC TRANSPOSE statement to

```
PROC TRANSPOSE DATA=SUBJECTS OUT=TRANSPOSED PREFIX=INFO;
```

Re-run the program and observe the names of the columns.

TABLE 16.4. Example of transposed data

Obs	_NAME_	COL1	COL2	COL3	COL4	COL5
1	SUB1	12	13	15	15	M
2	SUB2	21	21	31	33	F
3	SUB3	13	12	23	21	F
4	SUB4	14	14	23	32	M

Using TRANSPOSE to Deal with Multiple Records per Subject

As a second example using PROC TRANSPOSE, suppose you have data that have several (and possibly differing numbers of) observations per subject, but you want to analyze the data by observation (a set of observations per row). You can use PROC TRANSPOSE to transpose the data by a key variable. For example, Figure 16.3 is a list of records in a simulated SAS data set named COMPLICATIONS. These are observed complications for accident victims. Notice that some subjects have more than one complication (subject 1921, for example).

FIGURE 16.3. *Data from the COMPLICATIONS data set*

	SUBJECT	COMPLICATION
1	1001	Heart Attack
2	1033	Heart Attack
3	1048	Heart Attack
4	1054	Heart Attack
5	1073	Heart Attack
6	1135	Wound Infection
7	1149	Compartment Syndrome
8	1368	Pneumonia
9	1379	Heart Attack
10	1536	Heart Attack
11	1545	Heart Attack
12	1615	Heart Attack
13	1643	Pancreatitis
14	1645	Pneumonia
15	1796	Coagulopathy
16	1859	Pneumonia
17	1921	Pneumonia
18	1921	Renal Failure
19	2023	Pneumonia
20	2039	Coagulopathy
21	2074	Coagulopathy
22	2076	Pneumonia
23	2076	Heart Attack
24	2076	Renal Failure
25	2173	Coagulopathy
26	2173	Wound Infection

HANDS-ON
EXAMPLE

This example uses PROC TRANSPOSE to rearrange the COMPLICATIONS data set so that there is only one subject per row and to output a data set for subjects with three or more complications.

1. In the Editor window, open the file DTRANSPOSE2.SAS.

```
PROC TRANSPOSE DATA="C:\SASDATA\COMPLICATIONS"
    OUT=COMP_OUT PREFIX=COMP;
```

(Continued)

```
      BY SUBJECT;
      VAR COMPLICATION;
RUN;
DATA MULTIPLE;SET COMP_OUT;
DROP _NAME_ ;
IF COMP3 NE '';
ODS HTML;
PROC PRINT DATA=MULTIPLE; VAR SUBJECT COMP1-COMP3;
FORMAT SUBJECT 10. COMP1-COMP3 $10.;
RUN;
ODS HTML CLOSE;
```

The PROC TRANSPOSE step outputs a data set named COMP_OUT. The BY
statement indicates that the transpose is by subject, so there will be one
subject per row. The PREFIX= option specifies the prefix for the new variables created for complications. That is, the first complication for a subject is
named COMP1, the second COMP2, and so on. The VAR statement indicates
which variable (COMPLICATION) will be used as the output variable (named
with the COMP prefix).

A second data set is created (MULTIPLE) that contains only records where
the value for COMP3 is not blank. Thus, only subjects that have three or
more complications are retained in the MULTIPLE data set. For example,

TABLE 16.5. **Output from PROC TRANSPOSE**

Obs	SUBJECT	COMP1	COMP2	COMP3	COMP4
1	2076	Pneumonia	Heart Atta	Renal Fail	
2	3585	DVT (Lower	Pneumonia	Renal Fail	
3	3630	DVT (Lower	Heart Atta	Pancreatit	Pneumonia
4	4585	Compartmen	Pneumonia	Skin Break	
5	4599	Aspiration	Pneumonia	Renal Fail	
6	4760	Acute Resp	Pneumonia	Renal Fail	
7	4775	Pneumonia	DVT (Lower	Pneumonia	Renal Fail
8	4795	Aspiration	DVT (Lower	Pneumonia	Renal Fail
9	5050	Aspiration	Pneumonia	Pneumothor	
10	5436	DVT (Lower	Pneumothor	Pulmonary	Renal Fail

subject 1921 has only two complications, so this subject is not included in the `MULTIPLE` data set, but subject 2076 does appear. The results are reported using a `PROC PRINT` statement.

2. Run this program. The abbreviated output shown in Table 16.5 presents the first few records. Note that each of subjects listed has at least three complications.

USING SAS MACROS

Macros, a powerful programming tool within SAS, allow you to set aside repetitive sections of code and to use them again and again when needed. The following brief and limited introduction to this topic illustrates some common ways to use SAS macros. For more information about macros, refer to the SAS documentation and the Going Deeper section of Chapter 11.

Creating and Using a SAS Macro Variable

If you are creating a program involving values that you will want to change (year, for example), you can program that variable as a macro, then use the macro to set and reset the variable to different values as needed.

For example, suppose you have a program that calculates values based on a given year. You can create a variable called `YEAR` using the statement

```
%LET YEAR=2009;
```

This type of macro statement typically appears at the beginning of your program. The general format for creating a macro variable is

```
%LET macro-variable-name = value;
```

The value does not need to include quotation marks even if the value is of character type. This was discussed in Chapter 2, the section "Understanding Three SAS Variable Types." Once you have created the variable, you can use it in a SAS statement by placing an `&` (ampersand) as a prefix to the variable name. Thus, once you define `YEAR` as a macro variable, you use it in a statement in the following way:

```
IND_DAY=MDY(7,4,&YEAR);
```

In this example, `IND_DAY` has been assigned the date value for July 4, 2009. Here is an example using a character macro:

```
%LET CITY = DALLAS;
```

Thus, within the program, the `TITLE` statement

```
TITLE "Analysis for Data from &CITY";
```

would print the title "Analysis for Data from DALLAS" in the output. Notice that when you use a macro variable within a quotation, you must use double quotes (" ") because a macro does not work on single-quoted statements.

Creating a Callable Macro Routine

Macros come in handy when you have repetitive code you want to use in a SAS program. You can define the code as a macro with one or more parameters (or no parameters) and then "call" the routine when you want those lines of codes used.

For example, the following program code prints out a short report on a requested subject from a data set. Because you may want to create these reports for a number of people, you can use a macro, then call it as many times as needed.

```
%MACRO REPORT(SUBJ=);
     DATA REPORT;SET "C:\SASDATA\SUBJECTS";
     IF SUBJ=&SUBJ;
     TITLE "REPORT ON SUBJECT # &SUBJ";
      PROC PRINT NOOBS DATA=REPORT;
          VAR GENDER TIME_EXPOSED DIAGNOSED;
       RUN;
%MEND REPORT;
*..................................REQUEST REPORTS;
ODS HTML STYLE=JOURNAL;
%REPORT(SUBJ=001)
%REPORT(SUBJ=017)
%REPORT(SUBJ=040)
RUN;
ODS HTML CLOSE;
```

The lines

```
%MACRO REPORT(SUBJ=);
```

and

```
%MEND REPORT;
```

begin and end the macro. The REPORT(SUBJ=); specifies the name of the macro (REPORT) and that it utilizes one parameter named SUBJ. This parameter is used to send the macro some value, which will then be used in the SAS code contained in the macro. In this case, a data set named REPORT is created that contains only information on the requested subject, and a PROC PRINT is used to create a brief report:

```
DATA REPORT;SET "C:\SASDATA\SUBJECTS";
IF SUBJ=&SUBJ;
TITLE "REPORT ON SUBJECT # &SUBJ";
```

```
PROC PRINT NOOBS DATA=REPORT;
     VAR GENDER TIME_EXPOSED DIAGNOSED;
RUN;
```

Notice within the macro code that &SUBJ is used twice, once in the IF statement and once in the TITLE statement. The lines

```
%REPORT(SUBJ=001)
%REPORT(SUBJ=017)
%REPORT(SUBJ=040)
```

call the REPORT macro three times, sending it a value for SUBJ, which is then used, and a separate report is generated for each subject, resulting in the output shown in Table 16.6.

Although this macro used only one parameter, you can use as many as are required for your application. There are a number of more sophisticated uses for macros, and many macros are available that calculate some particular statistic that is not yet included in SAS. You can often find these macros on the Web or in journal articles.

If you have multiple variables to input into a macro, separate the variables with commas. An example of a MACRO statement with multiple inputs might be

```
%MACRO MYMACRO(SUBJ=, DATASET=, YEAR=);
```

and a typical call might be

```
%MYMACRO(SUBJ=008, DATASET=MYDATA.SOMETHING,
YEAR=2009)
```

TABLE 16.6. **Output from macro program**

REPORT ON SUBJECT # 001

GENDER	TIME_EXPOSED	DIAGNOSED
M	23.31	1

REPORT ON SUBJECT # 017

GENDER	TIME_EXPOSED	DIAGNOSED
F	20.95	1

REPORT ON SUBJECT # 040

GENDER	TIME_EXPOSED	DIAGNOSED
F	18.1	0

HANDS-ON EXAMPLE

This example illustrates how to use a SAS macro program.

1. In the Editor window, open the program `AMACRO1.SAS`. This is the same code illustrated previously in this section.

2. In the section of the code that contains the macro calls

   ```
   %REPORT(SUBJ=001)
   %REPORT(SUBJ=017)
   %REPORT(SUBJ=040)
   ```

   change the `SUBJ=` values to 2, 10, and 20.

3. Run the program and observe the reports created for the requested subjects.

4. Alter the `VAR` statement to add `AGE` to the list of variables.
   ```
   VAR GENDER TIME_EXPOSED DIAGNOSED AGE;
   ```
   Re-run the program to see how this has changed the reports.

SUMMARY

This chapter provided additional information on common programming topics for the SAS language. The subjects covered are not exhaustive but were selected because they are often used for getting data ready for analysis. Many more topics could have been covered, and readers are encouraged to refer to the SAS documentation for additional information.

EXERCISES

16.1. Read an Excel file using DDE.

In this exercise, complete the code below to read the Excel file named `EXAMPLE.XLS` and perform a `PROC MEANS` on the numeric data. Use the `DDE3.SAS` example as a guide.

- The filename to open is `C:\SASDATA\EXAMPLE.XLS`.

- The data begin in row two, and there are seven columns of data to read.

- The names of the variables are `GROUP`, `AGE`, `TIME1`, `TIME2`, `TIME3`, `TIME4`, and `STATUS`. The `GROUP` variable is of character type, one character wide.

- This code is in the file `DDE_EXERCISE.SAS`.

```
OPTIONS _____ _____ ;
X '"_____"';
FILENAME MYFILE DDE 'Excel|C:\SASDATA\[sampledata.
xls]sheet1!R2C1:R_____';
DATA FROMXL;
     INFILE _____;
     INPUT GROUP $1. AGE _____;
PUT A PROC HERE;
RUN;
```

16.2. **Use** `PROC TRANSPOSE` **to summarize multiple records**.

Using `DTRANSPOSE2.SAS` as an example, complete the program below (`TRANS_EX.SAS`). The purpose of this program is to expand the `AMOUNTOWED` values onto one line for each `ID`, then to sum the rows and display the results. Use these guidelines:

■ Name the output file created by `PROC TRANSPOSE` as `EXPANDED`.

■ Use `AMT` as the prefix to the expanded variable.

■ Expand on the variable `AMOUNTOWED`.

■ Expand by `ID`.

■ Use `ODS HTML` to make the output into a table.

```
DATA OWED;
INPUT ID $3. AMOUNTOWED DOLLAR9.;
DATALINES;
001 $3,209
002 $29
002 $34.95
003 2,012
003 312.45
003 34.23
004 2,312
004 $3.92
005 .98
;
RUN;
PROC TRANSPOSE DATA=OWED OUT=_____ PREFIX=____;
     BY ___;
     VAR _____;
RUN;
DATA SUMMARIZE;SET EXPANDED;
TOTAL=SUM(of AMT1-AMT3);
DROP _NAME_;
RUN;
```

```
PROC PRINT DATA=SUMMARIZE;
RUN;
```

Your output should look like Table 16.7.

a. In the `DATA SUMMARIZE` data step, include the statement

    ```
    FORMAT TOTAL DOLLAR9.2;
    ```

    Re-run the program. How does that change the results?

b. Note that `SUM` (of list of variables) summed the data and ignored missing values. Change the `TOTAL=` statement to

    ```
    TOTAL = AMT1+AMT2+AMT3;
    ```
    Re-run the program. What is the difference in answers?

TABLE 16.7. Listing of transposed data

Obs	Id	Amt1	Amt2	Amt3	Total
1	001	3209.00	.	.	3209.00
2	002	29.00	34.95	.	63.95
3	003	2012.00	312.45	34.23	2358.68
4	004	2312.00	3.92	.	2315.92
5	005	0.98	.	.	0.98

16.3 Use a SAS macro.

Using `AMACRO1.SAS` as an example, complete the program below to create a report using the `CARS` data set. This code is in `EX_16.3.SAS`. Use this information:

- The name of the macro is `GETCARS`.
- The name of the SAS data set is `"C:\SASDATA\CARS"`. Use this in the `SET` statement.

- For the second and third reports, use FORD and TOYOTA. Note that the name must be in all caps.

- Place the macro variable named &CHOICE in the title.

```
%MACRO _____ (CHOICE=);
  DATA TEMP; SET "C:_____";
  IF BRAND=&CHOICE;
  TITLE "CAR SELECTION FOR _____";
  PROC PRINT; VAR BRAND MODEL CITYMPG;
  RUN;
%MEND GETCARS;
ODS HTML;
%GETCARS(CHOICE="SCION")
%GETCARS(CHOICE=_____)
%GETCARS(CHOICE=_____)
ODS HTML CLOSE;
```

a. Run the program and observe the results. It should create three reports, one for each brand of car.

b. Create a new call using VOLKSWAGEN.

c. To verify that case matters, do the following call:

```
%GETCARS(CHOICE="Honda")
```

Why didn't it produce a report?

d. Change the IF statement to

```
IF BRAND=UPCASE(&CHOICE);
```

Perform a call using

```
%GETCARS(CHOICE="Honda")
```

Why does it now work?

APPENDIX A

SAS GRAPH OPTIONS REFERENCE

This appendix is a brief reference to a number of SAS elements used in graphics and other procedures. These elements allow you visual control over many of the graphs produced in SAS procedures. Not all of the options for these elements are listed in this appendix. Refer to the SAS documentation for further information. The elements included in this appendix are:

- Fonts
- Color options
- Graph patterns
- Bar and block patterns
- Line styles
- Plot symbols

USING SAS FONTS

A selection of standard SAS fonts are illustrated in Figure A.1. These are the fonts loaded into Windows when you install SAS.

Use these fonts in any statement that allows the specification of a font. For example:

```
TITLE1 F="SWISS" "This is an example use of the SWISS font.";
```

In Windows, you can also specify any installed font on your machine. For example, the following statement uses the Times New Roman font.

```
TITLE1 F="TIMES" "This is an example use of the TIMES font.";
```

FIGURE A.1. *Standard SAS fonts*

ABCabc123 Example Brush

ABCabc123 Example Hersey

ABCabc123 Example Script

ABCabc123 Example Swiss

ABCabc123 Example Times

ABCabc123 Example Zapf

You can also specify height in such statements. (The default height is usually H=1.) For example:

```
TITLE1 F="COURIER" H=2 "Specify the height of the font.";
```

There are also bold, italic, and wide versions of some fonts. Refer to the SAS documentation for more information.

SPECIFYING SAS COLOR CHOICES

Color choices that can be used in SAS procedures include the following:

black	lilac	rose
blue	lime	salmon
brown	magenta	tan
cream	maroon	violet
cyan	orange	white
gold	pink	yellow
gray	purple	
green	red	

If you do not specifically indicate a color, the SAS default color is BLACK. You can modify these colors with prefixes such as LIGHT to create, for example, LIGHTBLUE. Other prefixes include:

brilliant	light	pale
dark	medium	strong
deep	moderate	vivid

Not all combinations work, so you may have to experiment to get the color you want.

Hundreds of other SAS colors are available. If you know a standard RGB specification for a color (often, institutions will have a specified RGB color for official documents), you can use that specification in a color option. An example would be CX3230B2 as the RGB code for "Brilliant Blue." Here are two examples (where H is the height option):

```
TITLE H=2 C=RED "This produces a Red title.";
TITLE2 H=1.5 C="CX3230B2" "This title is Brilliant Blue";
```

SPECIFYING PATTERNS FOR PROCS GPLOT AND PROC UNIVARIATE

In Chapter 6, "Evaluating Quantitative Data," you learned how to create a histogram from data. To display the histogram with a pattern rather than a solid color, you can use the PFILL=Mabcde option to specify a fill pattern for the histogram bars, where the codes are:

a
   from 1 to 5 (thickness/density of line)

b
   use X to denote crosshatch, N for no crosshatch

cde
   indicate starting angle (0 means no angle, 45 is 45 degree angle, etc.)

Thus, the program GPATTERN1.SAS:

```
PROC UNIVARIATE DATA="C:\SASDATA\SOMEDATA" NOPRINT;
   VAR AGE;
   HISTOGRAM /NORMAL PFILL=M3X45;
RUN;
```

produces a histogram using a crosshatch pattern at a 45 degree angle as shown in Figure A.2.

FIGURE A.2. *Example crosshatch pattern*

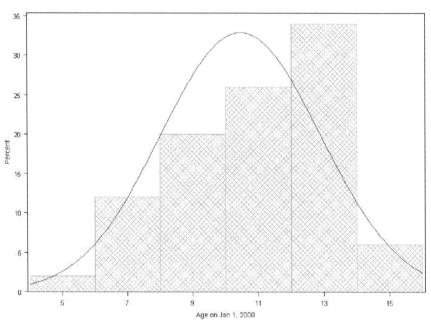

BAR AND BLOCK PATTERNS FOR BAR CHARTS, PIE CHARTS, AND OTHER GRAPHICS

Pattern choices can be used to specify colors and patterns for graphs in the PROC GCHART, PROC GPLOT, and PROC UNIVARIATE procedures with the PATTERN statement:

    PATTERNn options;

where *n* (ranging from 1 to 30) specifies the graph element in which the pattern is to be used. The following codes in the PATTERN statement allow you to specify colors and patterns.

E
    Empty pattern (empty box)

R1 to R5
    Right 45 degree stripes (light to heavy lines)

```
X1 to X5
```
Crosshatched patterns (light to heavy lines)

```
L1 to L5
```
Left 45 degree stripes (light to heavy lines)

For example, the SAS program GPATTERN2.SAS

```
TITLE;
ODS HTML ;
GOPTIONS RESET = ALL;
DATA BARS;
INPUT A B;
DATALINES;
1 1
2 2
3 3
4 4
5 5
;
PATTERN1 V=E C=BLUE;
PATTERN2 V=R1 C=BLACK;
PATTERN3 V=X2 C=BLACK;
PATTERN4 V=L3 C=BLACK;
PATTERN5 V=S C=BLACK;
PROC GCHART ;VBAR A
/DISCRETE WIDTH=10
SUBGROUP=B;
RUN;
QUIT;
ODS HTML CLOSE;
```

produces the graph in Figure A.3, which shows examples of the various patterns. Each PATTERN statement is applied to the bars—Pattern1 to the first bar, Pattern2 to the second, and so on.

SAS LINE STYLES

When drawing lines in a procedure such as PROC GPLOT, you can choose from one of the line styles shown in Figure A.4. These are specified within a SYMBOLn statement where n refers to lines in the order they are specified in the plot.

FIGURE A.3. *Example fill patterns*

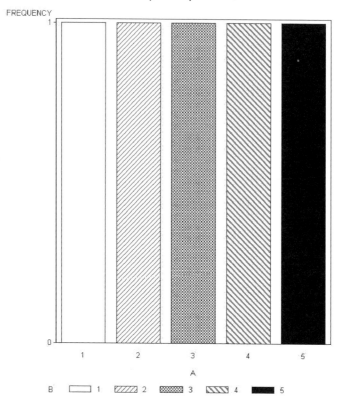

FIGURE A.4. *Line styles*

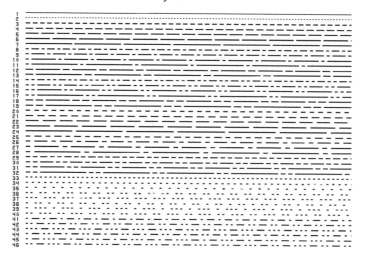

FIGURE A.5. *Select line style*

REGRESSION LINE TYPE SELECTED

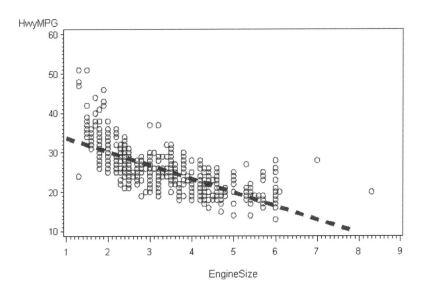

For example, the program `GLINE.SAS`:

```
goptions reset = all;
SYMBOL1 V=circle C=blue I=r L=2 w=5;
TITLE 'Regression Line Type Selected';
PROC GPLOT DATA="C:\SASDATA\CARS";
     PLOT hwympg*enginesize ;
RUN;
QUIT;
```

produces a scatterplot and regression line with line style `L=2` and width `W=5` for emphasis to illustrate the selected line style, as shown in Figure A.5.

USING SAS PLOTTING SYMBOLS

The symbol used for displaying a point on a graph such as a scatterplot in `PROC GPLOT` can be specified in a `SYMBOL` statement such as the following:

```
SYMBOL1 V=CIRCLE;
```

The standard SAS symbols you can select from are shown in Figure A.6.

FIGURE A.6. *Standard SAS symbols*

VALUE=	SYMBOL	VALUE=	SYMBOL
PLUS	+	%	♣
X	×	&	♧
STAR	✳	'	♠
SQUARE	□	=	☆
DIAMOND	◇	-	☉
TRIANGLE	△	@	☿
HASH	♯	*	♀
Y	Y	+	⊕
Z	Z	>	♂
PAW	⁝	. (DOT)	♃
POINT	⋅	<	♄
DOT	●	,	♆
CIRCLE	○	/	♅
	⌑	?	♌
¨	♤	(	☽
#	♡	)	♋
$	◇	:	✳

APPENDIX B

SAS FUNCTION REFERENCE

SAS functions can be used in a `DATA` statement to calculate new variables or as a part of a conditional statement. This appendix is more of a reference than a tutorial, but it does illustrate the use of a number of common functions in SAS. It is not an exhaustive list of functions, but it does include commonly used functions that are useful in manipulating data in preparation for analysis. Some examples are provided for functions whose use may not be apparent in a simple description. For a more extensive description of this material, please refer to the SAS documentation.

USING SAS FUNCTIONS

Here are some examples of how SAS functions are used:

```
DATA NEWDATA;SET OLDDATA;
TOTAL=SUM(A,B,C);
SQAGE=SQRT(AGE);
GENDER=UPCASE(SEX);
RUN;
```

Notice that in these cases the function on the right side of the $=$ sign does something to the argument(s) in the parentheses and returns a value, which is then assigned to the name on the left side of the $=$ sign.

The `SUM` function returns the total of the variables A, B, and C. The `SQRT` function returns the square root of the AGE variable. The `UPCASE` function makes all character values in the `SEX` variable uppercase. For example, if the `SEX` variable contains the value f, then the `GENDER` variable will contain the value F. The syntax for a function is:

```
NEWVARIABLE = FUNCTIONNAME(argument1, argument2...
argumentk);
```

where arguments can be constants, variables, expressions. or other functions. For functions that are not described in this appendix, refer to the SAS documentation.

ARITHMETIC/MATHEMATICAL FUNCTIONS

ABS(*x*)
> Absolute Value. Example: Y=ABS(-9) returns the value 9.

EXP(*x*)
> Exponentiation. Example: Y=EXP(1) returns the value 2.71828.

LOG(*x*)
> Natural Log. Example: Y=LOG(10) returns the value 2.30259.

LOG10(*x*)
> Log Base 10. Example: Y=LOG10 returns the value 1.0.

FACT(*x*)
> Factorial. Example: FACT(7) returns the value 5040, which is (7*6*5*4*3*2*1).

MAX(*x1,x2,x3...*)
> Returns maximum value in the list.

MEAN(*x1,x2,x3...*)
> Returns the arithmetic mean of nonmissing values in list. Example: MEAN(2,4,.,6) returns the value 4. (Note that the value dot . in the list represents a missing value.)

MEDIAN (*x1,x2,x3...*)
> Returns the median of nonmissing values in the list.

MIN(*x1,x2,x3 ...*)
> Returns the minimum in the list.

MOD(*x, k*)
> Remainder of *x/k*. Examples: MOD(5,3)=2, MOD(6,2)=0.

N(*x1,x2,x3...*)
> Returns the number of nonmissing values. Example: N(1,2,.,4) returns the value 3.

NMISS(*x1,x2,x3...*)
> Returns the number missing. Example: NMISS(1,2,.,4) returns the value 1.

ORDINAL(*k,x1,x2,x3...*)
> Finds the *k*th number in the sorted list.
> ORDINAL(2,11,6,9,3) = 6 because it is second in the ordered list.

`RANUNI(0)`
A different random number (uniform distribution) each time.

`RANUNI(x)`
Returns the same random sequence (uniform) each time for that particular seed, where x is a "seed" value you enter.

`RANNOR()`
A random number from a normal distribution with mean 0 and standard deviation 1. (See seed info for `RANUNI`.)

`SIGN(x)`
Returns the sign of x as a 1 or -1 value.

`SQRT(x)`
Square Root. Example: `Y=SQRT(9)` returns the value 3.

`SUM(x1,x2,x3...)`
Returns the sum of nonmissing values in list.

TRIGNOMETRIC FUNCTIONS

Each of these functions returns the specified trigonometric value for the value of the argument (in radians) entered into the function. For example,

`Y=COS(3.14);`
returns the value -1.000.

`ARCOS(argument):`
arccosine

`ARSIN(argument)`
arcsine

`ATAN(argument)`
arctangent

`COS(argument)`
cosine

`COSH(argument)`
hyperbolic cosine

SIN(*argument*)
  sine

SINH(*argument*)
  hyperbolic sine

TAN(*argument*)
  tangent

TANH(*argument*)
  hyperbolic tangent

DATE AND TIME FUNCTIONS

SAS date and time variables are stored as integers and indicate the number of days since 1/1/1960. A positive number indicates a date after 1/1/1960, and a negative number indicates a date before 1/1/1960. Date values that contain both date and time are stored in SAS as the number of seconds since midnight on 1/1/1960. Dates are typically displayed using a SAS date format such as MMDDYY8, which was first described in the Chapter 2 section "Reading Data Using Formatted Input" (see Table 2.4).

For these functions a SAS date is a variable designated as a date value. Here are two examples of how variables can be designated as dates:

- Assign a date value to a fixed date. A d at the end of the value tells SAS to interpret this quoted string as a date. For example (note that case does not matter either for the month abbreviation or for the "d"):

  ```
  BDATE = '12DEC1994'd;
  BEGINDATE ="1jan2011"D;
  EXAMDATE = '13-APR-2014'd;
  ```

- Read a value as a date in an INPUT statement. For example:

  ```
  INPUT BDATE MMDDYY8.;
  ```

In the following examples a "date" is a SAS value that contains only a date, and a "datetime" value contains date and time values.

When using date functions, beware of the "Y2K" problem. Any two-digit year lower than 20 is interpreted as being in the twenty-first century (e.g., the two-digit year 15 is interpreted as 2015) and two-digit years 20 or greater are interpreted as being in the twentieth century (e.g., the two-digit year 21 is interpreted as 1921). You can change this default using the statement YEARCUTOFF=19*XX* in your program. For example, if you specify YEARCUTOFF=1925, any two-digit year that is between 00 and 24 will be interpreted as being in the twenty-first century (e.g., 21 will be interpreted as 2021) and years from 25 to 99 will be interpreted as in the twentieth century (e.g., 44 will be interpreted as 1944).

DATDIF(*sdate,edate,basis*)

Returns the number of days between two dates. Basis is (default) `'30/360'`, `'ACT/ACT'`, `'ACT/360'`, or `'ACT/365'`. The BASIS option tells SAS what counting method to use to count days. (These are some day-count conventions used in investing, accounting, and other disciplines.) The `'30/360'` option means to use a 30-day month and a 360-day year. `'ACT/ACT'` means to use the actual number of days. `'ACT/360'` means to use the actual number of days in each month, and 360 days in a year; `'ACT/365'` means to use the actual number of days in each month and 365 days in a year.

For example,

DAYS=DATDIF(**'07JUL1976'd,'01JAN2013'd**,'30/360');

Returns the value (number of days) as 13134, whereas

DAYS=DATDIF(**'07JUL1976'd,'01JAN2013'd**,'ACT/ACT');

Returns the value (number of days) as 13327.

DATE()

Returns the current date (SAS date value).

DATEPART(*datetime*)

Extracts and returns only the date from a SAS datetime variable.

DATETIME()

Returns the current date and time of day from the computer's date and time values.

DAY(*date*)

Returns the day of month (a value from 1 to 31) from a SAS date.

DHMS(*date,hour,minute,second*)

Returns a SAS datetime value from the argument date, hour, minute, and second in the function.

HMS(*hour,minute,second*)

Creates a SAS time value from hour, minute, and second.

HOUR(<*time* | *datetime*>)

Returns the hour value from a SAS time or datetime variable.

INTCK('*interval*',*from,to*)

Returns the number of time intervals in a given time span, where *interval* can be:

Date Intervals: DAY, WEEKDAY, WEEK, TENDAY, SEMIMONTH, MONTH, QTR, SEMIYEAR, YEAR

Datetime Intervals: DTDAY, DTWEEKDAY, DTWEEK, DTTENDAY, DTSEM-IMONTH, DTMONTH, DTQTR, DTSEMIYEAR, DTYEAR

Time Intervals: HOUR, MINUTE, SECOND

For example,

WEEKS=INTCK('WEEK','07JUL1976'd,'01JAN2013'd);

Returns a value of 1904, indicating the number of weeks between the two indicated dates.

INTNX('*interval*',*start-from*,*increment*<,'*alignment*'>)
Advances a date, time, or datetime value by a given interval, and returns a date, time, or datetime value—see intervals above.

MDY(*month,day,year*)
Creates and returns a SAS date from month, day, year.

MINUTE(*time | datetime*)
Extracts and returns the minute value (1 to 60) from a SAS time or datetime variable.

MONTH(*date*)
Extracts and returns the month value (1 to 12) from a SAS date value.

QTR(*date*)
Extracts and returns the quarter value (1 to 4) of the year from a SAS date value.

SECOND(*time | datetime*)
Extracts and returns the value for seconds (1 to 60) from a SAS time or date-time value.

TIME()
Returns the current time of day as a datetime value (from the computer's system clock).

TIMEPART(*datetime*)
Extracts and returns the time value from a SAS datetime variable.

TODAY()
Returns the current date as a SAS date (from the computer's system clock).

WEEKDAY(*date*)
Extracts and returns the day of the week (1 to 7) from a SAS date value.

YEAR(*date*)
    Extracts and returns the year value (such as 2019) from a SAS date value.

YRDIF(*startdate,enddate,basis*)
    Returns the difference in years between two dates. Basis is '30/360', 'ACT/CT', 'ACT/360', or 'ACT/365'. (See descriptions of these basis values in the DATDIF function above.)

YYQ(*year,quarter*)
    Extracts and returns a SAS date from year and quarter.

CHARACTER FUNCTIONS

CAT(*text1, text2, ...*)
    Concatenates text without removing leading or trailing blanks. CATS removes leading and trailing blanks and CATT removes trailing blanks. For example,

RESULT=CAT("GEORGE"," WASHINGTON");
    Returns the value GEORGE WASHINGTON, and

RESULT=CATS("GEORGE"," WASHINGTON");
    Returns the value GEORGEWASHINGTON.

CATX (*separator, text1, text2, ...*)
    Removes leading and trailing blanks and inserts a separator between concatenated components. For example,

RESULT = CATX(":","GEORGE"," WASHINGTON");
    Returns the value GEORGE:WASHINGTON.

COMPBL(*text*)
    Removes multiple blanks between words in a character string.

COMPRESS(*text<,characters-to-remove>*)
    Removes specified characters from a character string.

DEQUOTE(*argument*)
    Removes quotation marks from text.

FIND(*text, texttofind <,'modifiers'> <,start>*)
    Finds an instance of the *texttofind* within the text. Start is an optional value indicating where in the text to start looking and modifiers are I for ignore case and T for ignore blanks. For example,

RESULT=FIND("aBcDef", "DEF","I")

Returns a value of 4 because DEF begins at the fourth character of ABCDEF (and case is ignored). If no match is found, a value of 0 is returned.

INDEX(*text,texttofind*)

Searches text for specified *texttofind* string and returns a number where the text begins, or 0.

LEFT(*text*)

Left-aligns a character string.

LENGTH(*text*)

Returns the length of a text string.

LOWCASE(*text*)

Converts all letters to lowercase.

QUOTE(*text*)

Adds double quotation marks to text.

REPEAT(*text,n*)

Repeats text *n* times.

REVERSE(*argument*)

Reverses a text expression.

RIGHT(*argument*)

Right-aligns text.

SCAN(*argument,n<,delimiters>*)

Returns the *n*th word from a text expression. Examples:

FIRST=SCAN("JOHN SMITH",1,' ');

Returns JOHN and

LAST=SCAN("JOHN SMITH",2,' ');

Returns SMITH.

SOUNDEX(*text*)

Turns text into a "sounds like" argument. Examples:

SOUNDEX("ALLEN")=SOUNDEX("ALAN");

matches, and

```
SOUNDEX("ALLEN")=SOUNDEX("MELON");
```
does not.

`SUBSTR(text,start<,n>)`
Searches for and replaces text. Examples:

```
VAR=SUBSTR("LINCOLN",3,2);
```
Returns VAR ="NC", and

```
SUBSTR("LINCOLN",3,2)= "XX";
```
Returns LIXX.

`TRANSLATE(text,to1,from1<,...ton,fromn>)`
Replaces characters in text with specified new characters. For example:

```
TRANSLATE('LINCOLN',"X","C");
```
Returns LINXOLN.

`TRANWRD(source,target,replacement)`
Replaces or removes all occurrences of a word in a text string. For example:

```
TRANWRD('SPECIAL WED MEAL','WED','MON');
```
Returns 'SPECIAL MON MEAL'.

`TRIM(argument)`
Removes trailing blanks from text. (Returns one blank if the expression is missing.)

`TRIMN(argument)`
Removes trailing blanks from text. (Returns a null string if the expression is missing.)

`UPCASE(argument)`
Converts text to uppercase.

`VERIFY(source,excerpt-1<,...excerpt-n)`
Searches text and returns the position of the first nonmatched character in the first argument. VERIFY("12345","54301") returns 2 because the second character doesn't match any character in the second argument.

TRUNCATION FUNCTIONS

CEIL(*value*)
Returns the smallest integer greater than or equal to the argument.

FLOOR(*value*)
Returns the largest integer less than or equal to the argument.

FUZZ(*value*)
Returns the nearest integer if value is within 1E-12.

INT(*value*)
Returns the decimal portion of the value of the argument.

ROUND(*value,roundoffunit*)
Rounds a value to the nearest roundoff unit. For example, ROUND(1.2345,.01) returns the value 1.23.

SPECIAL USE FUNCTIONS

These functions are used to convert data from one variable type to another.

INPUT(*string,informat*):
Example: s="1,212";x=input(s,comma5.); returns x=1212 (a numeric value)

Note: INPUTC(*string1,char-informat*) and INPUTN(*string1, num-informat*) are similar to INPUT(), but you can assign the format within the code.

PUT(*x1,format*)
Where *x1* is string or numeric and returns a character value. Example: x=PUT(1234,comma6.); returns the string value 1,234.

Note: PUTC(*x1,char-informat*) and PUTN(*x1,num-informat*) are similar to PUT(), but you can assign the format within the code.

CALL SYMPUT and CALL SYMPUTN
Not strictly functions, but these routines assign a value produced in a DATA step to a macro variable. The formats for these routines are:

CALL SYMPUT(macro-var,cval);
CALL SYMPUTN(macro-var,nval);

where cval is some character value or variable and nval is some numeric value or variable name. For example, to store the value of the character variable MYVAR into the macro variable named LEVEL, use the command

```
CALL SYMPUT('LEVEL',MYVAR);
```
You can then reference the variable as &LEVEL elsewhere in your SAS code.

HANDS-ON
EXAMPLE

This program demonstrates the INPUT and PUT functions and illustrates how you can convert character variables to numeric and numeric variables to character (DCONVERT.SAS).

```
DATA TEMP;
LENGTH CHAR4 $ 4;
INPUT NUMERIC CHAR4;
* CONVERT CHARACTER VARIABLE TO NUMERIC;
NEW_NUM=INPUT(CHAR4,BEST4.);
* CONVERT NUMERIC VARIABLE TO CHARACTER;
NEW_CHAR=PUT(NUMERIC,4.0);
DATALINES;
789.1 1234
009.2 0009
1.5 9999

;
PROC PRINT;
FORMAT NEW_NUM 6.1 NEW_CHAR $8.;
RUN;
```

Output is:

Obs	char4	numeric	new_num	new_char
1	1234	789.1	1234.0	789
2	0009	9.2	9.0	9
3	9999	1.5	9999.0	2

Notice that the converted numbers (new_char) have been rounded to integers because they were converted using a 4.0 format in the PUT statement.

FINANCIAL FUNCTIONS

IRR(*period,cash0,cash1,...*)

Returns the internal rate of return as a percentage.

MORT(*amount,payment,rate,number*)

When you set the PAYMENT variable to missing, this returns the payment for a loan calculation. For example, when you run DPAYMENT.SAS

```
DATA LOAN;
PAYMENT= MORT(30000,.,.06/12,48);
RUN;
PROC PRINT;RUN;
```

the value of (the monthly) PAYMENT is 704.55

NPV(*rate,period,cash0,cash1,...*)

Returns the net present value expressed as a percentage.

WORKING WITH PREVIOUS OBSERVATIONS

LAG*n*(*x*)

Returns the value of the *n*th previous observation. Example: If your data are x=10, 30, 15, then LAG2(x) for the third item would be 10. LAG() is the same as LAG1().

DIF*n*(*x*)

Returns the difference in the current value and the *n*th previous value. Example: If your data are x=10, 30, 15, then DIF2(x) of the third item would be 5 (15-10=5). DIF() is the same as DIF1().

MISCELLANEOUS FUNCTIONS

ZIPCITY(*zipcode*)

Converts a ZIP code to a city and state. For example, the expression

```
CITY=ZIPCITY(75137) ;
```

Where the *zipcode* (in this case 75137) is a character or numeric variable returns a value of "Duncanville, TX" for the CITY variable.

ZIPCITYDISTANCE(*zipcode1,zipcode2*)

Returns the distance (in miles) between the two ZIP codes.

ZIPSTATE(*zipcode*)

Converts a ZIP code to a two-letter state code. For example, the expression

```
STATE=ZIPSTATE("75137") ;
```

Where the *zipcode* (in this case "75137") is a character or numeric variable returns a value of "TX" for the STATE variable.

APPENDIX C

CHOOSING A SAS PROCEDURE

The guidelines in this appendix help you determine a proper analysis to perform on your data. Definitions used in the tables include:

- *Normal* indicates that the procedure is theoretically based on a normality assumption.

- *At least ordinal* indicates that your data have an order. This includes ordinal and quantitative data.

- In the Relational Analysis table, the term "Data type" applies to the dependent variable for regression procedures. For assessment of association (such as correlation or cross-tabulation), the data type applies to both variables.

DESCRIPTIVE STATISTICS

Make decision by reading from the left to right.

TABLE C.1. Decision table for descriptive statistics

	What is the data type?	Statistical procedures/SAS PROC
You want to describe a single variable.	Normal	Descriptive Statistics: Mean, standard deviation, etc. PROC MEANS, UNIVARIATE(Chapter 6)
	Quantitative	Descriptive Statistics, Median, Histogram, Stem-and-Leaf and boxplots PROC UNIVARIATE (Chapter 6 and 14)
	Categorical	Frequencies PROC FREQ, GCHART (BARCHARTs) (Chapters 7 and 14)
You want to describe two related or paired variables.	Both are normal	Pearson's Correlation PROC CORR, REG, GPLOT (Chapters 10 and 14)
	Both are at least ordinal	Spearman's Correlation PROC CORR, GPLOT (Chapters 10 and 14)
	Both are categorical	Crosstabulation Chapters 7 and 14)

COMPARISON TESTS

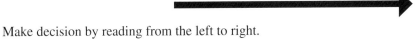

Make decision by reading from the left to right.

TABLE C.2. **Decision table for comparison tests**

	What is the data type?	Procedure to Use/SAS PROC
You are comparing a single sample to a norm (gold standard).	Normal	Single-sample *t*-test PROC MEANS, UNIVARIATE (Chapter 8)
	At least ordinal	Sign test PROC UNIVARIATE (Chapters 8 and 11)
	Categorical	Goodness-of-fit PROC FREQ (Chapter 7)
You are comparing data from two independent groups.	Normal	Two-sample *t*-test PROC TTEST (Chapter 8)
	At least ordinal	Mann-Whitney PROC NPAR1WAY(Chapter 11)
	Categorical	2 × c Test for Homogeneity Chi-Square PROC FREQ (Chapter 7)
You are comparing paired, repeated, or matched data	Normal	Paired *t*-test PROC TTEST, UNIVARIATE (on difference) (Chapter 8)
	At least ordinal	Sign test or Wilcoxon signed rank test PROC NPAR1WAY (Chapter 11)
	Binary (dichotomous)	McNemar PROC FREQ/AGREE (Chapter 7)

(Continued)

TABLE C.2. (Continued)

	What is the data type?	Procedure to Use/SAS `PROC`
More than two groups –INDEPENDENT	Normal	One-way ANOVA `PROC ANOVA, GLM` (Chapter 9)
	At least ordinal	Kruskal-Wallis `PROC NPAR1WAY` (Chapter 11)
	Categorical	r × c test for Homogeneity/Chi-Square, or Kappa for interrater reliability `PROC FREQ, FREQ/KAPPA` (Chapter 7)
More than two groups - REPEATED MEASURES	Normal	Repeated Measures `PROC GLM` (only for one-way) or `PROC MIXED` (Chapter 13)
	At least ordinal	Friedman ANOVA `PROC FREQ` (Chapter 11)
	Categorical	Cochran Q (not discussed)
Comparing means, model includes covariate adjustment	Normal	Analysis of covariance `PROC GLM` (Chapter 13)

RELATIONAL ANALYSES (CORRELATION AND REGRESSION)

Make decision by reading from the left to right.

TABLE C.3. Decision table for relational analysis

	What is the data type for the dependent (response) variable?	Procedure to use/SAS PROC
You want to analyze the relationship between two variables (if regression, one variable is classified as a response variable and one a predictor variable).	Normal	Pearson Correlation, Simple linear regression PROC CORR, REG (Chapter 10)
	At least ordinal	Spearman Correlation PROC CORR (Chapter 10)
	Categorical	r × c Contingency table analysis PROC FREQ (Chapter 7)
	Binary	Logistic regression PROC LOGISTIC (Chapter 12)
You want to analyze the relationship between a response variable and two or more predictor variables.	Normal	Multiple linear regression PROC REG (Chapter 10)
	Binary	Logistic regression PROC LOGISTIC (Chapter 12)

APPENDIX D

QUICK REFERENCE

This appendix provides a series of brief descriptions of basic SAS tasks. Most of the tasks are listed here without explanation, except for a reference to a chapter.

DATA step—Used to define and manipulate information in a SAS data set (Chapters 2–4)

```
DATA MYDATA; * Names and create a SAS data set;
```

Ways to name a data set—can be used whenever a dataset is named:

```
DATA SOMEDATA;      * create working/temporary data set;
DATA "C:\SASDATA\SOMEDATA"; *create permanent data set
                              in specified location;
LIBNAME MYSASLIB "C:\SASDATA"; * create a temporary
                                 SAS library;
DATA MYSASLIB.SOMEDATA;      * create permanent data set
                              in MYSASLIB library;
```

Versions of the INPUT statement:

```
* freeform input;
INPUT ID $ GENDER $ SBP DBP WEIGHT;
* column numbers specify location of data;
INPUT ID 1-4 SEX $ 5-5 AGE 6-9;
* specify beginning column, name, informat.
INPUT @1 ID 4. @5 SEX $1. @10 BDATE DATE9.;
```

Read date using format specification (see format table, Chapter 2):

```
DATA MYDATA;
INPUT @1 FNAME $11. @12 LNAME $12. @24 BDATE DATE9.;
DATALINES;
Bill       Smith        08JAN1952
;
RUN;
```

Ways to specify source of data or enter data set:

```
DATALINES;              * data are listed in the code
                          following this statement;
INFILE filename;        * data are in an ASCII file on disk;
SET dataset;            * data are in a SAS data file;
PROC IMPORT;            * imports data from a non-SAS filetype;
```

Common ways to manipulate data within the DATA step (Chapter 4):

```
IF AGE LE 0 then AGE = .;        * Conditionally specify
                                   missing value;
IF SBP GE 140 THEN HIGHBP=1; ELSE HIGHBP=0; * If-Then-Else;
IF GENDER="MALE";               * Subsetting if statement;
LABEL ID="Identification";      * Define label for a
                                  variable name;
AREA=LENGTH * WIDTH;            * Calculate a new variable;
```

Titles and footnotes (Chapter 5)

```
TITLE 'First title line';
TITLE2 'Up to 9 title lines';
FOOTNOTE 'First footnote line';
FOOTNOTE9 'Up to 9 footnote lines';
```

ODS—Output Delivery System (Chapter 15)

```
ODS TRACE ON;
ODS GRAPHICS ON;
ODS LISTING; *standard output;
ODS HTML [FILE='FILENAME.HTML'];
ODS PDF [FILE='FILENAME.PDF'];
ODS RTF [FILE='FILENAME.RTF'];
ODS PS [FILE='FILENAME.PS'];
   PROC MEANS * PUT PROCS HERE;
ODS TYPE CLOSE;
ODS TRACE OFF;
ODS GRAPHICS OFF;
```

PROC FORMAT—Used to define custom formats for values (Chapter 4)

```
PROC FORMAT;
VALUE $fmtsex 'F' = 'Female'
              'M' = 'Male';
VALUE  fmtyn  1='Yes'
              2='No';
PROC PRINT;     * apply a format to variables;
```

```
    FORMAT SEX $fmtsex.
          QUEST fmtyn.;
RUN;
```

PROC SORT—Sort a data set (Chapter 4)

```
PROC SORT DATA=dataset;
   BY AGE SBP descending;
RUN;
```

PROC PRINT—Create a listing of the data (Chapter 5)

```
PROC PRINT DATA=dataset;
   VAR varlist;
   SUM sumvar;
RUN;
```

PROC MEANS—Used to calculate statistics for quantitative data (Chapter 6)

```
PROC MEANS N MEAN MEDIAN MAXDEC=2 DATA=dataset;
   VAR varlist;
RUN;
```

```
PROC MEANS DATA=dataset;      * Means by group;
   CLASS groupvar;
   VAR varlist);
RUN;
```

PROC UNIVARIATE—Calculate detailed statistics on a variable (Chapter 6)

```
PROC UNIVARIATE DATA=dataset NORMAL PLOT;
   VAR SBP;
   HISTOGRAM SBP/NORMAL;
RUN;
```

PROC FREQ—Frequencies and cross-tabulations (Chapter 7)

```
PROC FREQ DATA=dataset; * basic frequency table;
   TABLES varlist;
RUN;
```

```
PROC FREQ DATA=dataset;
   TABLES var1*var2/CHISQ; * crosstabulation with
                             chi-square;
RUN;
```

PROC TTEST—Comparing means (Chapter 8)

```
PROC TTEST DATA=dataset HO=30; * Single sample t-test;
   VAR varname;
RUN;

PROC TTEST DATA=dataset;       * independent group
                                 t-test;
   CLASS groupvar;
   VAR varname;
RUN;

PROC TTEST DATA=dataset;       * paired t-test;
   PAIRED WBEFORE*WAFTER;
RUN;
```

PROC ANOVA, GLM, and MIXED—Comparing more than three means (Chapters 9 and 13)

```
PROC ANOVA DATA=dataset;     * one-way independent
                               group;
   CLASS groupvar;
   MODEL depvar= groupvar;
   MEANS groupvar /TUKEY;
RUN;

PROC GLM;                    * two fixed-factors;
  CLASS factor1var factor2var;
  MODEL RESPONSE= factor1var factor2var
factor1var*factor2var;
RUN;

PROC MIXED;                  * two-factor, one random;
  CLASS randomfactor fixedfactor;
  MODEL depvar = fixedfactor;
  RANDOM randomfactor randomfactor*fixedfactor;
RUN;
```

PROC CORR—Correlations between pairs of variables (Chapter 10)

```
PROC CORR DATA=SOMEDATA Spearman Pearson;
   VAR AGE TIME1-TIME4;
RUN;
```

PROC REG—Linear regression analysis (Chapter 10)

```
PROC REG DATA=dataset;       * simple linear regression;
    MODEL dependentvar = independentvar/R;
                             * examine residuals;
RUN;

PROC REG DATA=dataset;       * multiple linear regresson;
    MODEL dependentvar = ind1 ind2 ...etc
    /SELECTION=STEPWISE
     SLENTRY=0.05
     SLSTAY=0.05;
RUN;
```

Nonparametric comparisons (Chapter 11)

```
PROC NPAR1WAY DATA=dataset;
    CLASS GROUP;             * compare independent groups;
    VAR SALARY;
RUN;
```

Logistic regression (Chapter 12) (Note: You must output to an ODS format to get the ROC graph.)

```
PROC LOGISTIC DATA=dataset;
CLASS variables;
MODEL dependentvar = independentvar(s)
/ EXPB
  SELECTION=SETPWISE
  SLENTRY=0.05
  SLSTAY=0.1
  RISKLIMITS
  CTABLE
  OUTROC=ROC1;
RUN;
```

Scatterplot with regression line (Chapter 14)

```
GOPTIONS RESET=ALL;
SYMBOL1 V=STAR I=RL;
PROC GPLOT DATA=dataset;
  PLOT yvar*xvar;
RUN;
QUIT;
```

Barchart (Chapter 14)

```
PROC GCHART DATA=dataset;
  HBAR varname;
RUN;
```

Boxplot (Chapter 14)

```
PROC SORT DATA=dataset; BY groupvar;
PROC BOXPLOT DATA=dataset;
    PLOT varname*groupvar;
RUN;
```

REFERENCES

Cohen, J., Cohen, P., West, S.G., and Aiken, L.S. (2002). *Applied multiple regression/correlation analysis for the behavioral sciences* (3rd Edition). Mahwah, N.J.: Lawrence Erlbaum.

Desu, M. M., and Raghavarao, D. (2004). *Nonparametric Statistical Methods for Complete and Censored Data.* Boca Raton, Fla.: Chapman and Hall/CRC.

District of Columbia's 2005 Cities Crimes and Rates as reported in the FBI's September 2006 release of the "UCR for Metropolitan Statistical Areas," http://www.disastercenter.com/crime/dccrime.htm

Elliott, A. C., and Hynan, L. S. (2007). "A SAS Macro Implementation of a Multiple Comparison Post Hoc Test." Proceedings of the Joint Statistical Meetings.

Elliott, A. C., Hynan, L. S., Reisch, J. S., and Smith, J. P. (2006). "Preparing Data for Analysis Using Microsoft Excel." *J Investig Med* 54(6):334–41.

Elliott, A. C., and Woodward, W. A. (1986). Analysis of an unbalanced two-way ANOVA on the microcomputer. *Communications in Statistics*, Volume B15, Number 1, pp. 215–25.

Elliott, A. C., and Woodward, W. A. (2007). *Statistical Analysis Quick Reference Guidebook with SPSS Examples*. Thousand Oaks, Calif.: Sage.

Fleiss, J. L. (1981). *Statistical Methods for Rates and Proportions* (2nd Edition). New York: Wiley.

Hand, D., Daly, F., McConway, K., Lunn, D., and Ostrowski, E. (1994). *A Handbook of Small Data Sets*. Boca Raton, Fla.: Chapman and Hall.

Hosmer, D. W., and Lemeshow, S. (2000). *Applied Logistic Regression* (2nd Edition). New York: Wiley.

Landis, J. R., and Koch, G. G. (1977). The measurement of observer agreement for categorical data. *Biometrics* 33:159–74.

Littell, R. C., Milliken, G. A., Stroup, W. W., and Wolfinger, R. D. (1996). *SAS System for Mixed Models*. Cary, N.C.: SAS Institute, Inc.

Moore, D., and McCabe, G. (2006). *Introduction to the Practice of Statistics* (4th Edition). New York: Freeman.

SAS Institute, Inc. (2003). *SAS/STAT Software: Reference, Version 9.1*. Cary, N.C.: SAS Institute, Inc.

U.S. Department of Energy (2005). *Model 2005 Model Year Fuel Economy Data*, http://www.fueleconomy.gov/feg/FEG2005_GasolineVehicles.pdf.

Zar, J. H. (1999). *Biostatistics Analysis* (4th Edition), pp. 223–26. Upper Saddle River, N.J.: Prentice Hall.

INDEX